Apache Cookbook™

Other resources from O'Reilly

SECOND EDITION

Apache Cookbook™

Ken Coar and Rich Bowen

O'REILLY®

Beijing · Cambridge · Farnham · Köln · Paris · Sebastopol · Taipei · Tokyo

Apache Cookbook™, Second Edition
by Ken Coar and Rich Bowen

Published by O'Reilly Media, Inc., 1005 Gravenstein Highway North, Sebastopol, CA 95472

O'Reilly books may be purchased for educational, business, or sales promotional use. Online editions are also available for most titles (*http://safari.oreilly.com*). For more information, contact our corporate/institutional sales department: (800) 998-9938 or *corporate@oreilly.com*.

Editor: Tatiana Apandi	**Cover Designer:** Karen Montgomery
Production Editor: Sarah Schneider	**Interior Designer:** David Futato
Production Services: GEX, Inc.	**Illustrator:** Robert Romano and Jessamyn Reed

Printing History:

November 2003:	First Edition.
December 2007:	Second Edition.

RepKover™

This book uses RepKover™, a durable and flexible lay-flat binding.

ISBN-10: 0-596-52994-5
ISBN-13: 978-0-596-52994-9

[M]

Table of Contents

Preface

The Apache Web server is a remarkable piece of software. The basic package distributed by the Apache Software Foundation is quite complete and very powerful, and a lot of effort has gone into keeping it from suffering software bloat. One facet of the package makes it especially remarkable: it includes extensibility by design. In short, if the Apache package right out of the box does not do what you want, you can generally extend it so that it does. Dozens of extensions (called modules) are included as part of the package distributed by the Apache Software Foundation. And if one of these doesn't meet your needs, with several million users out there, there is an excellent chance someone else has already done your work for you, someone who has concocted a recipe of changes or enhancements to the server that will satisfy your requirements.

This book is a collection of these recipes. Its sources include tips from the firehose of the Usenet newsgroups, the Apache FAQ, Apache-related mailing lists, mail containing "how-to" questions, questions and problems posed on IRC chat channels, and volunteered submissions.

All of the items in this book come from real-life situations, encountered either by us or by other people who have asked for our help. The topics range from basic compilation of the source code to complex problems involving the treatment of URLs that require SSL encryption.

We've collected more than a hundred different problems and their solutions, largely based on how often they occurred, and have grouped them roughly by subject as shown in Recipe 1.

Primarily, these recipes are useful to webmasters who are responsible for the entire server; however, many are equally applicable to users who want to customize the behavior in their own Web directories through the use of *.htaccess* files.

We've written the Apache Cookbook to be a practical reference, rather than a theoretical discourse: reading it recipe by recipe, chapter by chapter, isn't going to reveal a plot ("Roy Fielding in the Library with an RFC!"*). It's intended to provide point solutions to specific problems, located through the table of contents or the index.

---

* An obscure reference to a board game called *Clue* and an obscure developer of HTTP.

What's in This Book

Because much of the material in this book is drawn from question-and-answer discussions and consultations, we have tried to make it as complete as possible. Of course, this means that we have included "recipes" for some questions to which there are currently no satisfactory answers (at least to our knowledge). This has not been done to tease, annoy, or frustrate you; such recipes are included to provide completeness, so that you will know those problems have been considered rather than ignored.

Very few problems remain insoluble forever, and these incomplete recipes are the ones that will receive immediate attention on the book's Web site and in revisions of the book. If a reader has figured out a way to do something the book mentions but doesn't explain, or omits mentioning entirely, our research team can be notified, and that solution will go on the Web site and in the next revision.

Who knows, you may be the one to provide such a solution!

Platform Notes

The recipes in this book are geared toward two major platforms: Unixish (such as Linux, FreeBSD, and Solaris) and Windows. There are many that have no platform-specific aspects, and for those, any mention of the underlying operating system or hardware is gratefully omitted. Because of the authors' personal preferences and experiences, Unixish coverage is more complete than that for the Windows platforms. However, contributions, suggestions, and corrections for Windows-specific recipes will be gladly considered for future revisions and inclusion on the Web site.

Other Books

There are a number of books currently in print that deal with the Apache Web server and its operation. Among them are:

- *Apache: The Definitive Guide*, Third Edition, by Ben and Peter Laurie (O'Reilly)
- *Pro Apache*, Third Edition, by Peter Wainwright (Apress)
- *Apache Administrator's Handbook* by Rich Bowen, et al. (Macmillan)

You can also keep an eye on a couple of Web pages that track Apache titles:

- *http://Apache-Server.Com/store.html*
- *http://httpd.apache.org/info/apache_books.html*

Other Sources

In addition to books, there is a wealth of information available online. There are Web sites, mailing lists, and Usenet newsgroups devoted to the use and management of the Apache Web server. The Web sites are limitless, but here are some active and useful sources of information:

- The *comp.infosystems.www.servers.unix* and *comp.infosystems.www.servers.ms-windows* Usenet newsgroups. Although these aren't dedicated to Apache specifically, there is a lot of traffic concerning it, and experienced Apache users hang out here. If you don't have access to news, or don't know how to reach Usenet, check out *http://groups.google.com/*.

- The *Apache Today* Web site, *http://apachetoday.com/*, run by Internet.com. This site regularly lists articles about the Web server and making the most of it.

- The *users@httpd.apache.org* mailing list is populated with people who have varying degrees of experience with the Apache software, and some of the Apache developers can be found there, too. Posting is only permitted to subscribed participants. To join the list, visit *http://httpd.apache.org/userslist.html*.

- The #apache IRC channel on the *irc.freenode.net* network—or on many other IRC networks, for that matter. However, your chances of encountering us are most likely on the freenode network.

We must point out that none of these are "official" support mediums for the Web server. In fact, there is no "official" support path, since the software is largely developed by volunteers and is free. However, these informal support forums successfully answer many questions.

How This Book Is Organized

This book is broken up into 13 chapters and 2 appendixes, as follows:

Chapter 1, *Installation*, covers the basics of installing the vanilla Apache software, from source on Unixish systems, and on Windows from the Microsoft Software Installer (MSI) package built by the Apache developers.

Chapter 2, *Adding Common Modules*, describes the details of installing some of the most common third-party modules, and includes generic instructions that apply to many others that have less complex installation needs.

Chapter 3, *Logging*, includes recipes about recording the visits to your Web site(s), and Apache's error logging mechanism.

Chapter 4, *Virtual Hosts*, tells you how to run multiple Web sites using a single Apache server and set of configuration files.

Chapter 5, *Aliases, Redirecting, and Rewriting*, describes how to manipulate URLs, how to control which files they refer to, how to change them from one thing to another, and how to make them point to other Web sites.

Chapter 6, *Security*, covers some of the basic issues of securing your Apache server against penetration and exposure by the nefarious elements on the Internet.

Chapter 7, *SSL*, addresses the issues of making your Apache Web server capable of handling secure transactions with SSL-capable browsers—a must if you're going to be handling sensitive data such as money transfers or medical records.

Chapter 8, *Dynamic Content*, tells you how to enhance your server with runtime scripts and make them operate as a particular user.

Chapter 9, *Error Handling*, describes how to customize the Web server's error messages to give your site its own unique flavor.

Chapter 10, *Proxies*, describes how to configure your Apache server to act as a proxy between users and Web pages and make the processes as transparent and seamless as possible.

Chapter 11, *Performance*, includes a number of recipes for addressing performance bottlenecks and improving the overall function of your Apache server.

Chapter 12, *Directory Listings*, describes how to customize the module for displaying a directory listing as a Web page.

Chapter 13, *Miscellaneous Topics*, covers a variety of miscellaneous topics that didn't seem to fit into any of the other chapters.

Appendix A, *Using Regular Expressions in Apache*, explains how regular expressions are used for pattern-matching in Apache directives.

Appendix B, *Troubleshooting*, covers some basic troubleshooting techniques, where to look for messages, common configuration problems, and so on.

Conventions Used in This Book

Throughout this book certain stylistic conventions are followed. Once you are accustomed to them, you can easily distinguish between comments, commands you need to type, values you need to supply, and so forth.

In some cases, the typeface of terms in the main text will be different and likewise in code examples. The details of what the different styles (italic, boldface, etc.) mean are described in the following sections.

Programming Conventions

In this book, most case examples of code will be in the form of excerpts from scripts, rather than actual application code. When commands need to be issued at a command-line prompt (such as an xterm for a Unixish system or a DOS command prompt for Windows), they will look something like this:

```
% find/usr/local -name apachectl -print
# /usr/local/apache/bin/apachectl graceful
C:>cd "\Program Files\Apache Group\Apache\bin"
C:\Program Files\Apache Group\Apache\bin>apache -k stop
```

On Unixish systems, command prompts that begin with # indicate that you need to be logged in as the superuser (root username); if the prompt begins with %, then the command can be used by any user.

Typesetting Conventions

The following typographic conventions are used in this book:

Italic
: Used for commands, filenames, abbreviations, citations of books and articles, email addresses, URLs, and Usenet group names.

Bold
: Used for labeling menu choices in a graphical interface.

`Constant Width`
: Used for function names, command options, computer output, environment variable names, literal strings, and code examples.

`Constant Width Bold`
: Used for user input in computer dialogues and examples.

`Constant Width Italic`
: Used for replaceable parameters, filesystem paths, and variable names.

 This icon signifies a tip, suggestion, or general note.

 This icon indicates a warning or caution.

Documentation Conventions

Because this book deals with a general topic rather than a specific one (such as the Perl language), there are additional sources of information to which it will refer you. The most common ones are as follows.

The online manual ("man") pages on a Unixish system

References to the manpages will appear something like, "For more information, see the *kill(1)* manpage." The number in parentheses is the manual section; you can access this page with a command such as:

```
% man   1 kill
```

The Apache Web server documentation

Such a reference may appear as "See the *mod_auth* documentation for details." This refers to a Web page like:

> *http://httpd.apache.org/docs/mod/mod_auth.html*

In some cases, the reference will be to a specific Apache directive rather than an actual module; in cases like this, you can locate the appropriate Web page by looking up the directive name on:

> *http://httpd.apache.org/docs/mod/directives.html*

This page lists all of the directives available in the standard Apache package. In some situations, the directive may be specific to a nonstandard or third-party module, in which case the documentation should be located wherever the module itself was found. The links above are for the documentation for Version 1.3 of the software. To access the documentation for Version 2.0, replace "*docs/*" with "*docs-2.0/*" in the URLs.

Using Code Examples

This book is here to help you get your job done. In general, you may use the code in this book in your programs and documentation. You do not need to contact us for permission unless you're reproducing a significant portion of the code. For example, writing a program that uses several chunks of code from this book does not require permission. Selling or distributing a CD-ROM of examples from O'Reilly books does require permission. Answering a question by citing this book and quoting example code does not require permission. Incorporating a significant amount of example code from this book into your product's documentation does require permission.

We appreciate, but do not require, attribution. An attribution usually includes the title, author, publisher, and ISBN. For example: "*Apache Cookbook*, Second Edition, by Ken Coar and Rich Bowen. Copyright 2008 Ken Coar and Rich Bowen, 978-0-596-52994-9."

If you feel your use of code examples falls outside fair use or the permission given above, feel free to contact us at *permissions@oreilly.com*.

We'd Like to Hear from You

We have tested and verified the information in this book to the best of our ability, but you may find that features have changed (which may in fact resemble bugs). Please let us know about any errors you find, as well as your suggestions for future editions, by writing to the following address.

Please address comments and questions concerning this book to the publisher:

O'Reilly Media, Inc.
1005 Gravenstein Highway North
Sebastopol, CA 95472
800-998-9938 (in the United States or Canada)
707-829-0515 (international or local)
707-829-0104 (fax)

We have a Web page for this book, where we list errata, examples, and any additional information. You can access this page at:

http://www.oreilly.com/catalog/9780596529949

To comment or ask technical questions about this book, send an email to:

bookquestions@oreilly.com

For more information about our books, conferences, Resource Centers, and the O'Reilly Network, see our Web site at:

http://www.oreilly.com

We have a Web site for the book, where we'll list errata and plans for future editions. Here you'll also find the source code from the book available for download so you don't have to type it all in:

http://apache-cookbook.com

Safari® Enabled

Safari When you see a Safari® Enabled icon on the cover of your favorite technology book, that means the book is available online through the O'Reilly Network Safari Bookshelf.

Safari offers a solution that's better than e-books. It's a virtual library that lets you easily search thousands of top tech books, cut and paste code samples, download chapters, and find quick answers when you need the most accurate, current information. Try it for free at *http://safari.oreilly.com*.

Acknowledgments

Originally, each recipe was going to be individually attributed, but that turned out to be logistically impossible.

Many people have helped us during the writing of this book, by posing a problem, providing a solution, proofreading, reviewing, editing, or just (!) providing moral support. This multitude, to each of whom we are profoundly grateful, includes Nat Torkington (our project editor and demonstrator of Herculean feats of patience), Sharco and Guy- from #apache on *irc.freenode.net*, Mads Toftum, Morbus Iff (known to the FBI under the alias Kevin Hemenway), and Andy Holman.

Ken Coar

I dedicate this book to my significantly better half, Cathy Coar, who has performed Heraclean feats of love and support on my behalf for more than two decades.

My sincere thanks go out to the crew at O'Reilly, for their deific patience and understanding. Thanks also to the WriterBase Authors Support Group and Cabal mailing lists, whereon much balm and advice was offered. Our technical reviewers provided much excellent feedback and helped make this a better book.

The people who have worked on the Apache Web server documentation, and the people who develop the software itself, get a big note of thanks, too; without the former, collating a lot of the information in this book would have been a whole lot more difficult, and without the latter, the book wouldn't have happened at all.

The users of the software, whose frequently challenging questions populate the mailing lists, the IRC channels, and our inboxes, deserve thanks for all the inspiration they unwittingly provided for the recipes in this book.

But foremost among those to whom I owe gratitude is my significantly better half, Cathy, without whose patience, support, and constructive criticism I would never have achieved what I have.

Rich Bowen

I dedicate this book to the experts on #apache who answer so many of these questions every day, and to the beginners, on their way to becoming experts, who ask them.

A huge thank you goes to all the many people involved in making this book a reality. Tatiana, thank you for your patience and persistent assistance throughout this process.

And, finally, thanks go to my wonderful family. To Sarah, who always looks for my books at the bookstore. To Isaiah, for all his boundless energy and tight hugs. And to my Best Beloved, for helping me discover so much Pointless Beauty.

## CHAPTER 1

Installation

For this Cookbook to be useful, you need to install the Apache Web server software. So what better way to start than with a set of recipes that deal with the installation?

There are many ways of installing this package; one of the features of open software like Apache is that anyone may make an installation kit. This allows vendors (such as Debian, FreeBSD, Red Hat, Mandrake, Hewlett-Packard, and so on) to customize the Apache file locations and default configuration settings so that these settings fit with the rest of their software. Unfortunately, one of the consequences of customization is that the various prepackaged installation kits are almost all different from one another, which means that when it comes to getting assistance, you need to find someone familiar with the kit *you're* using.

In addition to installing it from a prepackaged kit, of which the variations are legion, there's always the option of building and installing it from the source yourself. This has both advantages and disadvantages; on the one hand, you know *exactly* what you installed and where you put it, but, on the other hand, it's possible that binary add-on packages will expect files to be in locations other than those you have chosen.

If setting up the Web server is something you're going to do once and never again, using a packaged solution prepared by your system vendor is probably the way to go. However, if you anticipate applying source patches, adding or removing modules, or just fiddling with the server in general, building it yourself from the ground up is probably the preferred method. (The authors of this book, being confirmed bit-twiddlers, *always* build from source.)

This chapter covers some of the more common prepackaged installation varieties and also how to build the server from the source yourself.

Throughout the chapter, we assume that you will be using *dynamic shared objects* (DSOs) rather than building modules statically into the server. The DSO approach is highly recommended; it not only makes it easy to update individual modules without having to rebuild the entire server, but it also makes adding or removing modules from the server's configuration a simple matter of editing the configuration file.

DSOs on Unixish systems typically have a *.so* extension; on Windows, they end with a *.dll* suffix.

1.1 Installing from Red Hat Linux's Packages

Problem

You have a Red Hat Linux server and want to install or upgrade the Apache Web server on it using the packages that Red Hat prepares and maintains.

Solution

If you are a member of the Red Hat Network (RHN), Red Hat's subscription service, you can use Red Hat's *up2date* tool to maintain your Apache package:

```
# up2date -ui apache apache-devel apache-manual
```

If you're running a more recent version:

```
# up2date -ui httpd httpd-devel httpd-manual
```

If you aren't a member of RHN, you can still download the packages from one of Red Hat's servers (either *ftp://ftp.redhat.com* or *ftp://updates.redhat.com*), and install it with the following command:

```
# rpm -Uvh apache
```

Discussion

The -Uvh option to the *rpm* command tells it to:

- Upgrade any existing version of the package already on the system or install it for the first time if it isn't.
- Explain the process, so that you can receive positive feedback that the installation is proceeding smoothly.
- Display a pretty line of octothorpes (#) across the screen, marking the progress of the installation.

If you use the packages Red Hat maintains for its own platform, you will benefit from a simple and relatively standard installation. However, you can only update versions for which Red Hat has put together an RPM package, which typically means that you may be lagging weeks to months behind the latest stable version.

There is also the issue of platform compatibility; for instance, at some point the version of Apache provided for Red Hat Linux changed from 1.3 to 2.0, and newer versions of the operating system will probably only have the 2.0 packages available. Similarly, if you run an older version of Red Hat Linux, the newer packages will probably not install properly on your system.

It's a good idea to install the *apache-devel* package as well. It's quite small, so it won't have much impact on your disk usage; however, it includes files and features that a lot of third-party modules will need in order to install properly.

See Also

- Red Hat's full platform release archive at *ftp://ftp.redhat.com/*
- Red Hat's incremental update (errata) archive at *ftp://updates.redhat.com/*

1.2 Installing from Debian Packages

Problem

You have a computer running Debian, or one of the Debian-based distributions, such as Ubuntu, and wish to install Apache.

Solution

Using *apt-get*, install the *apache2* package:

```
# apt-get install apache2-mpm-prefork
```

Discussion

As with any package-based Linux distribution, it's usually best to stick with the packages supplied by that distribution in order to have ease of updates, and maximum interoperability with other packages installed on the same system. On Debian, this means using *apt-get*.

It's a good idea to install the *apache2-dev* package as well, as it provides utilities, such as *apxs*, which will be useful in installing third-party modules, should the need arise.

Debian has its own unique arragement of configuration files, which is unlike that of any other distribution. Both modules and sites (virtual hosts) are arranged in subdirectories so that they can be enabled or disabled at will using utilities that come with Debian's version of Apache. For example, to enable a particular module, you will use the a2enmod command, which makes the appropriate changes to the server configuration file to cause that module to be loaded. For example:

```
# a2enmod rewrite
```

For a full description of where Debian places its files and directories, you should consult *http://wiki.apache.org/httpd/DistrosDefaultLayout*.

See Also

- *http://wiki.apache.org/httpd/DistrosDefaultLayout*

- *man a2enmod*
- *man apt-get*

1.3 Installing Apache on Windows

Problem

You want to install the Apache Web server software on a Windows platform.

 If you already have Apache installed on your Windows system, remove it before installing a new version. Failure to do this results in unpredictable behavior. See Recipe 1.8.

Solution

Primarily, Windows is a graphically oriented environment, so the Apache install for Windows is correspondingly graphical in nature.

The simplest way to install Apache is to download and execute the Microsoft Software Installer (MSI) package from the Apache Web site at *http://httpd.apache.org/down load*. The following screenshots come from an actual installation made using this method.

Each step of the installation procedure is distinct in the process and you can revise earlier decisions, until the files are installed. The first screen (Figure 1-1) simply confirms what you're about to do and the version of the package you're installing.

The second screen (Figure 1-2) presents the Apache license. Its basic tenets boil down to the following: do what you want with the software, don't use the Apache marks (trademarks like the feather or the name Apache) without permission, and provide proper attribution for anything you build based on Apache software. (This only applies if you plan to distribute your package; if you use it strictly on an internal network, this isn't required.) You can't proceed past this screen until you agree to the license terms.

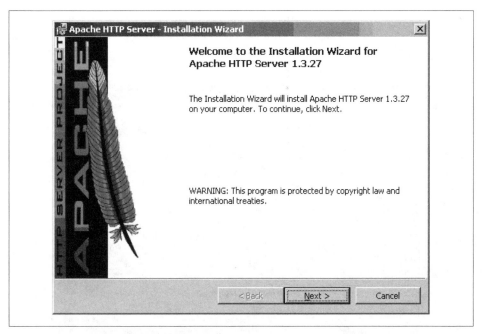

Figure 1-1. First screen of Apache MSI install

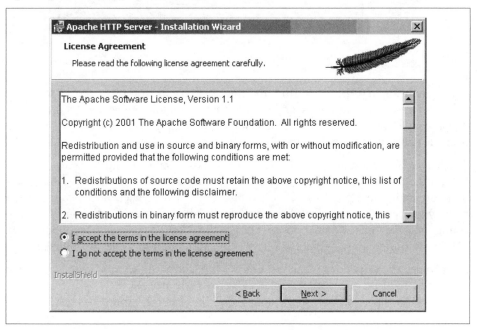

Figure 1-2. License agreement

Figure 1-3 shows the recommended reading for all new users of the Apache software. This describes special actions you should take, such as making configuration changes to close security exposures, so read it closely.

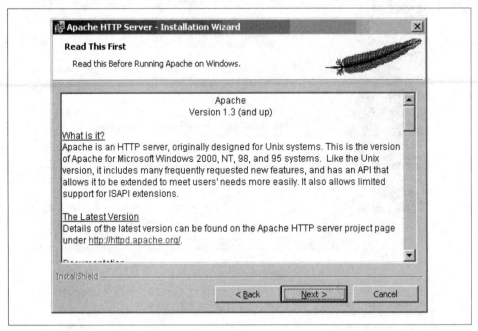

Figure 1-3. Recommended reading for new users

If you are installing Apache for the first time, the installation process asks for some information so that it can make an initial configuration for your server (Figure 1-4). If you already have a version of Apache installed, nothing you enter on this screen will override your existing configuration.

The Server Name in the figure is filled with the same value as the Network Domain field; this is a nod to the growing tendency to omit the "www" prefix of Web sites and use the domain name (e.g., *http://oreilly.com/* instead of *http://www.oreilly.com/*). What name you specify for the server is just advisory, allowing the installation process to configure some initial values; you can change them later by editing the configuration file. The important thing is that the Server Name value be resolvable into an IP address.

Next comes a screen asking what portions of the package you want to install, as shown in Figure 1-5. Just go with Typical unless you're an advanced user. The Custom option allows you to choose whether to install the Apache documentation.

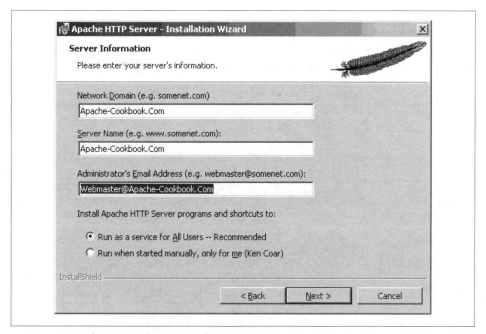

Figure 1-4. Initial server configuration information

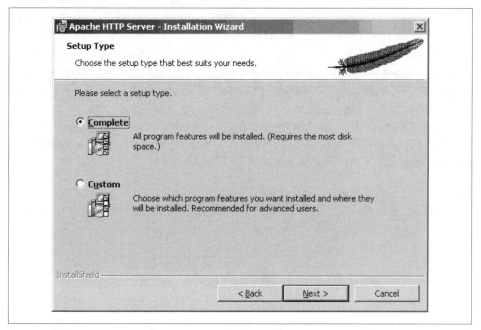

Figure 1-5. Installation type

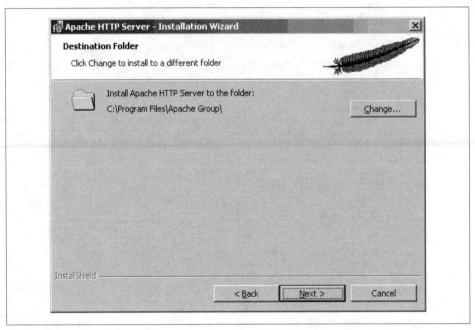

Figure 1-6. ServerRoot directory

Figure 1-6 asks where you want the software installed. The screenshot shows the default location, which will become the *ServerRoot*.

Once you've answered all the questions, a screen similar to Figure 1-7 will come up. This is your last chance to go back and change anything; once you click the Install button on this screen, the installation puts the pieces of the package in place on your system.

Figures 1-8 and 1-9 show the last screens for the Windows MSI install; they show the progress of the installation. When they're finished, Apache has been installed (and started, if you chose the "Run as a service" option shown in Figure 1-4).

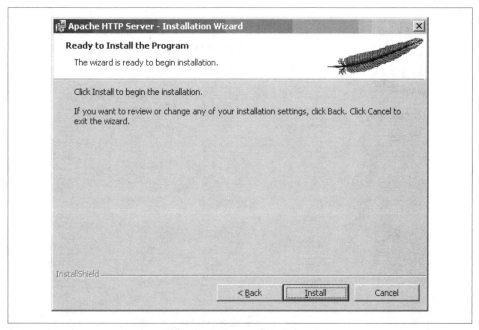

Figure 1-7. The last chance to change your mind

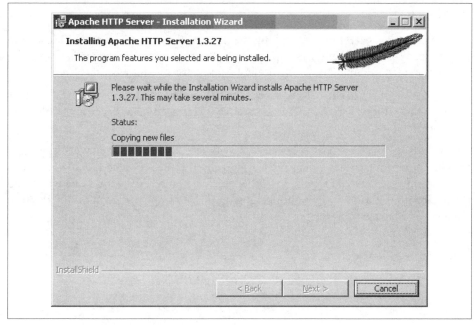

Figure 1-8. The installation progress

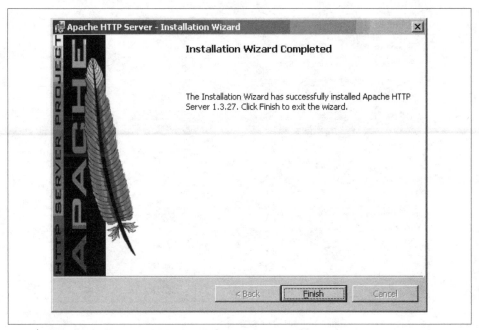

Figure 1-9. MSI installation finished

Discussion

A lot of effort has been put into making the Apache server run well on Windows and be managed like other Windows applications. As a consequence, the primary installation method (InstallShield or MSI) should be familiar to Windows users.

If you've never run Apache before, accept the defaults the first time you install it. This makes it easier for others to provide assistance if you need help, because the files will be in predictable locations.

If you chose to start the Apache server as a service (see Figure 1-4), then you can modify the conditions for it to start, such as the user it should run as or whether it should start automatically, just as you would any other service. Figure 1-10 shows one way to do this; bring up the window by right-clicking on the *My Computer* icon on the desktop and choose Manage from the pop-up menu.

See Also

- The Apache license at *http://www.apache.org/LICENSE*
- Recipe 1.8

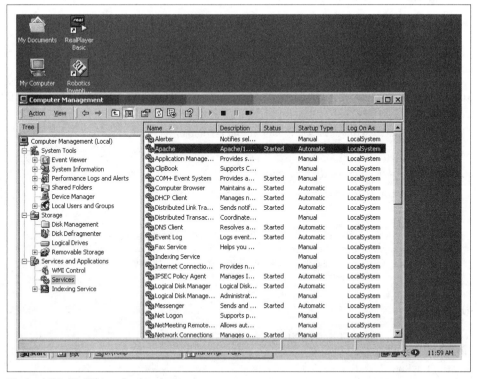

Figure 1-10. Modifying the Apache service

1.4 Downloading the Apache Sources

Problem

You want to build the Apache Web server yourself from the sources directly (see Recipe 1.5), but don't know how to obtain them.

Solution

There are a number of ways to obtain the sources. You can access the latest version in close to real-time by using Subversion (the tool used by the Apache developers for source control), you can download a release tarball, or you can install a source package prepared by a distributor, among others.

To install from a prepackaged tarball, download the tarball from *http://httpd.apache.org/download.cgi*, and then:

```
% tar xzvf httpd-2.0.59.tar.gz
```

If your version of `tar` doesn't support the z option for processing zipped archives, use this command instead:

```
% gunzip -c < httpd-2.0.59.tar.gz | tar xvf -
```

From the very latest up-to-the-minute Apache 2.0 source repository (not guaranteed to be completely functional), use:

```
% svn checkout http://svn.apache.org/repos/asf/httpd/httpd/branches/2.0.x/ httpd-2.0
```

You can fetch a particular release version instead of the bleeding edge code if you know the name the developers gave it. For example, this will pull the sources of the 2.0.59 release, which *is* expected to be stable, unlike the up-to-the-minute version:

```
% svn checkout http://svn.apache.org/repos/asf/httpd/httpd/tags/2.0.59/ httpd-2.0.59
```

You can find the names of the tags used in the source tree by visiting either *http://svn.apache.org/viewvc/httpd/httpd/tags/* or with:

```
% svn ls http://svn.apache.org/repos/asf/httpd/httpd/tags/
```

 All sorts of tags are used by the developers for various purposes. The tags used to label versions of files used for a release are always of the form *n.m.e*, so use these to work with a particular release version.

Discussion

No matter how you install the source, the directory tree will be ready for configuration and building. Once the source is in place, you should be able to move directly to building the package (see Recipe 1.5).

If you chose to install the sources using the Subversion method, you can keep your sources up-to-date by simply executing the following command from the top level of the source directory:

```
% svn update
```

This will update or fetch any files that have been changed or added by the developers since the last time you downloaded or updated.

If you update to the latest version of the sources, you're getting whatever the developers are currently working on, which may be only partially finished. If you want reliability, stick with the released versions, which have been extensively tested.

See Also

• Recipe 1.5

1.5 Building Apache from the Sources

Problem

You want to build your Apache Web server from the sources directly rather than installing it from a prepackaged kit.

Solution

Assuming that you already have the Apache source tree—whether you installed it from a tarball, Subversion, or some distribution package, the following commands—executed in the top directory of the tree, builds the server package with most of the standard modules as DSOs:

```
% ./buildconf
% ./configure --prefix=/usr/local/apache
> --with-layout=Apache --enable-modules=most --enable-mods-shared=all \
> --with-mpm=prefork
% make
# make install
```

If you want more detailed information about the various options and their meanings, you can use the following command:

```
% ./configure --help
```

Discussion

Building the server from the sources can be complex and time-consuming, but it's essential if you intend to make any changes to the source code. It gives you much more control over things, such as the use of shareable object libraries and the database routines available to modules. Building from source is also *de rigeur* if you're developing your own Apache modules.

If you want to build the modules statically into the server, replace any occurrences of `--enable-mods-shared=list` with `--enable-mods=list`.

The options to the *configure* script are many and varied; if you haven't used it before to build Apache, locate some online tutorials (such as those at *http://apache-server.com/tutorials/* or *http://httpd.apache.org/docs-2.0/install.html*) when you want to change the defaults. The default options generally produce a working server, although the filesystem locations and module choices may not be what you'd like; they may include modules you don't want or omit some you do. (See Chapter 2 for some examples.)

See Also

- Recipe 1.4
- *http://apache-server.com/tutorials/*
- *http://httpd.apache.org/docs-2.0/install.html*

1.6 Installing with ApacheToolbox

Problem

You have a complicated collection of modules you want to install correctly.

Solution

Download ApacheToolbox from *http://www.apachetoolbox.com/*. (Note that the version numbers will probably be different than these, which were the latest available when this section was written.) Unpack the file:

```
% bunzip2 Apachetoolbox-1.5.65.tar.bz2
% tar xvf Apachetoolbox-1.5.65.tar
```

(Depending on your version of `tar`, you may be able to combine these operations into a single *tar xjvf* command.)

Then run the installation script:

```
# cd Apachetoolbox-1.5.65
# ./install.sh
```

Discussion

ApacheToolbox is developed and maintained by Bryan Andrews. It is a shell script that assists in the configuration and installation of Apache. It includes support for over 100 commonly used or standard modules.

When you run the script, you select modules from lists appearing on various screens. Once you have decided on your list of modules, ApacheToolbox downloads the third-party modules you have selected and the tools that you don't have installed, and then runs the Apache *configure* script with any arguments needed to create the combination you have requested.

The main screen (see Figure 1-11) lists the most popular third-party modules that ApacheToolbox can install. Select or deselect a particular module by typing the number next to that module's name.

Typing **apache** moves you to the second screen (see Figure 1-12), which lists the standard Apache modules. Add or remove individual modules by typing the number next to their module names.

You can choose options for configuring the modules on additional menus, and you can build an RPM on your installation configuration, which you can then install on multiple machines without requiring that ApacheToolbox be installed.

Once you have made all your module selections, type **go** to tell ApacheToolbox to start the configuration process.

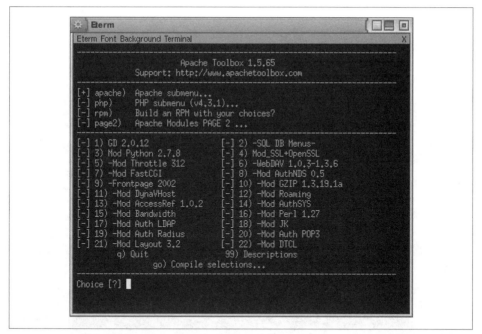

Figure 1-11. Main screen of ApacheToolbox install

Your preferences are saved to a file (*etc/config.cache*) so that if you want to reinstall Apache with the same configuration, you merely need to run ApacheToolbox again, and it will start up with the selections from the last run. To upgrade to a new version of Apache, get the latest version of ApacheToolbox, and ask it to run the installation script with your last selections (without going through the menu process), by typing the following commands:

```
# ./install.sh --update
# ./install.sh --fast
```

 The --update option requires that you have *lynx* installed.

Once ApacheToolbox has completed its work, you can edit the configuration script to insert or modify arguments. Once you are satisfied and ApacheToolbox has run the configuration script, go into the Apache source subdirectory and run *make* and *make install* to compile and install Apache:

```
# cd apache_1.3.27
# make
# make install
```

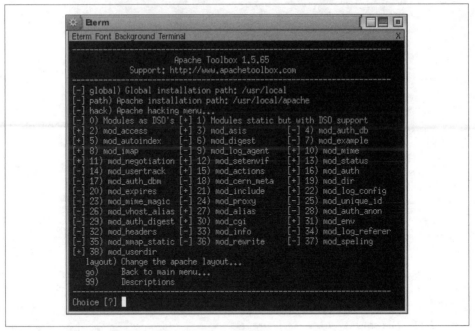

Figure 1-12. ApacheToolbox screen for standard Apache modules

 ApacheToolbox, as of this writing, is only available for Apache 1.3. We expect that it will be available for Apache 2.0 as soon as there are enough third-party modules to warrant the necessary development time.

See Also

- *http://apachetoolbox.com/*

1.7 Starting, Stopping, and Restarting Apache

Problem

You want to be able to start and stop the server at need, using the appropriate tools.

Solution

On Unixish systems, use the *apachectl* script; on Windows, use the options in the Apache folder of the Start menu.

Discussion

The basic Apache package includes tools to make it easy to control the server. For Unixish systems, this is usually a script called *apachectl*, but prepackaged distributions may replace or rename it. It can only perform one action at a time, and the action is specified by the argument on the command line. The options of interest are:

`apachectl start`
> This will start the server if it isn't already running. If it *is* running, this option has no effect and may produce a warning message.

`apachectl graceful`
> This option causes the server to reload its configuration files and gracefully restart its operation. Any current connections in progress are allowed to complete. The server will be started if it isn't running.

`apachectl restart`
> Like the `graceful` option, this one makes the server reload its configuration files. However, existing connections are terminated immediately. If the server isn't running, this command will try to start it.

`apachectl stop`
> This shuts the server down immediately. Any existing connections are terminated at once.

For Windows, the MSI installation of Apache includes menu items for controlling the server, as shown in Figure 1-13.

Both of the solutions shown (for Unixish and Windows systems) illustrate the basic server control operations: start, stop, and restart. The purpose of the start and stop functions should be self-evident. Any time you modify the server-wide configuration files (such as *httpd.conf*), you must restart the server for the changes to take effect.

See Also

- Recipe 1.1
- Recipe 1.3

1.8 Uninstalling Apache

Problem

You have the Apache software installed on your system, and you want to remove it.

Solution

On Red Hat Linux, to remove an Apache version installed with the RPM tool, use:

```
# rpm -ev apache
```

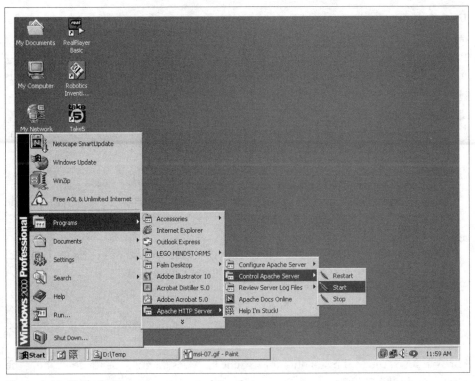

Figure 1-13. Using the Start menu to control Apache

Other packaging systems may provide some similar mechanism. If they don't, however, chances are that cleaning out all the files will require a lot of manual work.

On Windows, Apache can typically be removed like any other MSI-installed software (see Figure 1-14).

Discussion

Unfortunately, there is no generic works-for-all removal method for Apache installations on Unixish systems. Some packages, such as Red Hat's RPM, do remember what they installed so they can remove all the pieces, as shown in the solution. However, if the software was installed by building from the sources (see Recipe 1.5), the burden of knowing where files were put rests with the person who did the build and install. The same applies if the software was installed from source on a Windows system; it's only the MSI or InstallShield packages that make the appropriate connections to allow the use of the Add/Remove Software control panel.

For a Unixish system, if you have access to the directory in which the server was built, look for the `--prefix` option in the *config.nice* file. That will give you a starting point,

---

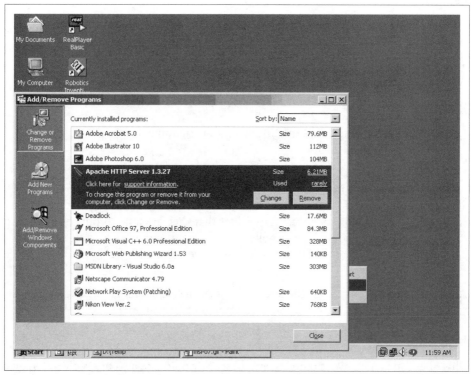

Figure 1-14. Uninstalling the Apache software

at least. Here is a list of the directories an Apache 2.0 installation usually puts somewhere on your disks:

bin
build
cgi-bin
conf
error
htdocs
icons
include
lib
logs
man
manual
modules

See Also

- Recipe 1.5

1.9 Which Version of Apache to Use

Problem

You want to know which version of Apache is the right one for you.

Solution

Although there is not necessarily one right answer for everyone, the Apache HTTP Server development team works very hard to ensure that every release of the software is the best, most stable, most secure product that they are able to put together, and each release of the product fixes problems that were found in earlier releases. So, it's always our position that the latest version of the server is the one that you should be running.

As of this writing, that means the latest release of the 2.2.x branch, which, right now, is 2.2.4. When 2.4 is released, we will recommend that you upgrade to 2.4.

Discussion

This question is not always quite as simple as we would like it to be. We want to give the One Right Answer, but there are sometimes very good reasons for sticking with an older version of the software. However, these reasons are less frequently valid than they were a few years ago.

The most common reason that people give for remaining on the 1.3 version of the server is that they are running *mod_something* and it's not available for 2.2 yet. In the early days of Apache 2, this was a valid reason for many people that were sticking with Apache 1.3, and it entered the commonly accepted wisdom that most modules weren't yet available for Apache 2.

However, as various major Linux distributions started including Apache 2 as the default Web server, more and more modules became available for Apache 2, or people developed alternative modules implementing the same functionality, and this became less and less true.

As of this writing, it seems to be that only a very few commercial modules still satisfy the "not available for Apache 2" category, and this reason is not nearly as believable as it once was.

Another common reason given is that a large installation, with many virtual hosts and complex configuration, is built on Apache 1.3, and it would be an enormous undertaking to migrate it to Apache 2. This is a much more compelling reason. However, it must also be factored in that Apache 1.3 is in maintenance-only mode, and will never get the new features that are being developed for the 2.x branch. Also, perhaps more importantly, the people who provide free online support for Apache are, for the most part, themselves using Apache 2, and their knowledge of Apache 1.3 is waning. So if you have a stable installation, and have no technical difficulties, and are content to slip gradually further and further behind in terms of new functionality, then perhaps staying with 1.3 is a valid solution in that case.

If, however, you are doing a new Web server installation, there is absolutely no good reason not to do with the latest version of the product. You'll benefit from the experience gained in the 1.3 days, and you'll get the new features that come with the 2.2 server, as well as the better-implemented old features.

See Also

- *http:/httpd.apache.org/docs/2.2/new_features_2_2.html*
- *http:/httpd.apache.org/docs/2.2/new_features_2_0.html*
- *http://www.oreilly.com/catalog/9780596529277*

1.10 Upgrading Using config.nice

Problem

You built your Apache Web server software from the source, and now you want to upgrade it while keeping all the same configuration options.

Solution

Unpack the source of the new version into a separate tree, and execute the *config.nice* script created by your build of the earlier version.

> This technique is primarily intended for use when upgrading within the same major version series, such as from 2.0.17 to 2.0.59, or from 2.2.0 to 2.2.4. Attempting to use it to apply older configuration options to a newer major version (such as from 2.0.17 to 2.2.4) may not work reliably.

For example, suppose you built and installed version 2.0.17 long ago, and you now want to upgrade your system to 2.0.59:

```
# cd /usr/local/build
# tar xvf /tmp/httpd-2.0.59.tat.gz
# cd httpd-20.0.59
# ../httpd-2.0.17/config.nice
# make
```

Discussion

When you execute the *configure* script to set up your compilation and installation preferences, it creates a file called *config.script* with all the options you chose. The file *config.nice* executes *configure* with all those options. This means you don't need to remember or write down all the options you specified when you finally got it working.

In addition, *config.nice* allows you to specify additional options, which it adds to those with which it invokes *configure*. When *configure* runs, it will create *config.nice* again with the complete new set of options.

See Also

- Recipe 1.5

1.11 Starting Apache at Boot

Problem

You want your Apache Web server to start automatically when your system boots up.

Solution

On a Windows system, if you installed Apache as a service, you can configure it to start automatically just as you would any other service. Go to the Services control panel and make the desired changes there.

On Unixish systems, how you set this up differs by platform. For Red Hat-based systems:

```
# cp path/to/apachectl /etc/rc.d/init.d/httpd
# vi /etc/rc.d/init.d/httpd    # add '# chkconfig 3 92 10'
# chkconfig --add httpd
# chkconfig --levels 35 httpd on
```

This will cause Apache to be started up (and shut down) as part of the normal sequence for runlevels 3 and 5.

Discussion

The solution provided is specific to Red Hat-based platforms such as Fedora Core or RHEL. For other platforms or distributions you may instead need to edit */etc/rc.local*, or copy the *apachectl* script into */etc/rc3.d*, or something similar. Consult your operating system's documentation for specifics.

See Also

- Recipe 1.5

- Recipe 1.7

1.12 Useful configure Options

Problem

The *configure* script, that is used to set up a build from source, has many options, and it's not clear which ones are really important.

Solution

Here are some of the most important and useful options that you you might want to use:

`--prefix`
Specifies the top level of the directory tree into which files will be put. The default is usually `--prefix=`*/usr/local/apache2*, but different layouts can change this (see the `--enable-layout` option in this section).

`--enable-layout`
This allows you to select one of the predefined filesystem structures; that is, where *make install* should put all the files. To see where files will be put for a particular layout, examine the *config.layout* in the top level of the source tree.

Currently the predefined layouts include:
> Apache
> beos
> BSDI
> Darwin
> Debian
> FreeBSD
> GNU
> Mac OS X Server
> OpenBSD
> opt
> RedHat
> Solaris
> SuSE

To use one of the layout names that contains spaces, you must enclose it in quotation marks:

```
% ./configure --enable-layout="Mac OS Server"
```

`--enable-mods-shared`
This option controls which modules will be built as DSOs rather than being linked statically into the server. An excellent shortcut value is *most*.

`--enable-ssl`

If you're going to be running a secure server, you will need to include this option, as the SSL module is *not* activated by default.

`--enable-suexec`

Use this option if you want the *suexec* utility to be built. Because of the degree to which it depends on the rest of the server build, you should specify this when configuring the main server build, and not try to build *suexec* later.

`--with-apr, --with-apr-util`

If you have multiple versions of the Apache Portable Runtime library and utilities installed—as you might if you build Apache on a system with Subversion installed—you can use these options to ensure that the Apache server is built with a compatible APR version.

`--with-included-apr`

This option is a nice shorthand way of specifying the compatible bundled version of APR should be used. The option is not available prior to Apache version 2.2, though.

`--with-mpm`

The Multi-Processing Model, or MPM, defines how the server handles requests by setting the relationship between threads and child processes. Usually the *configure* script will choose one appropriate for the platform on which you're building, but sometimes you may want to override this. For example, if you're going to be using the PHP scripting module, you need to use the *prefork* MPM in order to avoid problems.

`--with-port`

This option is useful if you are building the server under a non-*root* username but intend to run it as a system daemon. The *configure* script chooses a different default for the port number depending upon whether it's being run by *root* or not. With this option you can override this behaviour. The most common use of this option is:

```
--with-port=80
```

Discussion

Minimal documentation for all of the *configure* options is available from the script itself:

```
% ./configure --help
```

However, for more detailed understanding you need to consult the Apache documentation itself—or look at the source code.

See Also

- *http://httpd.apache.org/docs/2.0/install.html*

1.13 Finding Apache's Files

Problem

You've installed the Apache Web server, whether from source or an installation kit, but you're not sure where all the files have been put. (This is useful to know if you want to *un*install it later.)

Solution

If you installed the software from a source kit, look at the *config.layout* file in the top level of the source directory. Look for a *<Layout>* stanza that matches the `--enable-layout` option given to the *configure* script. (If none was supplied, the *Apache* layout will have been used.)

If you installed the software from an RPM package, use the `-ql` option to see where the files have been installed:

```
% rpm -ql httpd
```

If you installed from a kit prepared by a distributor, such as Ubuntu, check with the distribution documentation to find out where the files are stored.

Discussion

One of the advantages—and disadvantages—of open software is that everyone can build an installation kit. And everyone pretty much chooses options different from everyone else.

The Apache source package includes a list of "common" layouts, and most installation kits use one or another of these.

See Also

- *http://httpd.apache.org/docs/2.0/programs/configure.html*

## CHAPTER 2

Adding Common Modules

There are a number of extremely popular modules for the Apache Web server that are not included in the basic distribution. Most of these are separate because of licensing or support reasons; some are not distributed by the Apache Software Foundation because of a decision by the Apache developers; and some are integral parts of other projects. For instance, *mod_ssl* for Apache 1.3 is developed and maintained separately, not only because of the U.S. export control laws (which were more restrictive when the package was originally developed), but also because it requires changes to the core software that the Apache developers chose not to integrate.

This chapter provides recipes for installing some of the most popular of these third-party modules; when available, there are separate recipes for installation on Unixish systems and on Windows.

The most comprehensive list of third-party modules can be found in the Apache Module Registry at *http://modules.apache.org*. Some modules are so popular—or complex—that they have entire sites devoted to them, as do the ones listed in this chapter.

Although hundreds of third-party modules are available, many module developers are only concerned with their single module. This means that there are potentially as many different sets of installation instructions as there are modules. The first recipe in this chapter describes an installation process that should work with many Apache 1.3 modules, but you should check with the individual packages' instructions to see if they have a different or more detailed process.

Many of the modules are available from organizations that prepackage or distribute Apache software, such as in the form of an RPM from Mandrake or Red Hat, but such prebuilt module packages include the assumptions of the packager. In other words, if you build the server from source and use custom locations for the files, don't be surprised if the installation of a packaged module fails.

All of the modules described in this chapter are supported with Apache 1.3 on Unixish systems. Status of support with Apache 2.0 on Windows is shown in Table 2-1.

Table 2-1. Module support status

Module name	Windows	Support on Apache 2.0
mod_dav	Yes	Included; no installation necessary
mod_perl	Yes	Yes
mod_php	Yes	Yes
mod_ssl	No	Included; no installation necessary

2.1 Installing a Generic Third-Party Module

Problem

You have downloaded a third-party module that isn't listed in this chapter, and you want to install it.

Solution

Move to the directory where the module's source file was unpacked, and then:

```
% /path/to/apache/bin/apxs -cia module.c
```

Discussion

In the case of a third-party module that consists of a single *.c* file, there is a good chance that it can be built and installed using the Solution. Modules that involve multiple source files should provide their own installation instructions.

The `-cia` options mean to compile, install, and activate. The first is pretty straightforward; install means put the *.so* file in the place Apache expects to find it; and activate means to add the module to the *httpd.conf* file.

See Also

*   The *apxs* manpage, typically *ServerRoot/man/man8/apxs.8*

2.2 Installing mod_dav on a Unixish System

Problem

You want to add or enable WebDAV capabilities to your server. WebDAV permits specific documents to be reliably and securely manipulated by remote users without the need for FTP, to perform such tasks as adding, deleting, or updating files.

Solution

If you're using Apache 2.0 or later, *mod_dav* is automatically available, although you may need to enable it at compile time with `--enable-dav`.

If you are using Apache 1.3, download and unpack the *mod_dav* source package from *http://webdav.org/mod_dav/*, and then:

```
% cd mod_dav-1.0.3-1.3.6
% ./configure --with-apxs=/usr/local/apache/bin/apxs
% make
# make install
```

Restart the server, and be sure to read Recipe 6.18.

Discussion

The *mod_dav* source package is an encapsulated and well-behaved module that is easily built and added to an existing server. To test that it has been properly installed, you need to enable some location on the server for WebDAV management and verify access to that location with some WebDAV-capable tool. We recommend *cadaver*, which is an open source command-line WebDAV tool. (The URL for the *cadaver* tool is found at the end of this recipe.)

To enable your server for WebDAV operations, you need to add at least two directives to your *httpd.conf* file. The first identifies the location of the locking database used by *mod_dav* to keep WebDAV operations from interfering with each other; it needs to be in a directory that is writable by the server. For example:

```
# cd /usr/local/apache
# mkdir var
# chgrp nobody var
# chmod g+w var
```

Now add the following line to your *httpd.conf* file, outside any containers:

```
<IfModule mod_dav.c>
    DAVLockDB var/DAVlock
</IfModule>
```

 The *DAVLockDB* location *must not* be on an NFS-mounted filesystem because NFS doesn't support the sort of locking *mod_dav* requires. Putting the lock database on an NFS filesystem may result in unpredictable results.

Next, create a temporary directory for testing WebDAV functionality:

```
# cd /usr/local/apache
# mkdir htdocs/dav-test
# chgrp nobody htdocs/dav-test
# chmod g+w htdocs/dav-test
```

Add a stanza to your *httpd.conf* file that will enable this directory for WebDAV operations:

```
<Directory "/usr/local/apache/htdocs/dav-test">
    DAV On
</Directory>
```

Now restart your server. It should be ready to handle WebDAV operations directed to the */dav-test* local URI. To test it with the *cadaver* tool, try the following commands; your output should look very similar to that shown:

```
% cd /tmp
% echo "Plain text" > dav-test.txt
% cadaver
dav:!> open http://localhost/dav-test
Looking up hostname... Connecting to server... connected.
dav:/dav-test/> put dav-test.txt
Uploading dav-test.txt to '/dav-test/dav-test.txt': (reconnecting...done)
Progress: [= == == == == == == == == == == == == == ==>] 100.0% of 11
    bytes succeeded.
dav:/dav-test/> propset dav-test.txt MyProp 1023
Setting property on 'dav-test.txt': (reconnecting...done) succeeded.
dav:/dav-test/> propget dav-test.txt MyProp
Fetching properties for 'dav-test.txt':
Value of MyProp is: 1023
dav:/dav-test/> propdel dav-test.txt MyProp
Deleting property on 'dav-test.txt': succeeded.
dav:/dav-test/> close
Connection to 'localhost' closed.
dav:!> exit
% rm dav-test.txt
```

Properties are attributes of a WebDAV resource. Some are managed by the system, such as the resource's size, but others can be arbitrary and added, changed, and removed by the user.

Once you have verified that *mod_dav* is working correctly, remove the *htdocs/dav-test* directory, and the corresponding <Directory> stanza in your *httpd.conf* file, and follow the guidelines in Recipe 6.18.

See Also

- Recipe 6.18
- *http://webdav.org/mod_dav*
- *http://webdav.org/cadaver*

2.3 Installing mod_dav on Windows

Problem

You want to enable WebDAV capabilities on your existing Apache 1.3 server with *mod_dav*.

Solution

Apache 2.0 includes *mod_dav* as a standard module, so you do not need to download and build it.

Download and unpack the *mod_dav* Windows package from *http://webdav.org/mod_dav/win32*. Verify that your Apache installation already has the *xmlparse.dll* and *xmltok.dll* files in the *ServerRoot* directory; if they aren't there, check through the Apache directories to locate and copy them to the *ServerRoot*. *mod_dav* that requires the *Expat* package, which is included with versions of the Apache Web server after 1.3.9; these files hook into *Expat*, which *mod_dav* will use.

Put the *mod_dav* DLL file into the directory where Apache keeps its modules:

```
C:\>cd mod_dav-1.0.3-dev
C:\mod_dav-1.0.3-dev>copy mod_dav.dll C:\Apache\modules
C:\mod_dav-1.0.3-dev>cd \Apache
```

Add the following line to your *httpd.conf* file:

```
LoadModule dav_module modules/mod_dav.dll
```

You may also need to add an *AddModule* line if your *httpd.conf* file includes a *ClearModuleList* directive and re-adds the other modules. Alternatively, you can insert the *LoadModule* for *mod_dav* after the *ClearModuleList* directive.

Discussion

The *mod_dav* Package is an encapsulated and well-behaved module that is easily built and added to an existing server. To test that it has been properly installed, you need to enable some location on the server for WebDAV management and verify access to that location with some WebDAV-capable tool, or browse to it in *Windows Explorer*, which knows how to access WebDAV locations (as of Windows 2000), or access it from a different system where *cadaver* or another WebDAV tool is available.

To enable your server for WebDAV operations, you need to add at least two directives to your *ServerRoot/conf/httpd.conf* file. The first identifies the location of the locking database used by *mod_dav* to keep WebDAV operations from interfering with each other; it needs to be in a directory that is writable by the server. For example:

```
C:\Apache-1.3>mkdir var
```

Now add the following lines to your *httpd.conf* file to enable WebDAV:

```
<IfModule mod_dav.c>
    DAVLockDB "C:/Apache-1.3/var/dav-lock"
</IfModule>
```

Create a temporary directory for testing *mod_dav*'s ability to function:

```
C:\Apache-1.3>mkdir htdocs\dav-test
```

Modify the <*IfModule*> container to enable WebDAV operations for this test directory:

```
<IfModule mod_dav.c>
    DAVLockDB "C:/Apache-1.3/var/dav-lock"
    <Directory "C:/Apache-1.3/htdocs/dav-test">
        DAV On
    </Directory>
</IfModule>
```

Now restart your server and try accessing the */dav-test* location with a WebDAV client. If you're using *cadaver* from another system, see Recipe 2.2 for detailed instructions. If you want to use *Windows Explorer* to test *mod_dav*, read the following section.

Using Windows Explorer to test mod_dav

After enabling the *htdocs\dav-test* directory for WebDAV operations and restarting your server, start up *Windows Explorer*. Follow the steps below to access the directory using WebDAV. This can be done on the local system or on another Windows system that can access your server system.

1. Click on Network Places.
2. In the righthand pane of the *Windows Explorer* window, you should see an item named "Add Network Place." Double-click on this item.
3. When prompted for a location, enter:

   ```
   http://127.0.0.1/dav-test/
   ```

   If you are executing these steps on a different system, replace the 127.0.0.1 with the correct name of the server on which you installed *mod_dav*.
4. After clicking on Next, give this location any name you like or keep the default.
5. After completing the dialog, *Windows Explorer* should open a new window with the name you selected in the previous step. The window should be empty, which makes sense because the directory is.
6. In the main *Windows Explorer* window, navigate to a directory (any directory) with files in it.
7. Ctrl-drag a file (any file) from the main *Windows Explorer* window to the window that was opened by step 5.
8. Windows should briefly display a progress dialog window, and then the file should appear in the destination window.

Congratulations! The file was uploaded to your Web server using WebDAV.

After your testing is complete, don't forget to remove the *htdocs\dav-test* directory and the *<Directory "C:/Apache-1.3/htdocs/dav-test">* stanza in your configuration file, or else anyone can upload files to your server.

See Also

- Recipe 6.18
- *http://webdav.org/mod_dav/*

2.4 Installing mod_perl on a Unixish System

Problem

You want to install the *mod_perl* scripting module to allow better Perl script performance and easy integration with the Web server.

Solution

For Apache 1.3, download and unpack the *mod_perl* 1.0 source package from *http://perl.apache.org/*. Then use the following command:

```
% perl Makefile.PL \
>     USE_APXS=1 \
>     WITH_APXS=/usr/local/apache/bin/apxs \
>     EVERYTHING=1 \
>     PERL_USELARGEFILES=0
% make
% make install
```

Restart your server.

For Apache 2.0 and later, the process is similar. Download and unpack the *mod_perl* 2.0 source package, then use the following command:

```
% perl Makefile.PL MP_APXS=/usr/local/apach2/bin/apxs
```

Discussion

The *mod_perl* source package is quite a complex module, and there are several different ways to add it to your server. This recipe is the fastest and lowest-impact one; if it doesn't suit your needs, check the various *README.** files in the package directory after unpacking. Because its primary language is Perl rather than C, the installation instructions are significantly different from those for most other modules.

Once you have restarted your server successfully, *mod_perl* should be available and configured as part of it. You can test it by making some changes to the *httpd.conf* file, adding a few scripts, and seeing whether the server processes them correctly. Here is a sample set of steps to test *mod_perl*'s operation:

1. Create a directory where your *mod_perl* scripts can live:

```
# cd ServerRoot
# mkdir lib lib/perl lib/perl/Apache
```

2. Create a file named *startup.pl* in your server's *conf/* directory that will give *mod_perl* some startup instructions:

```
#! /usr/bin/perl
BEGIN {
    use Apache ( );
    use lib Apache->server_root_relative('lib/perl');
}
use Apache::Registry ( );
use Apache::Constants ( );
use CGI qw(-compile :all);
use CGI::Carp ( );
1;
```

3. Next, create the *lib/perl/Apache/HelloWorld.pm* file that will be used for our test:

```
package Apache::HelloWorld;
use strict;
use Apache::Constants qw(:common);
sub handler {
    my $r = shift;
    $r->content_type('text/plain; charset=ISO-8859-1');
    $r->send_http_header;
    $r->print("Hello, world!  Love, mod_perl.\n");
    return OK;
}
1;
```

4. Next, edit the server's configuration file to add the directives that will enable *mod_perl* to locate all the pieces it needs, and tell it when to invoke the test script. Add the following lines to the *httpd.conf* file:

```
<IfModule mod_perl.c>
    PerlRequire conf/startup.pl
    <Location /mod_perl/howdy>
        SetHandler perl-script
        PerlHandler Apache::HelloWorld
    </Location>
</IfModule>
```

5. Now restart your server and then request the script using *http://localhost/mod_perl/howdy*.

If your configuration is valid, the response should be a page containing simply the words, "Hello, world! Love, mod_perl."

See Also

- *http://perl.apache.org*
- *Writing Apache Modules with Perl and C* by Doug MacEachern and Lincoln Stein (O'Reilly)

- *mod_perl Developer's Cookbook* by Geoffrey Young, Paul Lindner, and Randy Kobes (Sams)

2.5 Installing mod_php on a Unixish System

Problem

You want to add the *mod_php* scripting module to your existing Apache Web server.

Solution

Download the *mod_php* package source from the Web site at *http://php.net* (follow the links for downloading) and unpack it. Then:

```
% cd php-5.2.3
% ./configure \
>     --with-apxs2=/usr/local/apache/bin/apxs
% make
# make install
```

Restart the server.

Discussion

To test that your installation was successful, create a file named *info.php* in your server's *DocumentRoot*; the file should contain the single line:

```
<?php phpinfo(); ?>
```

Add the following lines to your server's *httpd.conf* file:

```
<IfModule mod_php4.c>
    AddHandler application/x-httpd-php .php
</IfModule>
```

After restarting your server, try fetching the document *info.php* using a browser. You should see a detailed description of the PHP options that are active. If you do, indicating a successful installation, remove the *info.php* file.

There are numerous additional options and extensions available for PHP; the recipe given here is only for the most basic installation.

See Also

- Recipe 8.16
- Recipe 8.17
- *http://php.net*

2.6 Installing mod_php on Windows

Problem

You want to add the *mod_php* scripting module to your existing Apache server on Windows.

Solution

This recipe needs to be described largely in terms of actions rather than explicit commands to be issued.

1. Download the PHP Windows binary *.zip* file with API extensions (not the *.exe* file) from *http://php.net*.

2. Unpack the *.zip* file into a directory where you can keep its contents indefinitely (such as *C:\PHP4*). If you use *WinZip*, be sure to select the *Use folder names* checkbox to preserve the directory structure inside the *.zip* file.

3. Copy the *PHP4\SAPI\php4apache.dll* file to the *\modules* directory under your Apache installation's *ServerRoot*.

4. In a command-prompt window, change to the *PHP4* directory where you unpacked the *.zip* file, and type:

   ```
   ...\PHP4>copy php.ini-dist %SYSTEMROOT%\php.ini
   ...\PHP4>copy php4ts.dll %SYSTEMROOT%
   ```

   (If installing on Windows 95 or Windows 98, use `%WINDOWS%` instead of `%SYSTEMROOT%`.)

5. Edit the *%SYSTEMROOT%\php.ini* file, locate the line that starts with `extensions_dir`, and change the value to point to the *PHP4\extensions* directory. For instance, if you unpacked the *.zip* file into *C:\PHP4*, this line should look like:

   ```
   extensions_dir = C:\PHP4\extensions
   ```

6. Edit the *conf\httpd.conf* file under the Apache *ServerRoot* and add the following lines near the other *LoadModule* lines:

   ```
   LoadModule php4_module modules/php4apache.dll
   ```

   Add the following lines in some scope where they will apply to your *.php* files:

   ```
   <IfModule mod_php4.c>
       AddType application/x-httpd-php .php
   </IfModule>
   ```

7. Restart the Apache server, and the PHP module should be active.

Discussion

The PHP module installation on Windows requires a lot of nitpicky manual steps. To test that your installation was successful, create a file named *info.php* in your server's *DocumentRoot*; the file should contain the single line:

```
<?php phpinfo(); ?>
```

After restarting your server, try fetching the document *info.php* from it using a browser. You should see a detailed description of the PHP options that are active.

There are numerous additional options and extensions available for PHP; the recipe given here is only the most basic installation. See the *install.txt* file in the *PHP4* directory and the documentation on the Web site for more details.

See Also

- *http://php.net*

2.7 Installing mod_ssl

Problem

You want to add SSL support to your Apache server with the *mod_ssl* secure HTTP module.

Solution

Windows

There is a discussion of installing SSL on Windows in Recipe 7.2, but the short form is, you should get XAMPP from ApacheFriends.org, unless you are very experienced with building source code on the Microsoft Windows platform.

Apache 2.0

mod_ssl is included with 2.0, although it is not automatically compiled nor installed when you build from source. You need to include the **--enable-ssl** option on your *./configure* line, and enable it with *LoadModule* and *AddModule* directives.

Apache 1.3

To install *mod_ssl* on a Unixish system, download the tarball package from the *http://www.modssl.org* Web site and unpack it. Then:

```
% cd mod_ssl-2.8.14-1.3.27
% ./configure \
>     --with-apache=../apache_1.3.27 \
>     --with-ssl=SYSTEM \
>     --prefix=/usr/local/apache
% cd ../apache_1.3.27
% make
% make certificate
```

Discussion

The *mod_ssl* package requires source-level changes to the base Apache code, and so the version of the *mod_ssl* package you install must match the version of the Apache distribution you have. If your Apache installation doesn't include the source, such as if you installed a binary-only RPM or other vendor distribution, you won't be able to add *mod_ssl* to it.

In addition to the Apache source, *mod_ssl* requires that you have Perl and the OpenSSL libraries installed. The `--with-ssl` option on the build configuration statement indicates where this is located; if it is in a vendor-distributed directory, the special keyword `SYSTEM` tells the build to look for it, and you don't have to find it yourself.

Unlike most other Apache modules, when adding *mod_ssl* you run the *./configure* script that's in *mod_ssl*'s directory, rather than the one in the Apache source directory; the module's script makes changes to Apache's and then invokes it directly.

This recipe is the bare basics; there are many optional components and features that *mod_ssl* allows you to specify at configuration time. For more information, consult the *README* and *INSTALL* files in the *mod_ssl* source directory, or the *mod_ssl* Web site at *http://www.modssl.org*.

See Also

- Recipe 7.3
- *http://www.modssl.org*

2.8 Finding Modules Using modules.apache.org

Problem

You're looking for Apache modules with a particular functionality, or by name, and you've heard about the Apache Module Registry.

Solution

Visit *http://modules.apache.org* and search for keywords related to the functionality you want, or portions of the module name.

Discussion

The Apache modules registry is an unofficial site at which module authors can voluntarily register their work for easy location.

By no means are all third-party modules registered on this site; many are on SourceForge or on their authors' home systems. If you don't find what you're looking for at *http://modules.apache.org*, try SourceForge (*http://sourceforge.net*), FreshMeat (*http://freshmeat.net*), or just search the Web with Google or the search engine of your choice.

See Also

- *http://sourceforge.net*
- *http://freshmeat.net*

2.9 Installing mod_security

Problem

You want to install the *mod_security* module to take advantage of its simple and powerful filtering mechanisms.

Solution

1. Download *mod_security* and the core rules from *http://modsecurity.org/download*.

   After downloading, you should verify the PGP signature to make sure the file hasn't been altered. See the *mod_security* Web site for details.

2. Unpack the kit (not the rules) into a working directory:

   ```
   % cd /usr/local/build
   % tar xzf /usr/local/kits/modsecurity-apache_2.1.1
   ```

3. Move into the unpacked directory, and build the package using the supplied *Makefile*. Specify the value of your *ServerRoot* on the *make* command line:

   ```
   % cd /usr/local/build/modsecurity-apache_2.1.1/apache2
   % make top_dir=/usr/local/apache2
   # make top_dir=/usr/local/apache2 install
   ```

   Unlike many other third-party modules, *mod_security* needs to be built using its own mechanism rather than a simple invocation of Apache's *apxs* tool.

4. Unpack the core rules into a subdirectory under your *ServerRoot*:

   ```
   # cd /usr/local/apache2/conf
   # mkdir mod_security
   ```

```
# cd mod_security
# tar xzf /tmp/modsecurity-core-rules_2.1-1.4.tar.gz
```

5. Edit your *httpd.conf* file to add the following lines in the appropriate places:

   ```
   LoadModule security_module modules/mod_security2.so

   Include conf/mod_security/*.conf
   ```

6. Restart your server.

Discussion

The *Makefile* included with the *mod_security* package will do the building of the module and put it in the right place, but activating it in your server is your responsibility. Recent versions of the package include a set of core rules for handling things like blog spam and common attacks, and the rules are also available as a separate tarball, which may or may not be updated more frequently than the ones bundled with the software.

The current version of *mod_security* only supports version 2 of the Apache Web server. There is an older version that supports the 1.3 versions, but it is unlikely to be maintained for long.

See Also

- The *mod_security* Web site at *http://modsecurity.org*

2.10 Why Won't This Module Work?

Problem

You are trying to install a third-party module, but the Apache Web server refuses to recognize it.

Solution

Consult the sources for the module, or its documentation, or ask the author, in order to determine which version of Apache the package supports.

Discussion

As significant changes are made to the Apache Web server, sometimes compatibility suffers as the API is changed. Although efforts are made to keep this sort of thing to a minimum, sometimes it is unavoidable.

To keep an incompatible module from being loaded and crashing the Web server when used, both modules and the server have a built-in "magic" number that is recorded when they're built, and that relates to the version of the API. When the server tries to load a module DSO, it compares the module's magic number with the server's own, and if they aren't compatible, the server refuses to load it.

The development team tries to keep the magic number compatibility within major version numbers, but not across them. That is, a module built for Apache 1.3 *should* work with almost any 1.3 version of the server built after the module was, but it definitely won't work with a 2.0 server. Contrariwise, a 2.0 module won't work with a 1.3 server under any circumstances.

See Also

- The Apache Modules Registry at *http://modules.apache.org*

## CHAPTER 3

Logging

Apache can, and usually does, record information about every request it processes. Controlling how this is done and extracting useful information out of these logs after the fact is at least as important as gathering the information in the first place.

The logfiles may record two types of data: information about the request itself, and possibly one or more messages about abnormal conditions encountered during processing (such as file permissions). You, as the Webmaster, have a limited amount of control over the logging of error conditions, but a great deal of control over the format and amount of information logged about request processing (*activity logging*). The server may log activity information about a request in multiple formats in multiple logfiles, but it will only record a single copy of an error message.

One aspect of activity logging you should be aware of is that the log entry is formatted and written *after* the request has been completely processed. This means that the interval between the time a request begins and when it finishes may be long enough to make a difference.

For example, if your logfiles are rotated while a particularly large file is being downloaded, the log entry for the request will appear in the new logfile when the request completes, rather than in the old logfile when the request was started. In contrast, an error message is written to the error log as soon as it is encountered.

The Web server will continue to record information in its logfiles as long as it's running. This can result in extremely large logfiles for a busy site and uncomfortably large ones even for a modest site. To keep the file sizes from growing ever larger, most sites rotate or *roll over* their logfiles on a semi-regular basis. Rolling over a logfile simply means persuading the server to stop writing to the current file and start recording to a new one. Because of Apache's determination to see that no records are lost, cajoling it to do this according to a specific timetable may require a bit of effort; some of the recipes in this chapter cover how to accomplish the task successfully and reliably (see Recipes 3.8 and 3.9).

The log declaration directives, *CustomLog* and *ErrorLog*, can appear inside *<VirtualHost>* containers, outside them (in what's called the *main* or *global server*, or sometimes the *global scope*), or both. Entries will only be logged in one set or the other; if a *<VirtualHost>* container applies to the request or error and has an applicable log directive, the message will be written only there and won't appear in any globally declared files. By contrast if no *<VirtualHost>* log directive applies, the server will fall back on logging the entry according to the global directives.

However, whichever scope is used for determining what logging directives to use, all *CustomLog* directives in that scope are processed and treated independently. That is, if you have a *CustomLog* directive in the global scope and two inside a *<VirtualHost>* container, *both* of these will be used. Similarly, if a *CustomLog* directive uses the env= option, it has no effect on what requests will be logged by other *CustomLog* directives in the same scope.

Activity logging has been around since the Web first appeared, and it didn't take long for the original users to decide what items of information they wanted logged. The result is called the *common log format* (CLF). In Apache terms, this format is:

```
"%h %l %u %t \"%r\" %>s %b"
```

That is, it logs the client's hostname or IP address, the name of the user on the client (as defined by RFC 1413 and if Apache has been told to snoop for it with an *IdentityCheck On* directive), the username with which the client authenticated (if weak access controls are being imposed by the server), the time at which the request was received, the actual HTTP request line, the final status of the server's processing of the request, and the number of bytes of content that were sent in the server's response.

Before long, as the HTTP protocol advanced, the common log format was found to be wanting, so an enhanced format—called the *combined log format*—was created:

```
"%h %l %u %t \"%r\" %>s %b \"%{Referer}i\" \"%{User-agent}i\""
```

The two additions were the Referer (it's spelled incorrectly in the specifications) and the User-agent. These are the URL of the page that linked to the document being requested, and the name and version of the browser or other client software making the request.

Both of these formats are widely used, and many logfile analysis tools assume log entries are made in one or the other.

The Apache Web server's standard activity logging module allows you to create your own formats; it is highly configurable and is called (surprise!) *mod_log_config*. Apache 2.0 has an additional module, *mod_logio*, which enhances *mod_log_config* with the ability to log the number of bytes actually transmitted or received over the network. If these don't meet your requirements, though, there are a significant number of third-party modules available from the module registry at *http://modules.apache.org/*.

The status code entry in the common and combined log formats deserves some mention because its meaning is not immediately clear. The status codes are defined by the HTTP protocol specification documents (currently RFC 2616, which you can access by going to *ftp://ftp.isi.edu/in-notes/rfc2616.txt*). Table 3-1 gives a brief description of the codes defined in the HTTP specification at the time of this writing; other specifications (such as that for WebDAV) define additional staus conditions, but we're not going to include them here because they're more advanced and there are lots of them.

Table 3-1. HTTP status codes

Code	Abstract
Informational 1xx	
100	Continue
101	Switching protocols
Successful 2xx	
200	OK
201	Created
202	Accepted
203	Nonauthoritative information
204	No content
205	Reset content
206	Partial content
Redirection 3xx	
300	Multiple choices
301	Moved permanently
302	Found
303	See other
304	Not modified
305	Use proxy
306	(Unused)
307	Temporary redirect
Client error 4xx	
400	Bad request
401	Unauthorized
402	Payment required
403	Forbidden
404	Not found
405	Method not allowed
406	Not acceptable
407	Proxy authentication required
408	Request timeout

Code	Abstract
409	Conflict
410	Gone
411	Length required
412	Precondition failed
413	Request entity too large
414	Request-URI too long
415	Unsupported media type
416	Requested range not satisfiable
417	Expectation failed
Server error 5xx	
500	Internal server error
501	Not implemented
502	Bad gateway
503	Service unavailable
504	Gateway timeout
505	HTTP version not supported

The one-line abstracts shown in Table 3-1 are sometimes terse to the point of being confusing, but they should at least give you an inkling of what the server thinks happened. The first digit is used to separate the codes into classes or categories; for example, all codes starting with 5 indicate there is a problem handling the request, and the server thinks the problem is on its end rather than on the client's end.

For a complete description of the various status codes, you'll need to read a document about the HTTP protocol or the RFC itself.

3.1 Getting More Details in Your Log Entries

Problem

You want to add a little more detail to your access log entries.

Solution

Use the *combined* log format, rather than the *common* log format:

```
CustomLog logs/access_log combined
```

Discussion

The default Apache logfile enables logging with the *common* log format, but it also provides the *combined* log format as a predefined *LogFormat* directive.

The *combined* log format offers two additional pieces of information not included in the *common* log format: the `Referer` (where the client linked from) and the `User-agent` (what browser they are using).

Every major logfile parsing software package is able to handle the *combined* format as well as the *common* format, and many of them give additional statistics based on these added fields. So you lose nothing by using this format and potentially gain some additional information.

See Also

- *http://httpd.apache.org/docs/2.1/mod/mod_log_config.html*
- *http://httpd.apache.org/docs/2.2/mod/mod_log_config.html*

3.2 Getting More Detailed Errors

Problem

You want more information in the error log in order to debug a problem.

Solution

Change (or add) the *LogLevel* line in your *httpd.conf* file. There are several possible arguments, which are enumerated here.

For example:

```
LogLevel Debug
```

Discussion

There are several hierarchical levels of error logging available, each identified by its own keyword. The default value of *LogLevel* is *warn*. Listed in descending order of importance, the possible values are:

emerg
:   Emergencies; Web server is unusable

alert
:   Action must be taken immediately

crit
:   Critical conditions

error
  Error conditions

warn
  Warning conditions

notice
  Normal but significant condition

info
  Informational

debug
  Debug-level messages

emerg results in the least information being recorded and debug in the most. However, at debug level a lot of information will probably be recorded that is unrelated to the issue you're investigating, so it's a good idea to revert to the previous setting when the problem is solved.

Even though the various logging levels are hierarchical in nature, one oddity is that notice level messages are *always* logged regardless of the setting of the *LogLevel* directive.

The severity levels are rather loosely defined and even more loosely applied. In other words, the severity at which a particular error condition gets logged is decided at the discretion of the developer who wrote the code—your opinion may differ.

Here are some sample messages of various severities:

```
[Thu Apr 18 01:37:40 2002] [alert] [client 64.152.75.26] /home/smith/public_html/
    test/.htaccess: Invalid command 'Test', perhaps mis-spelled or defined by a
    module not included in the server configuration
[Thu Apr 25 22:21:58 2002] [error] PHP Fatal error:  Call to undefined function:
    decode_url(  ) in /usr/apache/htdocs/foo.php on line 8
[Mon Apr 15 09:31:37 2002] [warn] pid file /usr/apache/logs/httpd.pid overwritten --
    Unclean shutdown of previous Apache run?
[Mon Apr 15 09:31:38 2002] [info] Server built: Apr 12 2002 09:14:06
[Mon Apr 15 09:31:38 2002] [notice] Accept mutex: sysvsem (Default: sysvsem)
```

These are fairly normal messages that you might encounter on a production Web server. If you set the logging level to Debug, however, you might see many more messages of cryptic import, such as:

```
[Thu Mar 28 10:29:50 2002] [debug] proxy_cache.c(992): No CacheRoot, so no caching.
    Declining.
[Thu Mar 28 10:29:50 2002] [debug] proxy_http.c(540): Content-Type: text/html
```

These are exactly what they seem to be: debugging messages intended to help an Apache developer figure out what the proxy module is doing.

See Also

At the time of this writing, there is an effort underway to provide a dictionary of Apache error messages, what they mean, and what to do about the conditions they report, but it doesn't have anything concrete to show at this point. When it does, it should be announced at the Apache server developer site:

http://httpd.apache.org/dev

It will be mentioned on this book's companion Web site, as well:

http://apache-cookbook.com

In addition, see the detailed documentation of the *LogLevel* directive at the Apache site:

http://httpd.apache.org/docs/2.2/mod/core.html#loglevel

3.3 Logging POST Contents

Problem

You want to record data submitted with the POST method, such as from a web form.

Solution

Ensure that *mod_dumpio* is installed and enabled, and put the following in your configuration file:

```
# DumpIOLogLevel notice - 2.3.x and later
LogLevel debug
DumpIOInput On
```

Or, with *mod_security*:

```
SecAuditLogType Concurrent
SecAuditLogStorageDir /var/www/audit_log/data/
SecAuditLog /var/www/audit_log/index
SecAuditLogParts ABCFHZ
```

Discussion

mod_dumpio is a new module in Apache 2.0 (that is to say, it's not available for Apache 1.3) that allows the complete input and output of each HTTP transaction to be logged. In the example above, we're enabling input logging only, using the *DumpIOInput* directive.

On Apache 2.0 and 2.2, *LogLevel* needs to be set to *debug* in order for these records to be logged. In 2.3 and later, there's a new directive *DumpIOLogLevel* that allows you to set the *LogLevel* at which the entries will be logged. For example, if you set *DumpIOLogLevel* to *notice*, then these entries will be logged when *LogLevel* is set to *notice* or higher.

Log entries for POST data will look like:

```
[Sun Feb 11 16:49:27 2007] [debug] mod_dumpio.c(51): mod_dumpio:

dumpio_in (data-HEAP): 11 bytes
[Sun Feb 11 16:49:27 2007] [debug] mod_dumpio.c(67): mod_dumpio:

dumpio_in (data-HEAP): foo=example
```

In the log entry shown here, the form value *foo* was set to *example*.

The output from *mod_dumpio* is very noisy. A typical request may generate somewhere between 30 and 50 lines of log entries. The entry shown here is just a tiny part of what was logged with the *POST*.

mod_security also permits the logging of request data. In the *mod_security* configuration shown in the recipe above, a logfile is created containing all available request headers, and the request body itself.

See Also

- *http://modsecurity.org*
- *http://httpd.apache.org/docs/2.2/mod/mod_dumpio.html*

3.4 Logging a Proxied Client's IP Address

Problem

You want to log the IP address of the actual client requesting your pages, even if they're being requested through a proxy.

Solution

None.

Discussion

Unfortunately, the HTTP protocol itself prevents this from being possible. From the client side, proxies are intended to be completely transparent; from the side of the origin server, where the content actually resides, they are meant to be almost utterly opaque, concealing the identity of a request.

Your best option is to log the IP address from which the request came. If it came directly from a browser, it will be the client's address; if it came through one or more proxy servers, it will be the address of the one that actually contacts your server.

Both the `combined` and `common` log formats include the `%h` format effector, which represents the (remote) client's identity. However, this may be a hostname rather than an address, depending on the setting of your *HostNameLookups* directive, among other things. If you always want the client's IP address to be included in your logfile, use the %a effector instead.

See Also

- The HTTP protocol specification at *ftp://ftp.isi.edu/in-notes/rfc2616.txt*

3.5 Logging Client MAC Addresses

Problem

You want to record the MAC (hardware) address of clients that access your server.

Solution

This cannot be logged reliably in most network situations and not by Apache at all.

Discussion

The MAC address is not meaningful except on local area networks (LANs) and is not available in wide area network transactions. When a network packet goes through a router, such as when leaving a LAN, the router will typically rewrite the MAC address field with the router's hardware address.

See Also

- The TCP/IP protocol specifications (see *http://www.rfc-editor.org/cgi-bin/ rfcsearch.pl* and search for "TCP" in the title field)

3.6 Logging Cookies

Problem

You want to record all the cookies sent to your server by clients and all the cookies your server asks clients to set in their databases; this can be useful when debugging Web applications that use cookies.

Solution

To log cookies received from the client:

```
CustomLog logs/cookies_in.log "%{UNIQUE_ID}e %{Cookie}i"
CustomLog logs/cookies2_in.log "%{UNIQUE_ID}e %{Cookie2}i"
```

To log cookie values set and sent by the server to the client:

```
CustomLog logs/cookies_out.log "%{UNIQUE_ID}e %{Set-Cookie}o"
CustomLog logs/cookies2_out.log "%{UNIQUE_ID}e %{Set-Cookie2}o"
```

In versions before to 2.0.56, using the %{Set-Cookie}o format effector for debugging is not recommended if multiple cookies are (or may be) involved. Only the first one will be recorded in the logfile. See the Discussion text for an example.

Discussion

Cookie fields tend to be very long and complex, so the previous statements will create separate files for logging them. The cookie log entries can be correlated against the client request access log using the server-set UNIQUE_ID environment variable (assuming that *mod_unique_id* is active in the server and that the activity log format includes the environment variable with a %{UNIQUE_ID}e format effector).

At the time of this writing, the Cookie and Set-Cookie header fields are most commonly used. The Cookie2 and corresponding Set-Cookie2 fields are newer and have been designed to correct some of the shortcomings in the original specifications, but they haven't yet achieved much penetration.

Because of the manner in which the syntax of the cookie header fields has changed over time, these logging instructions may or may not capture the complete details of the cookies.

Bear in mind that these logging directives will record all cookies, and not just the ones in which you may be particularly interested. For example, here is the log entry for a client request that included two cookies, one named RFC2109-1 and one named RFC2109-2:

```
PNCSUsCoF2UAACI3CZs RFC2109-1="This is an old-style cookie, with space characters
    embedded"; RFC2109-2=This_is_a_normal_old-style_cookie
```

Even though there's only one log entry, it contains information about two cookies.

On the cookie-setting side, here are the Set-Cookie header fields sent by the server in its response header:

```
Set-Cookie: RFC2109-1="This is an old-style cookie, with space characters embedded";
    Version=1; Path=/; Max-Age=60; Comment="RFC2109 demonstration cookie"
Set-Cookie: RFC2109-2=This_is_a_normal_old-style_cookie; Version=1; Path=/; Max-
    Age=60; Comment="RFC2109 demonstration cookie"
```

And here's the corresponding log entry for the response (this was all one line in the logfile, so line wrapping was added to make it all fit on the page):

```
eCF1vsCoF2UAAHB1DMIAAAAA RFC2109-1=\"This is an old-style cookie, with space
    characters embedded\"; Version=1; Path=/; Max-Age=60; Comment=\"RFC2109
    demonstration cookie\", RFC2109-2=This_is_a_normal_old-style_cookie;
    Version=1; Path=/; Max-Age=60; Comment=\"RFC2109 demonstration cookie\"
```

 Before version 2.0.56, Apache *httpd* didn't log multiple cookies correctly; it would only log one.

See Also

- RFC 2109, "*HTTP State Management Mechanism*" (IETF definition of Cookie and Set-Cookie header fields) at *ftp://ftp.isi.edu/in-notes/rfc2109.txt*

- RFC 2965, "*HTTP State Management Mechanism*" (IETF definition of Cookie2 and Set-Cookie2 header fields) at *ftp://ftp.isi.edu/in-notes/rfc2965.txt*

- The original Netscape cookie proposal at *http://home.netscape.com/newsref/std/cookie_spec.html*

3.7 Not Logging Image Requests from Local Pages

Problem

You want to log requests for images on your site, except when they're requests from one of your own pages. You might want to do this to keep your logfile size down, or possibly to track down sites that are hijacking your artwork and using it to adorn their pages.

Solution

Use *SetEnvIfNoCase* to restrict logging to only those requests from outside of your site:

```
<FilesMatch \.(jpg|gif|png)$>
    SetEnvIfNoCase Referer "^http://www.example.com/" local_referrer=1
</FilesMatch>
CustomLog logs/access_log combined env=!local_referrer
```

Discussion

In many cases, documents on a Web server include references to images also kept on the server, but the only item of real interest for log analysis is the referencing page itself. How can you keep the server from logging all the requests for the images that happen when such a local page is accessed?

The *SetEnvIfNoCase* will set an environment variable if the page that linked to the image is from the *www.example.com* site (obviously, you should replace that site name with your own) and the request is for a GIF, PNG, or JPEG image.

 SetEnvIfNoCase is the same as *SetEnvIf* except that variable comparisons are done in a case-insensitive manner.

The *CustomLog* directive will log all requests that do not have that environment variable set, i.e., everything except requests for images that come from links on your own pages.

This recipe only works for clients that actually report the referring page. Some people regard the URL of the referring page to be no business of anyone but themselves, and some clients permit the user to select whether to include this information or not. There are also "anonymizing" sites on the Internet that act as proxies and conceal this information.

See Also

- Recipe 6.5

3.8 Rotating Logfiles at a Particular Time

Problem

You want to automatically roll over the Apache logs at specific times without having to shut down and restart the server.

Solution

Use *CustomLog* and the *rotatelogs* program:

```
CustomLog "| /path/to/rotatelogs /path/to/logs/access_log.%Y-%m-%d 86400" combined
```

Discussion

The *rotatelogs* script is designed to use an Apache feature called *piped logging*, which is just a fancy name for sending log output to another program rather than to a file. By inserting the *rotatelogs* script between the Web server and the actual logfiles on disk, you can avoid having to restart the server to create new files; the script automatically opens a new file at the designated time and starts writing to it.

The first argument to the *rotatelogs* script is the base name of the file to which records should be logged. If it contains one or more % characters, it will be treated as a strftime(3) format string; otherwise, the rollover time (in seconds since 1 January 1970), in the form of a 10-digit number, will be appended to the base name. For example, a base name of foo would result in logfile names like *foo.1020297600*, whereas a base name of foo.%Y-%m-%d would cause the logfiles to be named something like *foo. 2002-04-29*.

The second argument is the interval (in seconds) between rollovers. Rollovers will occur whenever the system time is a multiple of this value. For instance, a 24-hour day contains 86,400 seconds; if you specify a rollover interval of 86400, a new logfile will be created every night at midnight—when the system time, which is based at representing midnight on 1 January 1970, is a multiple of 24 hours.

Note that the rollover interval is in actual clock seconds elapsed, so when time changes because of daylight savings, this does not in any way affect the interval between rollovers.

See Also

- The *rotatelogs* manpage; try:

```
% man -M /path/to/ServerRoot/man rotatelogs.8
```

replacing the */path/to/ServerRoot* with the actual value of your installation's *ServerRoot* directive in *httpd.conf* or view the documentation online at *http:// httpd.apache.org/docs/2.2/programs/rotatelogs.html*

3.9 Rotating Logs on the First of the Month

Problem

You want to close the previous month's logs and open new ones on the first of each month.

Solution

The Apache distribution doesn't come with a script that does this, but there is a free program that provides this and many other useful features. It is called Cronolog, and may be obtained from *http://cronolog.org*.

Obtain and install Cronolog, and then place the following in your configuration file:

```
CustomLog "|/usr/bin/cronolog /www/logs/access%Y%m.log" combined
```

Discussion

Cronolog has been around for a long time, and provides many of the features that people wished were available in the standard *rotatelogs* utility. Over the years, *rotatelogs* has improved, but Cronolog has a number of other useful features that are of interest to sites with rapidly growing logfiles.

One of these is the ability to automatically rotate logfiles by day, week, month, or year, based on the format of the filename specified in the *CustomLog* directive.

In the example given, the logfile is rotated at the start of a new month, because the logfile name given contains only the year and month variables (%Y and %m, respectively).

See Also

- *http://httpd.apache.org/docs/logs.html#piped*

- *http://httpd.apache.org/docs/2.2/programs/rotatelogs.html*
- *http://cronolog.org*

3.10 Logging Hostnames Instead of IP Addresses

Problem

You want to see hostnames in your activity log instead of IP addresses.

Solution

You can let the Web server resolve the hostname when it processes the request by enabling runtime lookups with the Apache directive:

```
HostnameLookups On
```

Or you can let Apache use the IP address during normal processing and let a piped logging process resolve them as part of recording the entry:

```
HostnameLookups Off
CustomLog "| /path/to/logresolve -c >> /path/to/logs/access_log.resolved" combined
```

Or you can let Apache use and log the IP addresses, and resolve them later when analyzing the logfile. Add this to *http.conf*:

```
CustomLog /path/to/logs/access_log.raw combined
```

And analyze the log with:

```
% /path/to/logresolve -c < access_log.raw > access_log.resolved
```

Discussion

The Apache activity logging mechanism can record either the client's IP address or its hostname (or both). Logging the hostname directly requires that the server spend some time to perform a DNS lookup to turn the IP address (which it already has) into a hostname. This can have some serious impact on the server's performance, however, because it needs to consult the name service in order to turn the address into a name; and while a server child or thread is busy waiting for that, it isn't handling client requests. One alternative is to have the server record only the client's IP address and resolve the address to a name during logfile postprocessing and analysis. At the very least, defer it to a separate process that won't directly tie up the Web server with the resolution overhead.

In theory, this is an excellent choice; in practice, however, there are some pitfalls. For one thing, the *logresolve* application included with Apache (usually installed in the *bin/* subdirectory under the *ServerRoot*) will only resolve IP addresses that appear at the very beginning of the log entry, and so it's not very flexible if you want to use a nonstandard format for your logfile. For another, if too much time passes between the collection and resolution of the IP addresses, the DNS may have changed sufficiently so that misleading or incorrect results may be obtained. This is especially a problem with dynamically allocated IP addresses such as those issued by ISPs. Although, for these dynamically allocated IP addresses, the hostnames tend not to be particularly informative anyway.

An additional shortcoming becomes apparent if you feed your log records directly to *logresolve* through a pipe: as of Apache 1.3.24 at least, *logresolve* doesn't flush its output buffers immediately, so there's the possibility of lost data if the logging process or the system should crash.

In practice, however, all log analysis software provides hostname resolution functionality, and it generally makes most sense to use that functionality than trying to resolve the IP addresses in the logfile before that stage.

See Also

- The *logresolve* manpage:

    ```
    % man -M /path/to/ServerRoot/man/logresolve.8
    ```

- *http://httpd.apache.org/docs/2.2/programs/logresolve.html*

3.11 Maintaining Separate Logs for Each Virtual Host

Problem

You want to have separate activity logs for each of your virtual hosts, but you don't want to have all the open files that multiple *CustomLog* directives would use.

Solution

Use the *split-logfile* program that comes with Apache. To split logfiles after they've been rolled over (replace */path/to/ServerRoot* with the correct path):

```
# cd /path/to/ServerRoot
# mv logs/access_log logs/access_log.old
# bin/apachectl graceful
[wait for old logfile to be completely closed]
# cd logs
# ../bin/split-logfile < access_log.old
```

To split records to the appropriate files as they're written, add this line to your *httpd.conf* file:

```
CustomLog "| /path/to/split-logfile /usr/local/Apache/logs" combined
```

Discussion

In order for *split-logfile* to work, the logging format you're using must begin with "%v" (note the blank after the v). This inserts the name of the virtual host at the beginning of each log entry; *split-logfile* will use this to figure out to which file the entry should be written. The hostname will be removed from the record before it gets written.

There are two ways to split your access logfile: after it's been written, closed, and rolled over, or as the entries are actually being recorded. To split a closed logfile, just feed it into the *split-logfile* script. To split the entries into separate files as they're actually being written, modify your configuration to pipe the log messages directly to the script.

Each method has advantages and disadvantages. The rollover method requires twice as much disk space (for the unsplit log plus the split ones) and that you verify that the logfile is completely closed. (Unfortunately there is no guaranteed, simple way of doing this without actually shutting down the server or doing a graceless restart; it's entirely possible that a slow connection may keep the old logfile open for a considerable amount of time after a graceful restart.) Splitting as the entries are recorded is sensitive to the logging process dying—although Apache will automatically restart it, log messages waiting for it can pile up and constipate the server.

See Also

- Recipe 3.10

3.12 Logging Proxy Requests

Problem

You want to log requests that go through your proxy to a different file than the requests coming directly to your server.

Solution

Use the *SetEnv* directive to earmark those requests that came through the proxy server, in order to trigger conditional logging:

```
<Directory proxy:*>
    SetEnv is_proxied 1
</Directory>
CustomLog logs/proxy_log combined env=is_proxied
```

Or, for 2.x, use a *<Proxy>* block:

```
<Proxy *>
    SetEnv is_proxied 1
    </Proxy>
CustomLog logs/proxy_log combined env=is_proxied
```

Discussion

Apache 1.3 has a special syntax for the *<Directory>* directive, which applies specifically to requests passing through the proxy module. Although the * makes it appear that wildcards can be used to match documents, it's misleading; it isn't really a wildcard. You may either match explicit paths, such as *proxy:http://example.com/foo.html*, or use * to match *everything*. You cannot do something like *proxy:http://example.com/*.html*.

If you want to apply different directives to different proxied paths, you need to take advantage of another module. Because you're dealing with requests that are passing through your server rather than being handled by it directly (i.e., your server is a *proxy* rather than an *origin server*), you can't use *<Files>* or *<FilesMatch>* containers to apply directives to particular proxied documents. Nor can you use *<Location>* or *<LocationMatch>* stanzas because they can't appear inside a *<Directory>* container. You can, however, use *mod_rewrite*'s capabilities to make decisions based on the path of the requested document. For instance, you can log proxied requests for images in a separate file with something like this:

```
<Directory proxy:*>
    RewriteEngine On
    RewriteRule "\.(gif|png|jpg)$" "-" [ENV=proxied_image:1]
    RewriteCond "%{ENV:proxied_image}" "!1"
    RewriteRule "^" "-" [ENV=proxied_other:1]
</Directory>
CustomLog logs/proxy_image_log combined env=proxied_image
CustomLog logs/proxy_other_log combined env=proxied_other
```

Directives in the *<Directory proxy:*>* container will only apply to requests going through your server. The first *RewriteRule* directive sets an environment variable if the requested document ends in *.gif*, *.png*, or *.jpg*. The *RewriteCond* directive tests to see if that envariable isn't set, and the following *RewriteRule* will set a different envariable if so. The two *CustomLog* directives send the different types of requests to different logfiles according to the environment variables.

See Also

- The *mod_rewrite* and *mod_log_config* documentation

3.13 Logging Errors for Virtual Hosts to Multiple Files

Problem

Unlike access logs, Apache only logs errors to a single location. You want Apache to log errors that refer to a particular virtual host to the host's error log, as well as to the global error log.

Solution

There are at least two possible ways of doing this:

1. Use piped logging to send entries to a custom script that will copy and direct error messages to the appropriate files.
2. Use piped logging to duplicate log entries:

```
ErrorLog "| tee logfile1 | tee logfile2 > logfile3"
```

Discussion

Unlike activity logs, Apache will log error messages only to a single location. If the error is related to a particular virtual host and this host's *<VirtualHost>* container includes an *ErrorLog* entry, the error will be logged only in this file, and it won't appear in any global error log. If the *<VirtualHost>* does not specify an *ErrorLog* directive, the error will be logged only to the global error log. (The global error log is the last *ErrorLog* directive encountered that isn't in a *<VirtualHost>* container.)

Currently, the only workaround to this is to have the necessary duplication performed by a separate process (i.e., by using piped logging to send the error messages to the process as they occur). Of the two solutions given earlier, the first, which involves a custom script you develop yourself, has the most flexibility. If all you want is simply duplication of entries, the second solution is simpler but requires that your platform have a *tee* program (Windows does not). It also may be subject to lagging messages if your *tee* program doesn't flush its buffers after each record it receives. This could also lead to lost messages if the pipe breaks or the system crashes.

An alternate approach may be to send the error log to syslog, and then have your syslog server log entries to multiple places.

See Also

- *http://httpd.apache.org/docs/logs.html#piped*

3.14 Logging Server IP Addresses

Problem

You want to log the IP address of the server that responds to a request, possibly because you have virtual hosts with multiple addresses each.

Solution

Use the %A format effector in a *LogFormat* or *CustomLog* directive:

```
CustomLog logs/served-by.log "%A"
```

Discussion

The %A effector signals the activity logging system to insert the local IP address—that is, the address of the server—into the log record at the specified point. This can be useful when your server handles multiple IP addresses. For example, you might have a configuration that includes elements such as the following:

```
Listen 10.0.0.42
Listen 192.168.19.243
Listen 263.41.0.80
<VirtualHost 192.168.19.243>
    ServerName Private.Example.Com
</VirtualHost>
<VirtualHost 10.0.0.42 263.41.0.80>
    ServerName Foo.Example.Com
    ServerAlias Bar.Example.Com
</VirtualHost>
```

This might be meaningful if you want internal users to access *Foo.Example.Com* using the 10.0.0.42 address rather than the one published to the rest of the network (such as to segregate internal from external traffic over the network cards). The second virtual host is going to receive requests aimed at both addresses even though it has only one *ServerName*; using the %A effector in your log format can help you determine how many hits on the site are coming in over each network interface.

See Also

- The *mod_log_config* documentation

3.15 Logging the Referring Page

Problem

You want to record the URL of pages that refer clients to yours, perhaps to find out how people are reaching your site.

Solution

Add the following effector to your activity log format:

```
%{Referer}i
```

Discussion

One of the fields that a request header may include is called the `Referer`. `Referer` is the URL of the page that linked to the current request. For example, if file *a.html* contains a link such as:

```
<a href="b.html">another page</a>
```

When the link is followed, the request header for *b.html* will contain a `Referer` field that has the URL of *a.html* as its value.

The *Referer* field is not required nor reliable; some users prefer software or anonymizing tools that ensure that you can't tell where they've been. However, this is usually a fairly small number and may be disregarded for most Web sites.

See Also

- Recipe 3.17
- Recipe 6.5

3.16 Logging the Name of the Browser Software

Problem

You want to know the software visitors use to access your site, for example, so you can optimize its appearance for the browser that most of your audience uses.

Solution

Add the following effector to your activity log format:

```
%{User-Agent}i
```

Discussion

Request headers often include a field called the `User-agent`. This is defined as the name and version of the client software being used to make the request. For instance, a `User-agent` field value might look like this:

```
User-Agent: Mozilla/4.77 [en] (X11; U; Linux 2.4.4-4GB i686)
```

This tells you that the client is claiming to be Netscape Navigator 4.77, run on a Linux system and using X-windows as its GUI.

The `User-agent` field is neither required nor reliable; many users prefer software or anonymizing tools that ensure that you can't tell what they're using. Some software even lies about itself so it can work around sites that cater specifically to one browser or another; users have this peculiar habit of thinking it's none of the Webmaster's business which browser they prefer. It's a good idea to design your site to be as browser-agnostic as possible for this reason, among others. If you're going to make decisions based on the value of the field, you might as well believe it hasn't been faked—because there's no way to tell if it has.

See Also

- Recipe 3.17

3.17 Logging Arbitrary Request Header Fields

Problem

You want to record the values of arbitrary fields clients send to their request header, perhaps to tune the types of content you have available to the needs of your visitors.

Solution

Use the %{...}i log format variable in your access log format declaration. For example, to log the Host header, you might use:

```
%{Host}i
```

Discussion

The HTTP request sent by a Web browser can be very complex, and if the client is a specialized application rather than a browser, it may insert additional metadata that's meaningful to the server. For instance, one useful request header field is the `Accept` field, which tells the server what kinds of content the client is capable of and willing to receive. Given a *CustomLog* line such as this:

```
CustomLog logs/accept_log "\"%{Accept}i\""
```

a resulting log entry might look like this:

```
PNb6VsCoF2UAAH1dAUo "text/html, image/png, image/jpeg, image/gif,
    image/x-xbitmap, */*"
```

This tells you that the client that made that request is explicitly ready to handle HTML pages and certain types of images, but, in a pinch, will take whatever the server gives it (indicated by the wildcard */* entry).

See Also

- Recipe 3.15
- Recipe 3.17

3.18 Logging Arbitrary Response Header Fields

Problem

You want to record the values of arbitrary fields the server has included in a response header, probably to debug a script or application.

Solution

Use the %{...}o log format variable in your access log format declaration. For example, to log the Last-Modified header, you would do the following:

```
%{Last-Modified}o
```

Discussion

The HTTP response sent by Apache when answering a request can be very complex, according to the server's configuration. Advanced scripts or application servers may add custom fields to the server's response, and knowing what values were set may be of great help when trying to track down an application problem.

Other than the fact that you're recording fields the server is *sending* rather than receiving, this recipe is analogous to Recipe 3.17 in this chapter; refer to that recipe for more details. The only difference in the syntax of the logging format effectors is that response fields are logged using an o effector, and request fields are logged using i.

See Also

- Recipe 3.17

3.19 Logging Activity to a MySQL Database

Problem

Rather than logging accesses to your server in flat text files, you want to log the information directly to a database for easier analysis.

Solution

Install the latest release of *mod_log_sql* from *http://www.outoforder.cc/projects/apache/mod_log_sql/* according to the modules directions (see Recipe 2.1), and then issue the following commands:

```
# mysqladmin create apache_log
# mysql apache_log < access_log.sql
# mysql apache_log
mysql> grant insert,create on apache_log.* to webserver@localhost identified by 'wwwpw';
```

Add the following lines to your *httpd.conf* file:

```
<IfModule mod_log_sql.c>
    LogSQLLoginInfo mysql://webserver:wwwpw@dbmachine.example.com/apache_log
    LogSQLCreateTables on
</IfModule>
```

Then, in your *VirtualHost* container, add the following log directive:

```
LogSQLTransferLogTable access_log
```

Discussion

Replace the values of *webserver* and *wwwpw* with a less guessable username and password when you run these commands.

Consult the documentation on the referenced Web site to ensure that the example here reflects the version of the module that you have installed, as the configuration syntax changed with the 2.0 release of the module.

See Also

- *http://www.outoforder.cc/projects/apache/mod_log_sql*

3.20 Logging to syslog

Problem

You want to send your log entries to syslog.

Solution

To log your error log to syslog, simply tell Apache to log to *syslog*:

```
ErrorLog syslog:user
```

 Some other *syslog* reporting class than `user`, such as `local1` might be more appropriate in your environment.

Logging your access log to syslog takes a little more work. Add the following to your configuration file:

```
CustomLog |/usr/local/apache/bin/apache_syslog combined
```

Where *apache_syslog* is a program that looks like the following:

```perl
#!/usr/bin/perl
use Sys::Syslog qw( :DEFAULT setlogsock );

setlogsock('unix');
openlog('apache', 'cons', 'pid', 'user');

while ($log = <STDIN>) {
    syslog('notice', $log);
}

closelog;
```

Discussion

There are several compelling reasons for logging to syslog. The first of these is to have many servers log to a central logging facility. The second is that there are many existing tools for monitoring syslog and sending appropriate notifications on certain events. Allow Apache to take advantage of these tools, and your particular installation may benefit. Also, in the event that your server is either compromised, or has some kind of catastrophic failure, having logfiles on a dfferent physical machine can be of enormous benefit in finding out what happened.

Apache supports logging your error log to syslog by default. This is by far the more useful log to handle this way, since syslog is typically used to track error conditions, rather than merely informational messages.

The syntax of the *ErrorLog* directive allows you to specify **syslog** as an argument, or to specify a particular syslog facility. In this example, the **user** syslog facility was specified. In your */etc/syslog.conf* file, you can specify where a particular log facility should be sent—whether to a file, or to a remote syslog server.

Because Apache does not support logging your access log to syslog by default, you need to accomplish this with a piped logfile directive. The program that we use to accomplish this is a simple Perl program using the *Sys::Syslog* module, which is a standard module with your Perl installation. Because the piped logfile handler is launched at server start-up, and merely accepts input on STDIN for the life of the server, there is no performance penalty for using Perl.

If you have several Web servers, and want to have all of them log to one central logfile, this can be accomplished by having all of your servers log to syslog, and pointing that syslog facility to a central syslog server. Note that this may cause your log entries to be in non-sequential order, which should not really matter, but may appear strange at first. This effect can be reduced by ensuring that your clocks are synchronized via NTP.

Consult your *syslogd* manual for further detail on setting up a networked syslog server.

Finally, depending on what particular operating system you are using, you may be able to use the *logger* utility to accomplish the same thing:

```
AccessLog "|/usr/bin/logger" combined
```

See Also

• The manages for *syslogd* and *syslog.conf*

3.21 Logging User Directories

Problem

You want each user directory Web site (i.e., those that are accessed via *http://server/ ~username*) to have its own logfile.

Solution

In *httpd.conf*, add the directive:

```
CustomLog "|/usr/local/apache/bin/userdir_log" combined
```

Then, in the file */usr/local/apache/bin/userdir_log*, place the following code:

```perl
#!/usr/bin/perl

my $L = '/usr/local/apache/logs'; # Log directory

my %is_open = (); # File handle cache
$|=1;
open(F, ">>$L/access_log"); # Default error log

while (my $log = <STDIN>) {
    if ($log =~ m!\s/~(.*?)/!) {
        my $u = $1;
        unless ($is_open{$u}) {
            my $fh;
            open $fh, '>>' . $L . '/'. $u;
            $is_open{$u} = $fh;
        }
        select ($is_open{$u});
        $|=1;
        print $log;
    }
    else {
        select F;
        $|=1;
        print F $log;
    }
}

close F;
foreach my $h (keys %is_open) {
    close $h;
}
```

Discussion

Usually, requests to user directory Web sites are logged in the main server log, with no differentiation between one user's site and another. This can make it very hard for a user to locate log messages for their personal Web site.

The recipe above allows you to break out those requests into one logfile *per* user, with requests not going to a userdir Web site going to the main logfile. The log handler can, of course, be modified to put all log messages in the main logfile as well as in the individual logfiles.

In order to lessen the amount of disk activity necessary, file handles are cached, rather than opened and closed with each access. This results in a larger number of file handles which are open at any given time. For sites with a very large number of user Web sites, this may cause you to run out of system resources.

Because Perl buffers output by default, we need to explicitly tell our script not to buffer the output, so that log entries make it into the logfile immediately. This is accomplished by setting the autoflush variable, $|, to a true value. This tells Perl not to buffer output to the most-recently selected file handle. Without this precaution, output will be buffered, and it will appear that nothing is being written to your logfiles.

An alternate approach might involve setting an environment variable using *mod_rewrite* and then adding that variable to your *LogFormat* directive:

```
RewriteRule ^/~([^/]+)/ - [E=userdir:$1]
LogFormat "%{userdir}e %h %l %u %t \"%r\" %>s %b" common
```

Having done this, you could then use the *split-logfile* script to split the logfile up into one file per individual user.

See Also

- *http://httpd.apache.org/docs/2.0/mod/mod_log_config.html*
- *http://httpd.apache.org/docs/2.2/mod/mod_log_config.html*
- *http://httpd.apache.org/docs/2.2/programs/other.html*

## CHAPTER 4

Virtual Hosts

As a person can be known by many names, so can a Web server support multiple Web sites. In the Apache configuration file, each alternate identity, and probably the "main" one as well, is known as a virtual host (sometimes written as vhost) identified with a *<VirtualHost>* container directive. Depending on the name used to access the Web server, Apache responds appropriately, just as someone might answer differently depending on whether she is addressed as "Miss Jones" or "Hey, Debbie!" If you want to have a single system support multiple Web sites, you must configure Apache appropriately—and you'll need to know a little bit about your system (such as the IP addresses assigned to it) in order to do it correctly.

There are two different types of virtual host supported by Apache. The first type, called address-based or IP-based, is tied to the numeric network address used to reach the system, rather like telephone numbers. Bruce Wayne never answered the parlour telephone with "Batman here!" nor did he answer the phone in the Batcave by saying, "Bruce Wayne speaking." However, it's the same person answering the phone, just as it's the same Web server receiving the request. Even if the caller had a wrong number and said, "Hi, Steve!," the phone was still answered the same way; nothing would convince Batman to admit on the Batphone that it was Bruce Wayne answering.

The other type of virtual host is called name-based because the server's response depends on the name by which it was called. To continue the telephone analogy, consider an apartment shared by multiple roommates; you call the same number whether you want to speak to Dave, Joyce, Amaterasu, or Georg. Just as multiple people may share a single telephone number, multiple Web sites can share the same IP address. However, all IP addresses shared by multiple Apache virtual hosts need to be declared with a *NameVirtualHost* directive.

In the most simple of Apache configurations, there are no virtual hosts. Instead, all of the directives in the configuration file apply universally to the operation of the server. The environment defined by the directives outside any *<VirtualHost>* containers is sometimes called the "default server," "main server," or perhaps the "global server."

There is no official name for it, but it can become a factor when adding virtual hosts to your configuration.

But what happens if you add a *<VirtualHost>* container to such a configuration? How are those directives outside the container interpreted, and what is their effect on the virtual host?

The answer is not a simple one: essentially, the effect is specific to each configuration directive. Some get inherited by the virtual hosts, some get reset to a default value, and some pretend they've never been used before. You'll need to consult the documentation for each directive to know for sure.

There are two primary forms of virtual hosts: IP-based virtual hosts, where each virtual host has its own unique IP address; and name-based virtual hosts, where more than one virtual host runs on the same IP address but with different names. This chapter will show you how to configure each one and how to combine the two on the same server. You'll also learn how to fix common problems that occur with virtual hosts.

 To avoid problems and confusing error messages, we strongly advise that you explicitly include the port number on directives specifying an IP address if they support supplying both the address and the port. For instance, use:

```
NameVirtualHost *:80
```

instead of:

```
NameVirtualHost *
```

Normal Web operations use port 80, and most SSL requests use port 443.

4.1 Setting Up Name-Based Virtual Hosts

Problem

You have only one IP address, but you want to support more than one Web site on your system.

Solution

Use the *NameVirtualHost *:80* directive in conjunction with *<VirtualHost>* sections:

```
ServerName 127.0.0.1
NameVirtualHost *:80

<VirtualHost *:80>
    ServerName TheSmiths.name
    DocumentRoot "C:/Apache/Sites/TheSmiths"
</VirtualHost>
```

```
<VirtualHost *:80>
    ServerName JohnSmith.name
    DocumentRoot "C:/Apache/Sites/JustJohnSmith"
</VirtualHost>
```

Discussion

With IP addresses increasingly hard to come by, name-based virtual hosting is the most common way to run multiple Web sites on the same Apache server. The previous recipe works for most users in most virtual hosting situations.

The *:80 in the previous rules means that the specified hosts run on all addresses. For a machine with only a single address, this means that it runs on that address but will also run on the *loopback*, or *localhost* address. Thus if you are sitting at the physical server system, you can view the Web site.

The argument to the *<VirtualHost>* container directive needs to match the argument in a *NameVirtualHost* directive. Putting the hostname here may cause Apache to ignore the virtual host on server startup, and requests to this virtual host may unexpectedly go somewhere else. If your name server is down or otherwise unresponsive at the time that your Apache server is starting up, then Apache can't match the particular *<VirtualHost>* section to the *NameVirtualHost* directive to which it belongs.

Requests for which there is not a virtual host listed will go to the first virtual host listed in the configuration file. In the case of the previous example, requests coming to the server using hostnames that are not explicitly mentioned in one of the virtual hosts will be served by the TheSmiths.name virtual host.

It is particularly instructive to run *httpd -S* and observe the virtual host configuration as Apache understands it, to see if it matches the way that you understand it. *httpd -S* returns the virtual host configuration, showing which hosts are name-based, which are IP-based, and what the defaults are.

Multiple names can be listed for a particular virtual host using the *ServerAlias* directive, as shown here:

```
ServerName TheSmiths.name
ServerAlias www.TheSmiths.name Smith.Family.name
```

It is important to understand that virtual hosts render the server listed in the main body of your configuration file (the "main" or "default" server mentioned earlier) no longer accessible—you must create a virtual host section explicitly for that host. List this host first, if you want it to be the default one.

Adding name-based virtual hosts to your Apache configuration does not magically add entries to your DNS server. You must still add records to your DNS server so that the names resolve to the IP address of the server system. When users type your server name (s) into their browser location bars, their computers first contact a DNS server to look up that name and resolve it to an IP address. If there is no DNS record, then their browsers can't find your server.

For more information on configuring your DNS server, consult the documentation for the DNS software you happen to be running, or talk to your ISP if you're not running your own DNS server.

See Also

- *http://httpd.apache.org/docs/2.2/vhosts*

4.2 Designating One Name-Based Virtual Host as the Default

Problem

You want all unmatched requests, whether they specify a name or use an IP address, to be directed to a default host, possibly with a "host not found" error message.

Solution

Add the following *<VirtualHost>* section, and list it before all of your other ones:

```
<VirtualHost *:80>
    ServerName default
    DocumentRoot /www/htdocs
    ErrorDocument 404 /site_list.html
</VirtualHost>
```

Discussion

Note that this recipe is used in the context of name-based virtual hosts, so it is assumed that you have other virtual hosts that are also using the *<VirtualHost *:80>* notation, and that there is also an accompanying *NameVirtualHost *:80* appearing above them. We have used the `default` name for clarity; you can call it whatever you want.

Setting the *ErrorDocument 404* to a list of the available sites on the server directs the user to useful content, rather than leaving him stranded with an unhelpful 404 error message. You may wish to set *DirectoryIndex* to the site list as well, so that users who go directly to the front page of this site also get useful information.

It's a good idea to list explicitly all valid hostnames either as *ServerName*s or *ServerAlias*es, so that nobody ever winds up at the default site. However, if someone accesses the site directly by IP address, or if a hostname is added to the address in question before the appropriate virtual host is created, the user still gets useful content.

See Also

- Recipe 4.4

4.3 Setting Up Address-Based Virtual Hosts

Problem

You have multiple IP addresses assigned to your system, and you want to support one Web site on each.

Solution

Create a virtual host section for each IP address you want to list on:

```
ServerName 127.0.0.1

<VirtualHost 10.0.0.1>
    ServerName Example.Com
    DocumentRoot "C:/Apache/Sites/Example.Com"
</VirtualHost>

<VirtualHost 10.0.0.2>
    ServerName JohnSmith.Example.Com
    DocumentRoot "C:/Apache/Sites/JustJohnSmith"
</VirtualHost>
```

Discussion

The virtual hosts defined in this example catch all requests to the specified IP addresses, regardless of what hostname is used to get there. Requests to any other IP address not listed go to the virtual host listed in the main body of the configuration file.

The *ServerName* specified is used as the primary name of the virtual host, when needed, but is not used in the process of mapping a request to the correct host. Only the IP address (not the Host header field) is consulted to figure out which virtual host to serve requests from.

See Also

*   *http://httpd.apache.org/docs/2.2/vhosts/*

4.4 Creating a Default Address-Based Virtual Host

Problem

You want to create a virtual host to catch all requests that don't map to one of your address-based virtual hosts.

Solution

Use the *_default_* keyword to designate a default host:

```
<VirtualHost _default_>
    DocumentRoot /www/htdocs
</VirtualHost>
```

Discussion

The _default_ keyword creates a virtual host that catches all requests for any *address:port* combinations for which there is no virtual host configured.

The _default_ directive may—and should—be used in conjunction with a particular port number, such as:

```
<VirtualHost _default_:443>
```

Using this syntax means that the specified virtual host catches all requests to port 443, on all addresses for which there is not an explicit virtual host configured. SSL virtual hosts are usually set up using the _default_ syntax, so you'll see this syntax used in the default SSL configuration file, along with the necessary directives to enable SSL.

default typically does not work as people expect in the case of name-based virtual hosts. It does not match names for which there are no virtual host sections, only *address:port* combinations for which there are no virtual hosts configured. If you wish to create a default name-based host, see Recipe 4.2.

See Also

- Recipe 4.2

4.5 Mixing Address-Based and Name-Based Virtual Hosts

Problem

You have multiple IP addresses assigned to your system, and you want to support more than one Web site on each address.

Solution

Provide a *NameVirtualHost* directive for each IP address, and proceed as you did with a single IP address:

```
ServerName 127.0.0.1
NameVirtualHost 10.0.0.1:80
NameVirtualHost 10.0.0.2:80

<VirtualHost 10.0.0.1:80>
    ServerName TheSmiths.name
    DocumentRoot "C:/Apache/Sites/TheSmiths"
</VirtualHost>

<VirtualHost 10.0.0.1:80>
    ServerName JohnSmith.name
```

```
        DocumentRoot "C:/Apache/Sites/JustJohnSmith"
    </VirtualHost>

    <VirtualHost 10.0.0.2:80>
        ServerName Example.Com
        DocumentRoot "C:/Apache/Sites/Example.Com"
    </VirtualHost>

    <VirtualHost 10.0.0.2:80>
        ServerName DoriFerguson.Example.Com
        DocumentRoot "C:/Apache/Sites/JustDoriFerguson"
    </VirtualHost>
```

Discussion

Using the address of the server, rather than the wildcard * argument, makes the virtual hosts listen only to that IP address. However, you should notice that the argument to *<VirtualHost>* still must match the argument to the *NameVirtualHost* with which the virtual hosts are connected.

See Also

*   *http://httpd.apache.org/docs/2.2/vhosts/*

4.6 Mass Virtual Hosting with mod_vhost_alias

Problem

You want to host many virtual hosts, all of which have exactly the same configuration.

Solution

Use *VirtualDocumentRoot* and *VirtualScriptAlias* provided by *mod_vhost_alias*:

```
    VirtualDocumentRoot /www/vhosts/%-1/%-2.1/%-2/htdocs
    VirtualScriptAlias  /www/vhosts/%-1/%-2.1/%-2/cgi-bin
```

Discussion

This recipe uses directives from *mod_vhost_alias*, which you may not have installed when you built Apache, as it is not one of the modules that is enabled by default.

These directives map requests to a directory built up from pieces of the hostname that was requested. Each of the variables represents one part of the hostname, so that each hostname is mapped to a different directory.

In this particular example, requests for content from *www.example.com* are served from the directory */www/vhosts/com/e/example/htdocs*, or from */www/vhosts/com/e/example/ cgi-bin* (for CGI requests). The full range of available variables is shown in Table 4-1.

Table 4-1. mod_vhost_alias variables

Variable	Meaning
%%	Insert a %
%p	Insert the port number of the virtual host
%M.N	Insert (part of) the name

M and N may have positive or negative integer values, the meanings of which are shown in Table 4-2.

Table 4-2. Meanings of variable values

Value	Meaning
0	The whole name
1	The first part of the name
-1	The last part of the name
2	The second part of the name
-2	The next-to-last part of the name
2+	The second, and all following, parts
-2+	The next-to-last, and all preceding, parts

When the value is placed in the first part of the argument—in the M part of %$M.N$—it refers to parts of the hostname itself. When used in the second part—the N—it refers to a particular letter from that part of the hostname. For example, in hostname *www.example.com*, the meanings of the variables are as shown in Table 4-3.

Table 4-3. Example values for the hostname www.example.com

Value	Meaning
%0	www.example.com
%1	www
%2	example
%3	com
%-1	com
%-2	example
%-3	www
%-2.1	e
%-2.2	x
%-2.3+	ample

Depending on the number of virtual hosts, you may wish to create a directory structure subdivided alphabetically by domain name, by top-level domain, or simply by hostname.

Note that *mod_vhost_alias* does not set the *DOCUMENT_ROOT* environment variable, and so applications that rely on this value may not work in this kind of virtual hosting environment.

See Also

- *http://httpd.apache.org/docs/2.2/mod/mod_vhost_alias.html*
- *http://httpd.apache.org/docs/2.2/vhosts*

4.7 Mass Virtual Hosting Using Rewrite Rules

Problem

Although there is a module—*mod_vhost_alias*—that is explicitly for the purpose of supporting large numbers of virtual hosts, it is very limiting and requires that every virtual host be configured exactly the same way. You want to support a large number of vhosts, configured dynamically, but at the same time, you want to avoid *mod_vhost_alias*.

Solution

Use directives from *mod_rewrite* to map to a directory based on the hostname:

```
RewriteEngine on
RewriteCond    "%{HTTP_HOST}"    "^(www\.)?([^.]+)\.com"
RewriteRule    "^(.*)$"          "/home/%2$1"
```

Discussion

mod_vhost_alias is useful, but it is best for settings where each virtual host is identical in every way but the hostname and document tree. Using *mod_vhost_alias* precludes the use of other URL-mapping modules, such as *mod_userdir*, *mod_rewrite*, and *mod_alias*, and it can be very restrictive. Using *mod_rewrite* is less efficient, but it is more flexible.

For example, when using *mod_vhost_alias*, you must do all of your hosts with *mod_vhost_alias*; with this alternate approach, you can do some of your hosts using the rewrite rules and others using conventional virtual host configuration techniques.

The directives in the Solution map requests for **www.something.com** (or without the **www**) to the directory */home/something*.

See Also

- Recipe 5.17
- *http://httpd.apache.org/docs/2.2/vhosts*
- *http://httpd.apache.org/docs/2.2/mod/mod_rewrite.html*

4.8 Logging for Each Virtual Host

Problem

You want each virtual host to have its own logfiles.

Solution

Specify *Errorlog* and *CustomLog* within each virtual host declaration:

```
<VirtualHost *:80>
    ServerName    waldo.example.com
    DocumentRoot /home/waldo/www/htdocs

    ErrorLog      /home/waldo/www/logs/error_log
    CustomLog     /home/waldo/www/logs/access_log combined
</VirtualHost>
```

Discussion

The various logging directives can be placed either in the main body of your configuration file or within a *<VirtualHost>* section. When they are placed within a virtual host, log entries for that virtual host go in the specified logfiles, rather than into the logfile(s) defined in the main server configuration.

Each logfile counts against the total number of files and network connections your server is allowed to have. If you have 100 virtual hosts, each with its own error and activity log, that's 200 open channels—and if the server's quota is 256, you can only handle 56 concurrent requests at any one time.

Those numbers are just examples; actual values for maximum open file quotas vary by platform, but are generally *much* larger. Consult your platform's documentation to find out your actual limit.

For this reason, we recommend that you have all your virtual hosts log to the same files, and split them apart later for analysis or examination.

In the recipe given here, the logfiles are placed within the home directory of a particular user, rather than in the main log directory. This gives you easier access to those files, but you still need to take adequate precautions to set the permissions on the directory in question. Consult Chapter 6 for a discussion on file permissions.

See Also

- Chapter 3
- Chapter 6
- Recipe 4.9

4.9 Splitting Up a Logfile

Problem

Because of a large number of virtual hosts, you want to have a single logfile for all of them and split it up afterward.

Solution

```
LogFormat "%v %h %l %u %t \"%r\" %>s %b" vhost
CustomLog logs/vhost_log vhost
```

Then, after rotating your logfile:

```
split-logfile < logs/vhost_log
```

Discussion

The *LogFormat* directive in this recipe creates a logfile that is similar to the common logfile format but additionally contains the name of the virtual host being accessed. The *split-logfile* utility splits up this logfile into its constituent virtual hosts.

See Also

- Recipe 3.11

4.10 Port-Based Virtual Hosts

Problem

You want to present different content for HTTP connections on different ports.

Solution

Explicitly list the port number in the *<VirtualHost>* declaration:

```
Listen 8080

<VirtualHost 10.0.1.2:8080>
    DocumentRoot /www/vhosts/port8080
</VirtualHost>
```

```
Listen 9090

<VirtualHost 10.0.1.2:9090>
    DocumentRoot /www/vhosts/port9090
<VirtualHost>
```

Discussion

Port-based virtual hosting is somewhat less common than other techniques shown in this chapter. However, there are a variety of situations in which it can be useful. If you have only one IP address, have no ability to add hostnames to DNS, or if your ISP blocks inbound traffic on port 80, it may be useful to run virtual hosts on other ports.

It also may be useful in development environments to run separate httpd instances on different ports for different developers or different setups.

Visitors to your Web site must list the port number in the URL that they use. For example, to load content from the second virtual host previously listed, the following URL might be used:

```
http://server.example.com:9090
```

See Also

- *http://httpd.apache.org/docs/2.2/vhosts*

4.11 Displaying the Same Content on Several Addresses

Problem

You want to have the same content displayed on two of your addresses.

Solution

Specify both addresses in the *<VirtualHost>* directive:

```
NameVirtualHost 192.168.1.1:80
NameVirtualHost 172.20.30.40:80

<VirtualHost 192.168.1.1:80 172.20.30.40:80>
    DocumentRoot /www/vhosts/server
    ServerName server.example.com
    ServerAlias server
</VirtualHost>
```

Discussion

This setup is most useful on a machine that has addresses that are internal to your network, as well as those that are accessible only from outside your network. If these are the only addresses, you could use the * notation introduced in Recipe 4.1. However, if there are more addresses, this allows you to specify what content appears on what address.

See Also

- *http://httpd.apache.org/docs/2.2/vhosts/*

4.12 Defining Virtual Hosts in a Database

Problem

You want to define virtual hosts in a database, rather than having to edit the configuration file each time.

Solution

Obtain *mod_vhost_dbi* from *http://www.outoforder.cc/projects/apache/mod_vhost_dbi* and use that to configure virtual hosts to be loaded out of the database:

```
PoolDbiDriver       Server1  mysql
PoolDbiHost         Server1  192.168.1.50
PoolDbiUsername     Server1  datauser
PoolDbiPassword     Server1  password
PoolDbiDBName       Server1  vhosts
PoolDbiConnMin      Server1  1
PoolDbiConnSoftMax  Server1  1
PoolDbiConnHardMax  Server1  5
PoolDbiConnTTL      Server1  30

<VirtualHost *:80>
  VhostDbiEnabled On
  VhostDbiConnName Server1
  VhostDbiQuery "SELECT ServerName, DocumentRoot, Username " \
       FROM vhost_info WHERE ServerName = &{RequestHostname}"
</VirtualHost>
```

Discussion

mod_vhost_dbi is a third-party module that provides the ability to put your virtual host configuration in a database and update those virtual hosts without having to modify your configuration file or restart Apache.

The full documentation and code for this module is available from the site *http://www.outoforder.cc/projects/apache/mod_vhost_dbi*. Using the sample configuration above, you can get virtual hosts running. You'll need to create records in the vhost_info table for each virtual host, containing *ServerName*, *DocumentRoot*, and *Username*, where *ServerName* and *DocumentRoot* have the obvious meanings, and *Username* refers to the user ID under which *suexec* will execute CGI processes.

Unfortunately, *mod_vhost_dbi* is a somewhat limited solution because it provides only these three configuration directives.

## CHAPTER 5

Aliases, Redirecting, and Rewriting

When Apache receives a request, it is assumed that the client will be served a file out of the *DocumentRoot* directory. However, there will be times when you want these resources to be served from some other location. For example, if you wanted to place a set of documents on your Web site, it may be more convenient to leave them where they are, rather than to move them to a new location.

In this chapter, we deal with three general categories of these sorts of cases. *Aliasing* refers to mapping a URL to a particular directory. *Redirecting* refers to mapping a URL to another URL. And *Rewriting* refers to using *mod_rewrite* to alter the URL in some way.

Other recipes in this chapter are related because they map URLs to resources that are at unexpected places in the filesystem.

These topics are particularly interesting to Webmasters who want to avoid link-rot or have sites that are periodically subject to upheaval (files or directories are moved around, or even moved from server to server). The redirection and rewriting capabilities of the Apache Web server allow you to conceal such ugly behind-the-scenes disturbances from the eyes of your Internet visitors.

5.1 Mapping a URL to a Directory

Problem

You want to serve content out of a directory other than the *DocumentRoot* directory. For example, you may have an existing directory of documents, which you want to have on your Web site but that you do not want to move into the Apache document root.

Solution

```
Alias "/desired-URL-prefix" "/path/to/other/directory"
```

Discussion

The given example maps URLs starting with *desired-URL-prefix* to files in the */path/to/other/directory* directory. For example, a request for the URL:

http://example.com/desired-URL-prefix/something.html

results in the file */path/to/other/directory/something.html* being sent to the client.

This same effect could be achieved on Unixish systems by simply creating a symbolic link from the main document directory to the target directory and turning on the *Options +FollowSymLinks* directive.* However, using *Alias* explicitly allows you to keep track of these directories more easily. Creating symlinks to directories makes it hard to keep track of the location of all of your content. Additionally, a stray symlink may cause you to expose a portion of your filesystem that you did not intend to.

You may also need to add a few configuration directives to permit access to the directory that you are mapping to. An error message (in your *error_log* file) saying that the request was "denied by server configuration" usually indicates this condition. It is fairly common—and recommended in the documentation (*http://httpd.apache.org/docs/2.2/misc/security_tips.html#protectserverfiles*)—to configure Apache to deny all access, by default, outside of the *DocumentRoot* directory. Thus, you must override this for the directory in question, with a configuration block as shown below:

```
<Directory "/path/to/other/directory">
    Order allow,deny
    Allow from all
</Directory>
```

This permits access to the specified directory.

Note that the *Alias* is very strict with respect to slashes. For example, consider an *Alias* directive as follows:

```
Alias "/puppies/" "/www/docs/puppies/"
```

This directive aliases URLs starting with */puppies/* but does *not* alias the URL */puppies* (i.e., without the trailing slash). This may result in a "trailing slash problem." That is, if a user attempts to go to the URL *http://example.com/puppies* he gets a 404 error, whereas if he goes to the URL *http://example.com/puppies/* with the trailing slash, he receives content from the desired directory. To avoid this problem, create *Alias*es without the trailing slash on each argument.

Finally, make sure that if you have a trailing slash on the first argument to *Alias*, you also have one on the second argument. Consider the following example:

```
Alias "/icons/" "/usr/local/apache/icons"
```

---

* See the documentation for the *Option* directive at *http://httpd.apache.org/docs/2.2/mod/core.html#options*.

A request for *http://example.com/icons/test.gif* results in Apache attempting to serve the file */usr/local/apache/iconstest.gif* rather than the expected */usr/local/apache/icons/test.gif*.

This is called "maintaining slash parity," which is a fancy way of saying, "If you end the alias with a slash, end the directory with one, too; if the alias doesn't end with a slash, the directory shouldn't, either."

See Also

- *http://httpd.apache.org/docs/2.2/mod/mod_alias.html*
- *http://httpd.apache.org/docs/2.2/mod/core.html#options*

5.2 Creating a New URL for Existing Content

Problem

You have an existing directory that you want to access using a different name.

Solution

Use an *Alias* directive in *httpd.conf*:

```
Alias "/newurl" "/www/htdocs/oldurl"
```

Discussion

Although *Alias* is usually used to map URLs to a directory outside of the *DocumentRoot* directory tree, this is not necessarily required. There are many times when it is desirable to have the same content accessible via a number of different names. This is typically the case when a directory has its name changed, and you wish to have the old URLs continue to work, or when different people refer to the same content by different names.

Remember that *Alias* only affects the mapping of a local URI (the */foo/bar.txt* part of *http://example.com/foo/bar.txt*); it doesn't affect or change the hostname part of the URL (the *http://example.com/* part). To alter that portion of the URL, use the *Redirect* or *RewriteRule* directives.

See Also

- Recipe 5.1
- *http://httpd.apache.org/docs/2.2/mod/mod_alias.html*
- *http://httpd.apache.org/docs/2.2/mod/mod_rewrite.html*

5.3 Giving Users Their Own URLs

Problem

You want to give each user on your system his own Web space.

Solution

If you want users' Web locations to be under their home directories, add this to your *httpd.conf* file:

```
UserDir public_html
```

To put all users' Web directories under a central location:

```
UserDir "/www/users/*/htdocs"
```

If you want to let users access their home directory without having to use a tilde (~) in the URL, you can use *mod_rewrite* to perform this mapping:

```
RewriteEngine On
RewriteCond "/home/$1/public_html" -d [NC]
RewriteRule "^/([^/]+)/(.*)" "/home/$1/public_html/$2"
```

Finally, if you have *mod_perl* installed, you can do something more advanced like this (again, added to your *httpd.conf* file):

```
<Perl>
# Folks you don't want to have this privilege
my %forbid = map { $_ => 1 } qw(root postgres bob);
opendir H, '/home/';
my @dir = readdir(H);
closedir H;
foreach my $u (@dir) {
    next if $u =~ m/^\./;
    next if $forbid{$u};
    if (-e "/home/$u/public_html") {
        push @Alias, "/$u/", "/home/$u/public_html/";
    }
}
</Perl>
```

Discussion

The first solution is the simplest and most widely used of the possible recipes we present here. With this directive in place, all users on your system are able to create a directory called *public_html* in their home directories and put Web content there. Their Web space is accessible via a URL starting with a tilde (~), followed by their usernames. So, a user named *bacchus* accesses his personal Web space via the URL:

```
http://www.example.com/~bacchus/
```

If you installed Apache from the standard source distribution, your default configuration file includes an example of this setup. It also contains a *<Directory>* section

---

referring to the directory */home/*/public_html*, with various options and permissions turned on. You need to uncomment that section in order for anyone to have access to these user Web sites. This section should look something like the following:

```
<Directory "/home/*/public_html">
    AllowOverride FileInfo AuthConfig Limit
    Options MultiViews Indexes SymLinksIfOwnerMatch IncludesNoExec
    <Limit GET POST OPTIONS PROPFIND>
        Order allow,deny
        Allow from all
    </Limit>
    <LimitExcept GET POST OPTIONS PROPFIND>
        Order deny,allow
        Deny from all
    </LimitExcept>
</Directory>
```

Make sure you understand what each of these directives is enabling before you uncomment this section in your configuration.

The second solution differs in that the argument to *UserDir* is given as a full pathname and so is not interpreted as relative to the user's home directory, but as an actual filesystem path. The * in the file path is replaced by the username. For example, *http://example.com/~smith/* is translated to */www/users/smith/htdocs*. This directory structure needs to be configured in a manner similar to the previous example.

The third solution is slightly more sophisticated, and provides *UserDir* functionality without having to use a tilde (~) in the URL.

Using the *RewriteCond* directive, we first check for the existence of the user's home directory, and, if it exists, we rewrite requests into that directory. Performing this check first ensures that other URLs continue to work correctly, and only those URLs starting with a valid username are rewritten to a user's home directory.

This rewrite ruleset takes advantage of a little-known fact about *mod_rewrite*—in particular, that a *RewriteRule* is always considered first, and, if it matches, the *RewriteCond* is evaluated after that. Consequently, we can use $1 in the *RewriteCond*, even though the value of that variable is set in the *RewriteRule* appearing on the following line.

The fourth and final solution requires *mod_perl* and provides alias mappings for all top directories under the */home* hierarchy (typically user directories). It differs from the first two by *not* including the tilde prefix; user smith's Web location would be specified as *http://example.com/smith/* instead of *http://example.com/~smith/*, but is still the filesystem location */home/smith/public_html*.

In each case, the directory in question, and directories in the path leading up to it, need to be readable for the Apache user (usually *nobody* or *www* or *httpd*), and also have the execute bit set for that user, so the Apache server can read content out of that directory. The execute bit is needed in order to get a directory listing. Thus, for user *bob*, the directories */*, */home*, */home/bob*, and */home/bob/public_html* (or the corresponding directory paths for the other solutions) all need to execute access, and the last one also requires read access.

On Unixish systems, you would set these permissions by issuing the following commands:

```
% chmod o+x / /home /home/bob
% chmod o+rx /home/bob/public_html
```

The files within the directory need only be readable:

```
% find /home/bob/public_html -type f | xargs chmod 644
```

This will recurse through subdirectories, and change the file permission on all files, but not on directories.

If you use the first solution, many users may be concerned about these file permissions, and rightly so, as it usually allows all other users read access to these directories. Make sure that your users are aware of this, and that they keep personal files in directories that are not world readable.

The advantage of the second solution over the previous one is that these files are stored in a location that is not inside the user's home directory, and so the user may keep sensible file permissions on her home directory. This lets her store personal files there without concern that other users may have free access to them.

The last Solution is completely different and requires that you have *mod_perl* installed. The list of directives previously mentioned goes in your configuration file, using the *<Perl>* configuration directive supplied by *mod_perl*, which allows you to put Perl code in your configuration file to dynamically add things to the configuration file at server startup.

At server startup, the code shown looks in the */home/* directory for any user that has a *public_html* directory and creates an *Alias* for them. This has the advantage over the previous two solutions because the URLs no longer contain that annoying tilde character, which people tend to think unprofessional. So user *bacchus* is now able to access his personal Web space via the URL *http://www.example.com/bacchus/*.

The %forbid list at the top of the code provides a list of users who should not be given this special alias for one reason or another. This allows you to eliminate users for which this feature may cause a security risk, such as *root*, or users who have shown that they can't be trusted with such privileges.

As with the previous examples, this should be accompanied by a *<Directory>* section that enables read access for the directory */home/*/public_html*.

And, of course, you can have this code point these aliases at any location, if you want to serve content out of some other location rather than the home directories of the users.

See Also

- *http://httpd.apache.org/docs/2.2/mod/mod_userdir.html*

5.4 Aliasing Several URLs with a Single Directive

Problem

You want to have more than one URL map to the same directory but don't want multiple *Alias* directives.

Solution

Use *AliasMatch* in *http.conf* to match against a regular expression:

```
AliasMatch "^/pupp(y|ies)" "/www/docs/small_dogs"
AliasMatch "^/P-([[:alnum:]])([^/]*)" "/usr/local/projects/$1/$1$2"
```

Discussion

The *AliasMatch* directive allows you to use regular expressions to match arbitrary patterns in URLs and map anything matching the pattern to the desired URL. Think of it as *Alias* with a little more flexibility.

The first *AliasMatch* causes URLs starting with */puppy*, as well as URLs starting with */puppies*, to be mapped to the directory */www/docs/small_dogs*. The second *AliasMatch* is designed to map to the appropriate project directory if they're organised under the first character of their names. For instance, project `Example`'s URI would be */P-Example/* and would be mapped to */usr/local/projects/E/Example/*.

Apache's regular expression syntax is discussed in much greater detail in Appendix A.

See Also

- Appendix A
- *Mastering Regular Expressions* by Jeffrey Friedl (O'Reilly)

5.5 Mapping Several URLs to the Same CGI Directory

Problem

You want to have a number of URLs map to the same CGI directory but don't want to have multiple *ScriptAlias* directives.

Solution

Use *ScriptAliasMatch* in *httpd.conf* to match against a regular expression:

```
ScriptAliasMatch "^/[sS]cripts?|cgi(-bin)?/" "/www/cgi-bin/"
```

Discussion

This is a more complicated recipe than the previous one and may require that you read Appendix A. This directive maps requests starting with */script/*, */scripts/*, */Script/*, */Scripts/*, */cgi/*, and */cgi-bin/* to the directory */www/cgi-bin/*, and it causes all files in that directory to be treated as CGI programs.

This kind of directive is generally used to clean up a mess that you have made. If you design your Web site well from the start, this sort of thing is never necessary, but the first time you redesign, or otherwise rearrange your Web site, you'll find the necessity for these sorts of contortions.

See Also

- Recipe 5.4
- Appendix A

5.6 Creating a CGI Directory for Each User

Problem

You want each user to have their own *cgi-bin* directory rather than giving them all access to the main server CGI directory.

Solution

Put this in your *httpd.conf*:

```
<Directory "/home/*/public_html/cgi-bin/">
    Options ExecCGI
    SetHandler cgi-script
</Directory>
ScriptAliasMatch "/~([^/]+)/cgi-bin/(.*)" "/home/$1/public_html/cgi-bin/$2"
```

Discussion

You can't use *ScriptAlias* in this case, because for each user, the first argument to *ScriptAlias* would be different. The *<Directory>* container and the *ScriptAliasMatch* directive are functionally equivalent.

This recipe lets each user put CGI scripts in her own personal Web space. Files accessed via URLs starting with:

```
http://www.example.com/~username/cgi-bin/
```

are treated as CGI scripts.

If you have *suexec* enabled, CGI programs run from this target directory will be run with the user ID of the user specified in the URL. For example, a CGI program accessed via the URL *http://www.example.com/~rbowen/cgi-bin/example.cgi* would be run as the user *rbowen*.

 Allowing users to set up their own scripts to be automatically executed without some sort of review is asking for trouble, either from malicious users (perish the thought!) or exploitable insecure scripts.

See Also

- Recipe 8.1

5.7 Redirecting to Another Location

Problem

You want requests to a particular URL to be redirected to another server.

Solution

Use a *Redirect* directive in *httpd.conf*, and give an absolute URL on the second argument:

```
Redirect "/example" "http://www2.example.com/new/location"
```

Discussion

Whereas *Alias* maps a URL to something in the local filesystem, *Redirect* maps a URL to another URL, usually on another server. The second argument is a full URL and is sent back to the client (browser), which makes a second request for the new URL.

It is also important to know that the *Redirect* directive preserves path information, if there is any. Therefore, this recipe redirects a request for *http://original.example.com/example/something.html* to *http://other.example.com/new/location/something.html*.

Redirections come in several different flavors, too; you can specify which particular type of redirect you want to use by inserting the appropriate keyword between the *Redirect* directive and the first URL argument. All redirects instruct the client where the requested document is *now*; the different types of redirection inform where the client should look for the document in the future. If no keyword is specified, the `temp` meaning is used by default:

temp

A `temporary` redirection is used when the document is not in the originally requested location at the moment, but is expected to be there again some time in the future. So the client remembers the URL it used on the original request and will use it on future requests for the same document.

permanent

A `permanent` redirection indicates that not only is the requested document not in the location specified by the client, but that the client should never look for it there again. In other words, the client should remember the *new* location indicated in the redirect response and look there in all subsequent requests for the resource.

gone

This keyword means that the document doesn't exist in this location, and it shouldn't bother asking any more. This differs from the `404 Not Found` error response in that the `gone` status admits that the document *was* once here, even though it isn't any more.

seeother

A `seeother` redirection tells the client that the original document isn't located here any more and has been superseded by another one in a different location. That is, the original request might have been for:

http://example.com/chapter2.html

but the server answers with a `seeother` redirection to:
http://bookname.com/edition-2/chapter2.html

indicating that the desired content can be gotten at a different URL, and that a second request should be made to get it.

 The semantics of the 303 `see other` status code suggest that you only use it if you're really familiar with it. Use the `temporary` keyword instead if you're not sure whether `see other` is appropriate.

By default, if no keyword is present, a `temporary` redirection is issued.

Here's an example of the various directive formats, including the HTTP status code number in case you want to use an *ErrorDocument* to customize the server's response text:

```
#
# These are equivalent, and return a response with a 302 status.
#
Redirect      /foo.html http://example.com/under-construction/foo.html
Redirect temp /foo.html http://example.com/under-construction/foo.html
RedirectTemp  /foo.html http://example.com/under-construction/foo.html
#
# These are equivalent to each other as well, returning a 301 status
#
Redirect permanent /foo.html http://example.com/relocated/foo.html
RedirectPermanent  /foo.html http://example.com/relocated/foo.html
#
# This tells the client that the old URL is dead, but the document
```

```
# content has been replaced by the specified new document.  It
# returns a 303 status.
#
Redirect seeother /foo.html http://example.com/relocated/bar.html
#
# Returns a 410 status, telling the client that the document has been
# intentionally removed and won't be coming back.  Note that there
# is no absoluteURL argument.
#
Redirect gone     /foo.html
```

See Also

- *http://httpd.apache.org/docs/2.2/mod/mod_alias.html*

5.8 Redirecting Several URLs to the Same Destination

Problem

You want to redirect a number of URLs to the same place. For example, you want to redirect requests for */fish* and */Fishing* to *http://fish.example.com/*.

Solution

Use *RedirectMatch* in *httpd.conf* to match against a regular expression:

```
RedirectMatch "^/[fF]ish(ing)?(/.*)?" "http://fish.example.com/$2"
```

Discussion

This recipe redirects requests on one server for URLs starting with fish or fishing, with either an upper-case or lower-case f, to a URL on another server, *fish.example.com*. As with *Redirect*, the path information, if any, is preserved. That is, a request for *http://original.server/Fishing/tackle.html* is redirected to *http://fish.example.com/tackle.html* so that existing relative links continue to work.

As with several of the earlier examples, *RedirectMatch* uses regular expressions to provide arbitrary text pattern matching.

See Also

- Appendix A

5.9 Permitting Case-Insensitive URLs

Problem

You want requested URLs to be valid whether uppercase or lowercase letters are used.

Solution

Use *mod_speling* to make URLs case-insensitive:

```
CheckSpelling On
```

Discussion

The *mod_speling* module is part of the standard Apache distribution but is not enabled by default, so you need to explicitly enable it.

In addition to making URLs case-insensitive, *mod_speling*, as the name implies, provides simple spellchecking capability. In particular, in the case of a "not found" error, *mod_speling* attempts to find files that may have been intended, based on similar spelling, transposed letters, or perhaps letters swapped with similar-looking numbers, like O for 0 and l for 1.

When *mod_speling* is installed, it may be turned on for a particular scope (such as a directory, virtual host, or the entire server) by setting the *CheckSpelling* directive to *On*.

And, yes, that is the correct spelling of the module name.

See Also

* *http://httpd.apache.org/docs/2.2/mod/mod_speling.html*

5.10 Showing Highlighted PHP Source without Symlinking

Problem

You want to be able to see the syntax-highlighted source to your PHP scripts without having to set up symbolic links for all of them.

Solution

Add a line such as the following to your *httpd.conf* or *.htaccess* file:

```
RewriteRule "^(.+\.php)s$" "$1" [T=application/x-httpd-php-source]
```

Or, for versions 2.2 and later:

```
RewriteRule "^(.+\.php)s$" "$1" [H=application/x-httpd-php-source]
```

Alternate Solution

Add a line such as the following to your *httpd.conf* file:

```
RewriteRule "^(.*\.php)s$" "/cgi-bin/show.php?file=$1" [PT,L]
```

Create a file named *show.php* as shown below, and put it in your server's */cgi-bin/* directory:

```php
<?php
/*
 * Show the highlighted source of a PHP script without a symlink or copy.
 */
if ((! isset($_GET))
    || (! isset($_GET['file']))
    || (! ($file = $_GET['file']))) {
    /*
     * Missing required arguments, so bail.
     */
    return status('400 Bad Request',
                  "Data insufficient or invalid.\r\n");
}

$file = preg_replace('/\.phps$/', '.php', $file);
if (! preg_match('/\.php$/', $file)) {
    return status('403 Forbidden',
                  "Invalid document.\r\n");
}
$docroot = $_SERVER['DOCUMENT_ROOT'];
if ((! preg_match(";^$docroot;", $file))
    || (! preg_match(";^/home/[^/]+/public_html;", $file))) {
    return status('403 Forbidden',
                  "Invalid document requested.\r\n");
}
Header('Content-type: text/html; charset=iso-8859-1');
print highlight_file($file);
return;

function status($msg, $text) {
    Header("Status: $msg");
    Header('Content-type: text/plain; charset=iso-8859-1');
    Header('Content-length: ' . strlen($text));
    print $text;
}
?>
```

Discussion

The PHP interpreter has a built-in function to display PHP source code syntax color-coded. Ordinarily, this function is invoked for *.phps* files when your configuration file contains the following line:

```
AddHandler application/x-httpd-php-source .phps
```

However, in order to take advantage of this functionality, you need to make a copy, or symbolic link, of each PHP file you wish to treat this way, replacing the *.php* file extension with a *.phps* file extension. This is impractical and inconvenient.

The recipe given removes the need to do this, by rewriting any request for a *.phps* file to that same filename, but with a *.php* file extension instead, and associating the *php-source* handler with that request.

The [H] flag to the *RewriteRule* directive is new in version 2.2, and so for earlier versions, you will need to use the [T] flag instead, which provides a similar functionality.

The script in the alternate solution uses a built-in PHP function to display the script's source in highlighted form. It's a more complex solution than the one-liner change in the first solution, but it allows you to change the behaviour without having to restart the server, just by altering the script. The *preg_match* against $docroot verifies the requested file is under the server's *DocumentRoot*. The next *preg_match* also permits files in users' *public_html* directories.

See Also

- Recipe 2.5

5.11 Replacing Text in Requested URLs

Problem

You want to change all occurrences of *string1* to *string2* in a request's URL.

Solution

```
RewriteRule "(.*)string1(.*)" "$1string2$2" [N,PT]
```

Discussion

The [N] flag tells Apache to rerun the rewrite rule. This rule will get run repeatedly until the *RewriteCond* fails. Thus, it will get rerun as long as the URL contains the string that you want to replace. As soon as all occurrences of this string have been replaced, the *RewriteCond* will fail, and the rule will stop. The [PT] tells *mod_rewrite* to pass the rewritten URL on to the rest of Apache for any additional processing once the rewriting is done.

Care should be taken to avoid infinite loops, such as might happen if *string1* is part of *string2*.

See Also

- Appendix A

5.12 Rewriting Path Information to CGI Arguments

Problem

You want to pass arguments as part of the URL but have these components of the URL rewritten as CGI QUERY_STRING arguments.

Solution

This is just an example, of course; make appropriate changes to the *RewriteRule* line to fit your own environment and needs:

```
RewriteEngine on
RewriteRule "^/book/([^/]*)/([^/]*)" "/cgi-bin/book.cgi?author=$1&subject=$2" [PT]
```

Discussion

One reason you might want or need to do this is if you're gluing together two legacy systems that do things in different ways, such as a client application and a vendor script.

For example, the *RewriteRule* in the Solution will cause:

```
http://www.example.com/book/apache/bowen
```

to be rewritten as:

```
http://www.example.com/cgi-bin/book.cgi?subject=apache&author=bowen
```

The [PT] flag on the *RewriteRule* directive instructs Apache to keep processing the URL even after it has been modified; without the flag, the server would directly try to treat the rewritten URL as a filename, instead of continuing to the step at which it determines it's a CGI script. It also allows multiple *RewriteRule* directives to make additional refinements to the URL.

If the URL being rewritten already has a query string, or might, change the [PT] to [QSA,PT]. The QSA means "query string add" and will cause the query string generated by the rewrite to be added to the query string in the original URL. Without QSA, the original query string will be replaced.

See Also

- *http://httpd.apache.org/docs/2.2/mod/mod_rewrite.html*

5.13 Denying Access to Unreferred Requests

Problem

You want to prevent other Web sites from using your images (or other types of documents) in their pages and allow your images to be accessed only if they were referred from your own site.

Solution

Put this in your *httpd.conf*:

```
RewriteEngine On
RewriteCond "%{HTTP_REFERER}" !=""
```

```
RewriteCond "%{HTTP_REFERER}" "!^http://mysite.com/.*$" [NC]
RewriteRule "\.(jpg|gif|png)$ - [F]
```

Discussion

This recipe is a series of *RewriteCond* directives, designed to determine whether an image file is requested from within a document on your site or if it is embedded in a page from another server. If the the latter, then the other site is stealing your images and needs to be stopped.

The first rule checks to see if the referer is even set. Some clients don't send a referer, and some browsers can be configured not to send referers. If we deny requests from all clients that don't send a referer, we'll deny a lot of valid requests; so we let these ones in.

Next, we check to see if the referer appears to be from some site other than our own. If so, we keep going through the rules. Otherwise, we'll stop processing the rewrite.

Finally, we check to see if this is a request for an image file. If the file is a nonimage file, such as an HTML file, then we want to allow people to link to these files from somewhere offsite.

If we've reached this point in the ruleset, we know that we have a request for an image file from within a page on another Web site. The *RewriteRule* matches a request and returns Forbidden to the client.

See Also

- *http://httpd.apache.org/docs/2.2/mod/mod_rewrite.html*
- Recipe 5.14

5.14 Redirecting Unreferred Requests to an Explanation Page

Problem

When a request comes to your server without a referring URL being mentioned, you want to redirect it to a page that explains why you're not satisfying it.

Solution

Add lines such as the following to your configuration files:

```
RewriteEngine On
RewriteCond "%{HTTP_REFERER}" "^$"
RewriteRule "(.*)" "/cgi-bin/need-referer" [PT,E=ORIG:$1]
```

Be sure to put these directives in an appropriate scope, or people won't be able to type in your site's URLs at all!

Discussion

The specific problem being addressed in the Solution is requests coming to your server with no information about where they got the URL (which is passed in the `Referer` request header field). This frequently indicates someone surfing directly to the page rather than following a link, and in the case of images informaltable may be the result of a "Save As" request on the user's part. If you want to only serve requests that came from links on your own site, you can change the *RewriteCond* directive to:

```
RewriteCond "%{HTTP_REFERER}" "!http://%{SERVER_NAME}/" [NC]
```

The *RewriteRule* will pass the request to a CGI script named *need-referer*, and will put the original URI into the environment variable `ORIG` for the script to reference. Note that only the local portion of the URI is included; the hostname will not be, for instance.

The lack of a `Referer` request header field does not always signify skulduggery. Some people consider it none of a site's business how they came to it, and don't care to have their surfing patterns recorded. However, there's no way Apache can tell *why* the header field was omitted, so your *need-referer* script should explain the situation.

See Also

- Recipe 5.13

5.15 Rewriting Based on the Query String

Problem

You want to translate one URI into another based on the value of the query string.

Solution

Put this in your *httpd.conf*:

```
RewriteCond "%{QUERY_STRING}"   "^user=([^=]*)"
RewriteRule "/people"           "http://%1.users.example.com/" [R]
```

Discussion

mod_rewrite does not consider the query string as part of the URI for matching and rewriting purposes, so you need to treat it separately. The given example translates requests of the form:

> *http://example.com/people?user=jones*
> *http://jones.users.example.com/*

The [R] tells *mod_rewrite* to direct the browser to the URL constructed by the *RewriteRule* directive.

See Also

- *http://httpd.apache.org/docs/2.2/mod/mod_alias.html*

5.16 Redirecting All—or Part—of Your Server to SSL

Problem

You want certain parts of your non-SSL Web space to be redirected to a secured area.

Solution

You can redirect everything that is attached to port 80 with the following *RewriteRule*:

```
RewriteCond "%{SERVER_PORT}"    "^80$"
RewriteRule "^(.*)$"            "https://%{SERVER_NAME}$1" [R,L]
```

You can redirect particular URLs to a secure version:

```
RewriteRule "^/normal/secure(/.*)" "https://%{HTTP_HOST}$1" [R,L]
```

You can check to see whether the HTTPS environment variable is set:

```
RewriteCond "%{HTTPS}" "!=on"
RewriteRule "^(/secure/.*)" "https://%{HTTP_HOST}$1" [R,L]
```

Or, you can simply use the *Redirect* directive in the http section of *httpd.conf* file to to cause a URL to be served as HTTPS:

```
Redirect "/" "https://secure.example.com/"
```

Make sure that this appears only in in the `http` scope and not in the `https` scope, or all `https` requests will loop.

Discussion

The first solution causes all requests that come in on port 80 (normally the unencrypted HTTP port) to be redirected to the same locations on the current server but accessed through SSL. Note the use of `SERVER_NAME`; because this is a complete site redirection, it's simplest to use the server's official name for itself.

The directive shown in the second solution causes all portions of the server's Web space under *http://myhost/normal/secure* to be redirected to the SSL location rooted at *https:// myhost/*. The use of `HTTP_HOST` rather than `SERVER_NAME` means that only the location and the scheme in the visitor's browser, not the server name.

Note that using HTTP_HOST might break here, because it may contain the port number, too. If you expect HTTP_HOST to contain the port number, therefore, you'll need to compensate for this in your ruleset.

Note that the paths to the SSL and non-SSL locations differ; if you want the paths to be the same except for the security, you can use something like the directives given in the third solution.

See Also

• *http://httpd.apache.org/docs/2.2/mod/mod_rewrite.html*

5.17 Turning Directories into Hostnames

Problem

You want to migrate pathnames under a single hostname to distinct hostnames.

Solution

Use *RewriteRule* in *httpd.conf*:

```
RewriteRule "^/(patha|pathb|pathc)(/.*)" "http://$1.example.com$2" [R]
RewriteRule "^/([^./]*)(/.*)" "http://$1.example.com$2" [R]
RewriteRule "^/~([^./]*)(/.*)" "http://$1.example.com$2" [R]
```

Discussion

The first recipe redirects requests of the form *http://example.com/pathseg/some/ file.html* to a different host, such as *http://pathseg.example.com/some/file.html*, but only for those requests in which *pathseg* is patha, pathb, or pathc.

The second recipe does the same thing, except that *any* top-level path segment is redirected in this manner.

The third recipe splits the difference, redirecting all "user" requests to distinct hosts with the same name as the user.

See Also

• *http://httpd.apache.org/docs/2.2/mod/mod_rewrite.html*

5.18 Redirecting All Requests to a Single Host

Problem

You want all requests made of your system to be redirected to a specific host.

Solution

Put this in your *httpd.conf*:

```
RewriteCond "%{HTTP_HOST}"   "!^www.example.com"        [NC,OR]
RewriteCond "%{SERVER_NAME}" "!^www.example.com"        [NC]
RewriteRule "(.*)"           "http://www.example.com$1" [R]
```

Discussion

Any request handled by your server within the scope of the directives in the Solution (which aren't directed to the www.example.com host) is redirected there.

The two different *RewriteCond* directives are used to catch all requests made by some host other than www.example.com, regardless of the redirection method.

The NC (No Case) flag makes the regular expression case-insensitive. That is, it makes it match regardless of whether letters are upper- or lowercase.

The OR flag is a logical "or," allowing the two conditions to be strung together so that either one being true is a sufficient condition for the rule to be applied.

Finally, the R flag causes an actual Redirect to be issued, so that the browser will make another request for the generated URL.

See Also

*   *http://httpd.apache.org/docs/2.2/mod/mod_rewrite.html*

5.19 Turning Document Names into Arguments

Problem

You want to redirect requests for documents to a CGI script, or other handler, that gets the document names as an argument.

Solution

Use *RewriteRule* in *httpd.conf*:

```
RewriteRule "^/dir/([^./]*)\.html" "/dir/script.cgi?doc=$1" [PT]
```

Discussion

This solution causes all requests for HTML documents in the specified location to be turned into requests for a handler script that receives the document name as an argument in the `QUERY_STRING` environment variable.

The `PT` flag should be included to allow any appropriate subsequent URL rewriting or manipulation to be performed.

See Also

- *http://httpd.apache.org/docs/2.2/mod/mod_rewrite.html*

5.20 Rewriting Elements between Path and Query String

Problem

You want to turn portions of a URL into query-string parameters, or vice versa.

Solution

To rewrite *http://example.com/path/to/5* to *http://example.com/path/to?id=5*:

```
RewriteRule "^(/path/to)/(\d+)" "$1?id=$2" [PT]
```

To go the other way:

```
RewriteCond "%{QUERY_STRING}" "\bid=(\d+)\b"
RewriteRule "(/path/to)" "$1/%2" [PT,QSA]
```

> Note that the arguments to the *RewriteRule* directives need to be structured differently if they occur in a *.htaccess* file. The above solution illustrates the syntax if they're put into the server-wide configuration files.

Discussion

It is quite common for sites to have to change the way URLs are structured, either moving portions into or out of the query-string portion. This often becomed necessary when the underlying software is changed—say, from one blogging package to another. The new software requires URLs to be in a different format, but you don't want to invalidate all the old-style URLs that might be bookmarked or otherwise spread around the Web.

This is a perfect application for *mod_rewrite*, and quite simple to accomplish as well, as demonstrated in the solution.

- *http://httpd.apache.org/docs/2.2/mod/mod_rewrite.html*

5.21 Rewriting a Hostname to a Directory

Problem

You want requests for *http://bogus.example.com/* to be turned into requests for *http://example.com/bogus/*.

Solution

```
RewriteCond "%{HTTP_HOST}" "^([^.]+)\.example\.com" [NC]
RewriteRule "(.*)" "http://example.com/%1$1" [R]"
```

To do this transparently, without a redirect:

```
RewriteCond "%{HTTP_HOST}" "^([^.]+)\.example\.com$" [NC]
RewriteRule "(.*)" "/%1$1" [PT]
```

Discussion

This technique is occasionally needed when wildcard hostnames are being supported. It gives the illusion that URLs are pointing to separate hosts rather than subdirectories on only one system. Of course, using the redirection ([R]) flag will void the illusion because the replacement URL will be visible to the end user. If you want it to be completely transparent to the user, you can use the second option to get the equivalent result with a rewrite internal to the server that the client never sees.

See Also

- *http://httpd.apache.org/docs/2.2/mod/mod_rewrite.html*

5.22 Turning URL Segments into Query Arguments

Problem

You want to turn requests of the form:

```
http://example.com/foo/bar.html
```

into something like this:

```
http://example.com/cgi-bin/remap?page=foo/bar.html
```

Solution

Add a line such as the following to your configuration file:

```
RewriteRule "/(.*)" "/cgi-bin/remap?page=$1" [QSA,PT]
```

Discussion

The solution performs the rewrite in a manner completely transparent to the user, since all the changes to how to find things are done within the server rather than giving the users's client a new URL to load.

The QSA option allows any query-string information that was on the original request to be retained and merged with the one being added by the *RewriteRule*. The PT option tells the server to continue processing the request rather than treating it as completely finished. This is necessary in order to have the new URL, which involves a CGI script, handled correctly.

See Also

- Recipe 5.21

5.23 Using AliasMatch, ScriptAliasMatch, and RedirectMatch

Problem

You want to use the basic functionality of the *Alias* or *Redirect* directives, but you need to handle a bunch of related cases without needing one directive for each.

Solution

Use the grouping syntax to manipulate the URI into filesystem paths:

```
AliasMatch "/users/(.*)/" "/home/webonly/$1/"
```

Force browsers to learn the new URLs for directories relocated to their own hosts:

```
RedirectMatch permanent "/projects/([^/]+)(/.*)" "http://$1.projectdomain.com$2"
```

Discussion

The *AliasMatch*, *ScriptAliasMatch*, and *RedirectMatch* directives use the same regular expression syntax as the rest of Apache's configuration language. They're not as powerful as the *mod_rewrite* directives, though, because they can't be made conditional and can't reference environment variables. However, they tend to have less of a performance impact on the server precisely because of their simpler syntax.

See Also

- Recipe 5.4
- Recipe 5.5

## CHAPTER 6

Security

In this chapter, security means allowing people to see what you want them to see and preventing them from seeing what you don't want them to see. Additionally, there are the issues of what measures you need to take on your server in order to restrict access via non-Web means. This chapter illustrates the precautions you need to take to protect your server from malicious access and modification of your Web site.

The most common questions ask how to protect documents and restrict access. Unfortunately, because of the complexity of the subject and the nature of the Web architecture, these questions also tend to have the most complex answers or often no convenient answers at all.

Normal security nomenclature and methodology separate the process of applying access controls into two discrete steps; in the case of the Web, they may be thought of as the server asking itself these questions:

- Are you really who you claim to be?
- Are you allowed to be here?

These steps are called *authentication* and *authorization*, respectively. Here's a real-world example: a flight attendant checks your photo identification (authentication) and your ticket (authorization) before permitting you to board an airplane.

Authentication can be broken down into what might be called *weak* and *strong*. Weak authentication is based on the correctness of credentials that the end user supplies (which therefore may have been stolen from the real owner—hence the name "weak"), whereas strong authentication is based on attributes of the request over which the end user has little or no control, and it cannot change from request to request—such as the IP address of his system.

Although checking authentication and authorization are clearly separate activities, their application gets a bit blurred in the context of the Apache Web server modules. Even though the main difference between the many security modules is how they store the credentials (in a file, a database, an LDAP directory, etc.), they nevertheless have to provide the code to retrieve the credentials from the store, validate those supplied by the client, and check to see if the authenticated user is authorized to access the resource. In other words, there's a lot of functionality duplicated from module to module, and although there are frequently similarities between their behavior and directives, the lack of shared code means that sometimes they're not quite as similar as you'd hope. This overloading of functionality has been somewhat addressed in the next version of the Web server after 2.0 (still in development at the time of this writing).

In addition to the matter of requiring a password to access certain content from the Web server, there is the larger issue of securing your server from attacks. As with any software, Apache has, at various times in its history, been susceptible to conditions that would allow an attacker to gain inappropriate control of the hosting server. For example, an attacker may have been able to access, or modify, files that the site administrator had not intended to give access to, or an attacker may have been able to execute commands on the target server. Thus, it is important that you know what measures need to be taken to ensure that your server is not susceptible to these attacks.

The most important measure that you can take is to keep apprised of new releases, and read the CHANGES file to determine if the new version fixes a security hole to which you may be subject. Running the latest version of the Apache server is usually a good measure in the fight against security vulnerabilities.

Recipes in this chapter show you how to implement some of the frequently requested password scenarios, as well as giving you the tools necessary to protect your server from external attacks.

Authentication and Authorization

When checking for access to restricted documents, there are actually two different operations involved: checking to see who you are, and checking to see if you're allowed to see the document.

The first part, checking to see who you are, is called *authentication*. The Web server doesn't know who you are, so you need to provide some proof of your identity, such as a username and matching password. When the server successfully compares these bits of information (called *credentials*) with those in its databases, the server will proceed, but if you're not in the list, or the information doesn't match, the server will turn you away with an error status.

Once you have convinced the server you are who you say you are, it will look at the list of people allowed to access the document and see if you're on it; this is called *authorization*. If you are on the list, access proceed normally; otherwise, the server returns an error status and denies access.

The two different operations do not differentiate in the errors they return; it is always a 401 (unauthorized) code, even if the failure was in authentication. This is to prevent would-be attackers from being able to tell when they have valid credentials.

6.1 Using System Account Information for Web Authentication

Problem

You want all the users on your Unixish system to be able to authenticate themselves over the Web using their already-assigned usernames and passwords.

Solution

Set up a realm using *mod_auth* and name */etc/passwd* as the *AuthUserFile*:

```
<Directory "/home">
    AuthType Basic
    AuthName HomeDir
    AuthUserFile /etc/passwd
    Require valid-user
    Satisfy All
</Directory>
```

Discussion

We must stress that using system account information for Web authentication is a very bad idea, unless your site is also secured using SSL. For one thing, any intruder who happens to obtain one of your users' credentials not only can access the protected files over the Web, but can actually log onto your system where it's possible to do significant damage. For another, Web logins don't have the same security controls as most operating systems; over the Web, an intruder can keep hammering away at a username with password after password without the system taking any defensive measures; all *mod_auth* will do is record a message in the Apache error log. However, most operating systems will enter a paranoid mode and at least ignore login attempts for a while after some number of failures.

If you still want to do this, either because you consider the risk acceptable or because it doesn't apply in your situation, the *httpd.conf* directives in the Solution will do the trick. The syntax and order of the fields in a credential record used by *mod_auth* happens (and not by accident) to match the standard layout of the */etc/passwd* lines. *mod_auth* uses a simple text file format in which each line starts with a username and password and may optionally contain additional fields, with the fields delimited by colons. For example:

```
smith:$apr1$GLWeF/..$8hOXRFUpHhBJHpOUdNFe51
```

mod_auth ignores any additional fields after the password, which is what allows the */etc/passwd* file to be used. Note that the password in the example is encrypted.

You can manage Apache *mod_auth* credential files with the *htpasswd* utility, but don't use this utility on the */etc/passwd* file! Use the normal account maintenance tools for that.

Note that this technique will not work if shadow passwords are in use, because the password field of */etc/passwd* contains nothing useful in that situation. Instead, the passwords are stored in the file */etc/shadow*, which is readable only by *root*, while Apache runs as an unprivileged user. Furthermore, most modern Unixish operating systems use the */etc/shadow* means of user authentication by default.

See Also

- The Authentication and Authorization sidebar, earlier in this chapter
- The HTTP, Browsers, and Credentials sidebar, later in this chapter
- The Weak and Strong Authentication sidebar, later in this chapter
- The *htpasswd* manpage
- The *passwd(5)* manpage

6.2 Setting Up Single-Use Passwords

Problem

You want to be able to provide credentials that will allow visitors into your site only once.

Solution

No solution is available with standard Apache features.

Discussion

As described in the HTTP, Browsers, and Credentials sidebar, the concept of being "logged in" to a site is an illusion. In order to achieve the desired one-time-only effect, the server needs to complete the following steps:

1. Note the first time the user successfully presents valid credentials.
2. Somehow, associate that fact with the user's "session."
3. Never allow those credentials to succeed again if the session information is different from the first time they succeeded.

The last step is not a simple task, and it isn't a capability provided in the standard Apache distribution. To complicate matters, there is the desire to start a timeout once the credentials have succeeded, so that the user doesn't authenticate once and then leave his browser session open for days and retain access.

Fulfilling this need would require a custom solution. Unfortunately, we are not aware of any open or public modules that provide this capability; however, search and watch the module registry for possible third-party implementations.

See Also

- Recipe 6.3
- *http://modules.apache.org*

6.3 Expiring Passwords

Problem

You want a user's username and password to expire at a particular time or after some specific interval.

Solution

No solution is available with standard Apache features, but a few third-party solutions exist.

Discussion

Refer to the HTTP, Browsers, and Credentials sidebar. In order for Apache to provide this functionality, it would need to store more than just the valid username and password; it would also have to maintain information about the credentials' expiration time. No module provided as part of the standard Apache distribution does this.

There are several third-party solutions to this problem, including the Perl module *Apache::Htpasswd::Perishable* and the *mod_perl* handler *Apache::AuthExpire*.

There are two slightly different ways to look at this problem, that will influence your choice of a solution. You may want a user's authentication to be timed out after a certain amount of time, or perhaps after a certain period of inactivity, forcing them to log in again. Or you may want a particular username/password pair to be completely expired after a certain amount of time, so that it no longer works. The latter might be used instead of a single-use password, which is impractical to implement in HTTP.

Apache::Htpasswd::Perishable partially implements the latter interpretation of the problem by adding expiration information to the password file. Inheriting from the *Apache::Htpasswd* module, it adds two additional methods, *expire* and *extend*, which set an expiration date on the password and extend the expiration time, respectively.

For example, the following code will open a password file and set an expiration date on a particular user entry in that file:

```
use Apache::Htpasswd::Perishable;

my $pass = Apache::Htpasswd::Perishable->new("/usr/local/apache/passwords/user.pass")
    or die "Could not open password file.";
$pass->expire('waldo', 5); # Set the expiration date 5 days in the future
```

Such a mechanism is only useful if expired passwords are removed from the password file periodically. This can be accomplished by running the following *cron* script every day. This will delete those users for whom the expiration date has passed:

```perl
#! /usr/bin/perl
use Apache::Htpasswd::Perishable;

my $password_file = '/usr/local/apache/passwords/user.pass';

open(F,$password_file) or die "Could not open password file.";
my @users;
while (my $user = <F>) {
    $user =~ s/^([^:])+:.*$/$1/;
    push @users, $user;
}
close F;

my $pass = Apache::Htpasswd::Perishable->new($password_file) or die
    "Could not open password file.";
foreach my $user (@users) {
    $pass->htDelete($user) unless $pass->expire($user) > 0;
}
```

Apache::AuthExpire, by contrast, implements timeouts on "login sessions." That is, a user must reauthenticate after a certain period of inactivity. This gives you protection against the user who steps away from her computer for a few moments, leaving herself "logged in."

As previously discussed, HTTP is stateless so it does not really have a concept of being logged in. However, by watching repeated connections from the same address, such a state can be simulated.

To use the expiring functionality offered by *Apache::AuthExpire*, download the module from CPAN, and install it:

```
# perl -MCPAN -e shell
cpan> install Apache::AuthExpire
```

Then configure your Apache server to use this module for your authentication handler:

```
PerlAuthenHandler Apache::AuthExpire
PerlSetVar DefaultLimit 7200
```

The given example will time out idle connections after 7,200 seconds, which is 2 hours.

See Also

- Recipe 6.2
- *http://modules.apache.org*
- *http://search.cpan.org/author/JJHORNER/Apache-AuthExpire/AuthExpire.pm*
- *http://search.cpan.org/author/ALLENDAY/Apache-Htpasswd-Perishable/Perishable.pm*

6.4 Limiting Upload Size

Problem

With more and more Web hosting services allowing customers to upload documents, uploads may become too large. With a little creativity, you can put a limit on uploads by using the security capabilities of the server.

Solution

Assume you want to put a limit on uploads of ten thousand (10,000) bytes. The simplest way to do this is to add a *LimitRequestBody* directive to the appropriate scope:

```
<Directory "/usr/local/apache2/uploads">
    LimitRequestBody 10000
</Directory>
```

If a user ties to send a request that's too large, he'll get an error message. However, the default Apache message may leave something to be desired so you can either tailor it with a *ErrorDocument 413* directive, or with some more complex (and more flexible) jiggery-pokery such as the following:

```
SetEnvIf Content-Length "^[1-9][0-9]{4,}" upload_too_large=1
<Location /upload>
    Order Deny,Allow
    Deny from env=upload_too_large
    ErrorDocument 403 /cgi-bin/remap-403-to-413
</Location>
```

You can tailor the response by making the */cgi-bin/remap-403-to-413* script look something like this:

```
#! /usr/local/bin/perl
#
# Perl script to turn a 403 error into a 413 IFF
# the forbidden status is because the upload was
# too large.
#
if ($ENV{'upload_too_large'}) {
    #
    # Constipation!
    #
    print <<EOHT
Status: 413 Request Entity Too Large
Content-type: text/plain; charset=iso-8859-1
Content-length: 84

Sorry, but your upload file exceeds the limits
set forth in our terms and conditions.
EOHT
}
else {
    #
```

```
              # This is a legitimate "forbidden" error.
              #
              my $uri = $ENV{'REDIRECT_REQUEST_URI'};
              my $clength = 165 + length($uri);
              print <<EOHT
Status: 403 Forbidden
Content-type: text/html; charset=iso-8859-1
Content-length: $clength

<html>
 <head>
  <title>Forbidden</title>
 </head>
 <body>
  <h1>Forbidden</h1>
  <p>
  You don't have permission to access $uri
  on this server.
  </p>
 </body>
</html>
EOHT
}
exit(0);
```

Discussion

This script is invoked when a request results in a `403 Forbidden` error (which is what the *Deny* directive causes if it's triggered). It checks to see if it's a real forbidden condition, or whether the upload file is too large, displaying an appropriate error page.

Note that both paths issue a `Status` CGI response header field; this is necessary to propagate the correct status back to the client. Without this, the status code would be 200 OK because the script would have been invoked successfully, which is hardly the appropriate status. An incorrect status code may cause the browser to report to the user that the file was uploaded successfully, which might generate confusion, as this may be in conflict with the message of the error page.

Actually, there is a status value that corresponds to "you sent me something too large" (413), so we remap the *Deny*'s 403 (Forbidden) status to it.

 The same `Content-length` field is used to indicate the amount of data included in a `POST` request, such as from a Web form submission, so be careful not to set your maximum too low or your forms may start getting this error!

See Also

• Chapter 9

6.5 Restricting Images from Being Used Off-Site

Problem

Other sites are linking to images on your system, stealing bandwidth from you and incidentally making it appear as though the images belong to them. You want to ensure that all access to your images is from documents that are on your server.

Solution

Add the following lines to the *.htaccess* file in the directory where the images are, or to the appropriate *<Directory>* container in the *httpd.conf* file. Replace the *myserver.com* with your domain name:

```
<FilesMatch "\.(jpg|jpeg|gif|png)$">
    SetEnvIfNoCase Referer "^http://([^/]*\.)?myserver.com/" local_referrer=1
    Order Allow,Deny
    Allow from env=local_referrer
</FilesMatch>
```

In fact, by using the following recipe, you can even go one step further, and return a different image to users accessing your images via an off-site reference:

```
SetEnvIfNoCase Referer "^http://([^/]*\.)?myserver.com/" local_referrer=1
RewriteCond "%{ENV:local_referer}" "!=1"
RewriteRule ".*" "/Stolen-100x100.png" [L]
```

Discussion

The first solution will cause all requests for image files to be refused with a `403 Forbidden` status unless the link leading to the request was in one of your own documents. This means that anyone linking to your images from a different Web site system will get the error instead of the image, because the referer does not match the approved server name.

Note that this technique can cause problems for requests that do not include a `Referer` request header field, such as people who visit your site through an anonymizing service or who have their browser configured not to send this information.

The second solution is similar to the first, except that it substitutes an image of your choice for the one requested, rather than denying the request. Using the values in the Solution, you can construct a *Stolen-100x100.png* that has whatever admonitory message or perhaps just some picture that will deter the visitor from "stealing" your images.

This technique has a tendency to get the problem fixed more quickly, since visitors to the thieving site will see "This Image Is Stolen!"—and that's typically not the impression the site's owners would like them to get. Simply returning a 403 (Forbidden) error will result in a broken-image icon on the referring page, and *everyone* is used to those nowadays and thinks nothing of them.

See Also

- Recipe 6.21

6.6 Requiring Both Weak and Strong Authentication

Problem

You want to require both weak and strong authentication for a particular resource. For example, you wish to ensure that the user accesses the site from a particular location and to require that he provides a password.

Solution

Use the *Satisfy* directive to require both types of authentication:

```
<Directory /www/htdocs/sensitive>

    # Enforce all restrictions
    Satisfy All

    # Require a password
    AuthType Basic
    AuthName Sensitive
    AuthUserFile /www/passwords/users
    AuthGroupFile /www/passwords/groups
    Require group salesmen

    # Require access from a certain network
    Order deny,allow
    Deny from all
    Allow from 192.168.1
</Directory>
```

Discussion

In this example, a user must provide a login, identifying him as a member of the salesmen group, and he must also use a machine on the 192.168.1 network.

The *Satisfy All* directive requires that all access control measures be enforced for the specified scope. A user accessing the resource from a nonmatching IP address will immediately receive a `Forbidden` error message in his browser, while, in the logfile, the following error message is logged:

```
[Sun May 25 15:31:53 2003] [error] [client 208.32.53.7] client denied by server
    configuration: /usr/local/apache/htdocs/index.html
```

Users who are in the required set of IP addresses, however, receive a password dialog box and are required to provide a valid username and password.

Looking forward a little bit, the syntax of this recipe will change somewhat with the 2.4 release of the Web server. The *Allow*, *Deny*, and *Satisfy* directives have long confused Apache admins, and so this syntax has been revised.

The new syntax will look something like the following, with the old syntax still being available to those who want it by use of the *mod_access_compat* module.

The *Satisfy All* command will look like:

```
<SatisfyAll>
    Require group salesmen
    Require ip 192.168.1
</SatisfyAll>
```

See also the *SatisfyOne* directive, which replaces the *Satisfy any* syntax.

See Also

- Recipe 6.9

6.7 Managing .htpasswd Files

Problem

You wish to create password files for use with Basic HTTP authentication.

Solution

Use the *htpasswd* utility to create your password file, as in Table 6-1.

Table 6-1. Managing password files with htpasswd

Command	Action
% `htpasswd -c` user.pass waldo	Create a new password file called *user.pass* with this one new entry for user waldo. Will prompt for password.
% `htpasswd` user.pass ralph	Add an entry for user ralph in password file *user.pass*. Will prompt for password.
% `htpasswd -b` user.pass ralph mydogspot	Add a user ralph to password file *user.pass* with password mydogspot.

Or, use the Perl module *Apache::Htpasswd* to manage the file programmatically:

```
use Apache::Htpasswd;
$pass = new Apache::Htpasswd("/usr/local/apache/passwords/user.pass") or
    die "Couldn't open password file.";

# Add an entry
$pass->htpasswd("waldo", "emerson");

# Delete entry
$pass->htDelete("waldo");
```

Discussion

The *htpasswd* utility, which comes with Apache, is located in the *bin* subdirectory.

 On some third-party distributions of Apache, the *htpasswd* program has been copied into a directory in your path, but ordinarily it will not be in your path; you will either have to put it there, or provide the full path to the program in order to run it, such as */usr/local/apache/bin/htpasswd*.

The first line of the Solution creates a new password file at the specified location. That is, in the example given, it creates a new password file called *user.pass*, containing a username and password for a user *waldo*. You will be prompted to enter the desired password, and then prompted to repeat the password for confirmation.

The -c flag creates a new password file, even if a file of that name already exists, so make sure that you only use this flag the first time. After that, using it causes your existing password file to be obliterated and replaced with the (almost empty) new one.

The second line in the Solution adds a password to an existing password file. As before, the user is prompted to enter the desired password, and then prompted to confirm it by typing it again.

The examples given here create a password file using the **crypt** algorithm by default on all platforms other than Windows, Netware, and TPF. On those platforms, the MD5 algorithm is used by default.

For platforms that use **crypt**, each line of the password file looks something like:

```
waldo:z32oW/ruTI8U
```

The portion of the line following the username and colon is the encrypted password. Other usernames and passwords appear one per line.

The *htpasswd* utility provides other options, such as the ability to use the MD5 algorithm to encrypt the password (the -m flag), provide the password on the command line rather than being prompted for it (the -b flag), or print the results to *stdout*, rather than altering the password file (the -n flag).

The -b flag can be particularly useful when using the *htpasswd* utility to create pass-words in some scripted fashion, rather than from an interactive prompt. The third line of the recipe above illustrates this syntax.

As of Apache 2.0.46, the -D flag lets you delete an existing user from the password file:

```
% htpasswd -D user.pass waldo
```

whereas in previous versions, you would need to use some alternate method to remove lines from the file. For example, you could remove a line using *grep*, or simply open the file in a text editor:

```
% egrep -v '^waldo:' user.pass >! user.pass
```

Apache::Htpasswd, written by Kevin Meltzer, is available from CPAN (*http://cpan.org*) and gives a Perl interface to Apache password files. This allows you to modify your password files from CGI programs or via other mechanisms, using just a few lines of Perl code as shown in the recipe.

In addition to the methods demonstrated in this recipe, there are also methods for checking a particular password against the contents of the password file, obtaining a list of users from the file, or retrieving the encrypted password for a particular user, among other things. See the documentation for this fine module for the full details on its many features.

One final note about your password file. We strongly recommend that you store your password file in some location that is not accessible through the Web (i.e., outside of your document directory). By putting it in your document directory, you run the risk of someone downloading the file and running a brute-force password-cracking algorithm against it, which will eventually yield your passwords for them to use.

See Also

- Recipe 6.8
- *http://search.cpan.org/author/KMELTZ/Apache-Htpasswd/Htpasswd.pm*

6.8 Making Password Files for Digest Authentication

Problem

You need to create a password file to be used for Digest authentication.

Solution

Use the following command forms to set up a credential file for a realm to be protected by Digest authentication:

```
% htdigest -c "By invitation only" rbowen
% htdigest "By invitation only" krietz
```

Discussion

Digest authorization, implemented by *mod_auth_digest*, uses an MD5 hash of the username, password, and authentication realm to check the credentials of the client. The *htdigest* utility, which comes with Apache, creates these files for you.

The syntax for the command is very similar to the syntax for the *htpasswd* utility, except that you must also specify the authentication realm that the password will be used for. The resulting file contains one line per user, looking something like the following:

```
rbowen:By invitation only:23bc21f78273f49650d4b8c2e26141a6
```

Note that, unlike entries in the password files created by *htpasswd*, which can be used anywhere, these passwords can be used only in the specified authentication realm, because the encrypted hash includes the realm.

As with *htpasswd*, the -c flag creates a new file, possibly overwriting an existing file. You will be prompted for the password and then asked to type it again to verify it.

htdigest does not have any of the additional options that *htpasswd* does.

See Also

- Recipe 6.7

6.9 Relaxing Security in a Subdirectory

Problem

There are times when you might want to apply a tight security blanket over portions of your site, such as with something like:

```
<Directory /usr/local/apache/htdocs/BoD>
    Satisfy All
    AuthUserFile /usr/local/apache/access/bod.htpasswd
    Require valid-user
</Directory>
```

Because of Apache's scoping rules, this blanket applies to all documents in that directory and in any subordinate subdirectories underneath it. But suppose that you want to make a subdirectory, such as *BoD/minutes*, available without restriction.

Solution

The *Satisfy* directive is the answer. Add the following to either the *.htaccess* file in the subdirectory or in an appropriate *<Directory>* container:

```
Satisfy Any
Order Deny,Allow
Allow from all
```

HTTP, Browsers, and Credentials

It is easy to draw incorrect conclusions about the behavior of the Web; when you have a page displayed in your browser, it is natural to think that you are still connected to that site. In actuality, however, that's not the case—once your browser fetches the page from the server, both disconnect and forget about each other. If you follow a link, or ask for another page from the same server, a completely new exchange has begun.

When you think about it, this is fairly obvious. It would make no sense for your browser to stay connected to the server while you went off to lunch or home for the day.

Each transaction that is unique and unrelated to others is called *stateless*, and it has a bearing on how HTTP access control works.

When it comes to password-protected pages, the Web server doesn't remember whether you've accessed them before or not. Down at the HTTP level where the client (browser) and server talk to each other, the client has to prove who it is every time; it's the *client* that remembers your information.

When accessing a protected area for the first time in a session, here's what actually gets exchanged between the client and the server:

1. The client requests the page.
2. The server responds, "You are not authorized to access this resource (a `401 unauthorized` status). This resource is part of authentication realm *XYZ*." (This information is conveyed using the `WWW-Authenticate` response header field; see RFC 2616 for more information.)
3. If the client isn't an interactive browser, at this point it probably goes to step 7. If it is interactive, it asks the user for a username and password, and shows the name of the *realm* the server mentioned.
4. Having gotten credentials from the user, the client reissues the request for the document—including the credentials this time.
5. The server examines the provided credentials. If they're valid, it grants access and returns the document. If they aren't, it responds as it did in step 2.
6. If the client receives the unauthorized response again, it displays some message about it and asks the user if he wants to try entering the username and password again. If the user says yes, the client goes back to step 3.
7. If the user chooses not to reenter the username and password, the client gives up and accepts the "unauthorized" response from the server.

Once the client has successfully authenticated with the server, it remembers the credentials, URL, and realm involved. Subsequent requests that it makes for the same document or one "beneath" it (e.g., */foo/bar/index.html* is "beneath" */foo/index.html*) causes it to send the same credentials automatically. This makes the process start at step 4, so even though the challenge/response exchange is still happening between the client and the server, it's hidden from the user. This is why it's easy to get caught up in the fallacy of users being "logged on" to a site.

This is how all HTTP weak authentication works. One of the common features of most interactive Web browsers is that the credentials are forgotten when the client is shut down. This is why you need to reauthenticate each time you access a protected document in a new browser session.

Discussion

This tells Apache that access is granted if the requirements of either the weak (user credentials) or strong protection (IP address) mechanisms are fulfilled. Then it goes on to say that the strong mechanism will always be happy regardless of the visitor's origin.

Be aware that this sets a new default security condition for all subdirectories below the one affected. In other words, you are not just unlocking the one subdirectory but all of its descendants as well.

See Also

- Recipe 6.6
- Recipe 6.10

6.10 Lifting Restrictions Selectively

Problem

You want most documents to be restricted, such as requiring a username and password, but want a few to be available to the public. For example, you may want *index.html* to be publicly accessible, whereas the rest of the files in the directory require password authentication.

Solution

Use the *Satisfy Any* directive in the appropriate place in your *.htaccess* or *httpd.conf* file:

```
<Files index.html>
    Order Deny,Allow
    Allow from all
    Satisfy Any
</Files>
```

You can locate this in a *.htaccess* file, or within a *<Directory>* container to limit its effect:

```
<Directory "/usr/local/apache/htdocs">
    Satisfy All
    Order allow,deny
    Deny from all
    <Files *.html>
        Order deny,allow
        Allow from all
        Satisfy Any
```

```
        </Files>
      </Directory>
```

Discussion

Regardless of what sorts of restrictions you may have on other files, or on the directory as a whole, the *<Files>* container in the solution makes the *index.html* file accessible to everyone without limitation. *Satisfy Any* tells Apache that any of the restrictions in place may be satisfied, rather than having to enforce any particular one. In this case, the restriction in force will be *Allow from all*, which permits access for all clients.

This method can be easily extended to apply to arbitrary filename patterns using shell global characters. To extend it to use regular expressions for the filename, use the *<FilesMatch>* directive instead.

Weak and Strong Authentication

The basic Apache security model for HTTP is based on the concepts of *weak* and *strong* authentication mechanisms. Weak mechanisms are those that rely on information volunteered by the user; strong ones use credentials obtained without asking him. For instance, a username and password constitute a set of weak credentials, whereas the IP address of the user's client system is regarded as a strong one.

One difference between the two types lies in how Apache handles an authentication failure. If invalid weak credentials are presented, the server will respond with a `401 Unauthorized` status, which allows the user to try again. In contrast, a failure to authenticate when strong credentials are required will result in a `403 Forbidden` status —for which there is no opportunity to retry.

In addition, strong and weak credentials can be required in combination; this is controlled by the *Satisfy* directive. The five possible requirements are:

- None; no authentication required.
- Only strong credentials are needed.
- Only weak credentials are required.
- Both strong and weak credentials are accepted; if either is valid, access is permitted.
- Both strong and weak credentials are required.

See Also

- Recipe 6.9
- Recipe 6.6
- *http://httpd.apache.org/docs/mod/mod_access.html*

6.11 Authorizing Using File Ownership

Problem

You wish to require user authentication based on system file ownership. That is, you want to require that the user that owns the file matches the username that authenticated.

Solution

Use the *Require file-owner* directive:

```
<Directory /home/*/public_html/private>
    AuthType Basic
    AuthName "MyOwnFiles"
    AuthUserFile /some/master/authdb
    Require file-owner
</Directory>
```

Discussion

The goal here is to require that username **jones** must authenticate in order to access the */home/jones/public_html/private* directory.

The user does not authenticate against the system password file but against the *AuthUserFile* specified in the example. Apache just requires that the name used for authentication matches the name of the owner of the file or directory in question. Note also that this is a feature of *mod_auth* and is not available in other authentication modules.

 This feature was added in Apache 1.3.22. In Apache 2.2, this functionality is provided by the module *mod_authz_owner*.

See Also

- The *Require file-group* keyword at *http://httpd.apache.org/docs/mod/mod_auth.html#require*

6.12 Storing User Credentials in a MySQL Database

Problem

You wish to use user and password information in your MySQL database for authenticating users.

Solution

For Apache 1.3, use *mod_auth_mysql*:

```
Auth_MySQL_Info db_host.example.com db_user my_password
Auth_MySQL_General_DB auth_database_name

<Directory /www/htdocs/private>
    AuthName "Protected directory"
    AuthType Basic
    require valid-user
</Directory>
```

For Apache 2.2 and later, use *mod_authn_dbi*:

```
AuthnDbiDriver Config1 mysql
AuthnDbiHost Config1 db.example.com
AuthnDbiUsername Config1 db_username
AuthnDbiPassword Config1 db_password
AuthnDbiName Config1 auth_database_name
AuthnDbiTable Config1 auth_database_table
AuthnDbiUsernameField Config1 user_field
AuthnDbiPasswordField Config1 password_field
AuthnDbiIsActiveField Config1 is_active_field

AuthnDbiConnMin Config1 3
AuthnDbiConnSoftMax Config1 12
AuthnDbiConnHardMax Config1 20
AuthnDbiConnTTL Config1 600

<Directory  "/www/htdocs/private">
  AuthType Digest
  AuthName  "Protected directory>
  AuthBasicProvider dbi
  AuthnDbiServerConfig Config1
  Require valid-user
</Directory>
```

Discussion

There are a number of modules called *mod_auth_mysql*. The module used in the previous example is the *mod_auth_mysql* from *http://www.diegonet.com/support/mod_auth_mysql.shtml*. For the full explanation of the database fields that you will need to create, and the additional options that the module affords, you should consult the documentation on the Web site.

If you are running Apache 2.2 or later, you will want to take advantage of the new authentication framework, and use the module *mod_authn_dbi*, available from *http://open.cyanworlds.com/mod_authn_dbi*. Because of the new authentication API in Apache 2.2, a number of things are possible that were not possible in earlier versions. For example, a single module, such as *mod_authn_dbi*, can be used for either Basic or Digest authentication, by simply changing the *AuthType* directive from *Basic* to

Digest. (*AuthBasicProvider* would also become *AuthDigestProvider* in the previous example.)

mod_authn_dbi uses *libdbi*, which is a generic database access library, allowing you to use your favorite database server to provide authentication services. *libdbi* drivers are available for most popular database servers. For a more complete description of *mod_authn_dbi*, you should consult the documentation on the Web site.

See Also

- *http://www.diegonet.com/support/mod_auth_mysql.shtml*
- *http://open.cyanworlds.com/mod_authn_dbi*

6.13 Accessing the Authenticated Username

Problem

You want to know the name of the user who has authenticated.

Solution

Some scripting modules, such as *mod_php*, provide a standard interface for accessing values set by the server. For instance, to obtain the username that was used to authenticate from within a PHP script, it would access a field in the `$_SERVER` superglobal array:

```
$auth_user = $_SERVER['REMOTE_USER'];
```

For a Perl or *mod_perl* script, use:

```
my $username = $ENV{REMOTE_USER};
```

In a Server-Side Include (SSI) directive, this may look like:

```
Hello, user <!--#echo var="REMOTE_USER" -->. Thanks for visiting.
```

Other scripting modules may provide specific means of accessing this information. For those that don't, or for nonscript applications, use the appropriate means to consult the `REMOTE_USER` environment variable.

Discussion

When a user has authenticated, the environment variable `REMOTE_USER` is set to the name with which she authenticated. You can access this variable in CGI programs, SSI directives, PHP files, and a variety of other methods. The value also will appear in your *access_log* file.

Note that although it is the convention for an authentication module to set this variable, there are reportedly some third-party authentication modules that do not set it but provide other methods for accessing that information.

See Also

- Recipe 6.14

6.14 Obtaining the Password Used to Authenticate

Problem

You want to get the password the user used to authenticate.

Solution

Standard Apache modules do not make this value available. It is, however, available from the Apache API if you wish to write your own authentication methods.

In the Apache 1.3 API, you need to investigate the `ap_get_basic_auth_pw` function. In the 2.0 API, look at the `get_basic_auth` function.

If you write an authentication handler with *mod_perl*, you can retrieve the username and password with the `get_username` function:

```
my ($username, $password) = get_username($r);
```

You can make this information available to CGI scripts executed by the server if you rebuild the package with the appropriate flag. For Apache 1.3 and 2.0:

```
% CFLAGS="$CFLAGS -DSECURITY_HOLE_PASS_AHTORIZATION"
```

Discussion

For security reasons, although the username is available as an environment variable, the password used to authenticate is *not* available in any simple manner. The rationale behind this is that it would be a simple matter for unscrupulous individuals to capture passwords so that they could then use them for their own purposes. Thus, the decision was made to make passwords near to impossible to obtain.

The only way to change this is to rebuild the server from the sources with a particular (strongly discouraged) compilation flag. Alternately, if you write your own authentication module, you would of course have access to this value, as you would need to verify it in your code.

See Also

- Recipe 6.13

6.15 Preventing Brute-Force Password Attacks

Problem

You want to disable a username when there are repeated failed attempts to authenticate using it, as if it is being attacked by a password-cracker.

Solution

There is no way to do this with standard Apache authentication modules. The usual approach is to watch your logfile carefully. Or you can use something like *Apache::BruteWatch* to tell you when a user is being attacked:

```
PerlLogHandler Apache::BruteWatch
PerlSetVar BruteDatabase      DBI:mysql:brutelog
PerlSetVar BruteDataUser      username
PerlSetVar BruteDataPassword  password

PerlSetVar BruteMaxTries      5
PerlSetVar BruteMaxTime       120
PerlSetVar BruteNotify        rbowen@example.com
```

Discussion

Because of the stateless nature of HTTP and the fact that users are not, technically, "logged in" at all (see the HTTP, Browsers, and Credentials sidebar, earlier in this chapter), there is no connection between one authentication attempt and another. Most Apache auditing tools, such as *mod_security*, work on a per-request basis, and have no way to compare one request to another to build a profile across multiple requests. This makes it possible to repeatedly attempt to log in with a particular username, without it being easily dectable by any automated tool.

Your best bet is to carefully watch the log files, or to have some process which watches the log files for you.

Apache::BruteWatch is one way to watch the logfile and send notification when a particular account is being targeted for a brute-force password attack. With the configuration shown above, if a given account fails authentication five times in two minutes, the server administrator will be notified of the situation, so that she can take appropriate measures, such as blocking the offending address from the site.

Apache::BruteWatch is available from CPAN (*CPAN.org*) and requires *mod_perl* to run.

We are not, at this time, aware of another module that does this in real time.

See Also

- The HTTP, Browsers, and Credentials sidebar, earlier in this chapter

6.16 Using Digest Versus Basic Authentication

Problem

You want to understand the distinction between the `Basic` and `Digest` authentication methods.

Solution

Use *AuthType Basic* and the *htpasswd* tool to control access using `Basic` authentication. Use *AuthType Digest* and the *htdigest* tool for the `Digest` method.

Discussion

`Basic` Web authentication is exactly that: primitive and insecure. It works by encoding the user credentials with a reversible algorithm (essentially base-64 encoding) and transmitting the result in plaintext as part of the request header. Anyone (or anything) that intercepts the transmission can easily crack the encoding of the credentials and use them later. As a consequence, `Basic` authentication should only be used in environments where the protected documents aren't truly sensitive or when there is no alternative.

In contrast, `Digest` authentication uses a more secure method that is much less susceptible to credential theft, spoofing, and replay attacks. The exact details don't matter; the essential ingredient is that no username or password traverses the network in plaintext.

Preparing a realm to use `Basic` authentication consists of simply storing the username/password pair and telling the server where to find them. The password may or may not be encrypted. The same credentials may be applied to any realm on the server, or even copied to a completely different server and used there. They may be stored in a variety of databases; multiple modules exist for storing `Basic` credentials in flat text files, GDBM files, MySQL databases, LDAP directories, and so on.

Setting up `Digest` authentication is a little more involved. For one thing, the credentials are not transportable to other realms; when you generate them, you specify the realm to which they apply. For another, the only storage mechanism currently supported directly by the Apache package is flat text files; if you want to keep your `Digest` credentials in an LDAP directory or Oracle database, you're going to have to look for third-party modules to do it or else write one yourself.

In addition to the more complex setup process, `Digest` authentication currently suffers from a lack of market penetration. That is, even though Apache supports it, not all browsers and other Web clients do; so you may end up having to use `Basic` authentication simply, because there's nothing else available to your users. However, this is less and less the case with the passage of time, and there are very few Web clients in the wild any more that don't support `Digest` authentication.

See Also

- Recipe 6.18

6.17 Accessing Credentials Embedded in URLs

Problem

You know people access your site using URLs with embedded credentials, such as *http://user:password@host/*, and you want to extract them from the URL for validation or other purposes.

Solution

None; this is a nonissue that is often misunderstood.

Discussion

Embedding the username and password in the URL gives a way to distribute a link to your users to access a password-protected site directly without being prompted for the password. However, what tends to be misunderstood about this is that the username and password are actually sent to the server in the ordinary way (i.e., via the WWW-Authenticate header) and not as part of the URL. The browser dissects the URL and turns it into the appropriate request header fields to send to the server.

See Also

- The HTTP, Browsers, and Credentials sidebar, earlier in this chapter

6.18 Securing WebDAV

Problem

You want to allow your users to upload and otherwise manage their Web documents with WebDAV but without exposing your server to any additional security risks.

Solution

Require authentication to use WebDAV:

```
<Directory "/www/htdocs/dav-test">
    Order Allow,Deny
    Deny from all
    AuthDigestFile "/www/acl/.htpasswd-dav-test"
    AuthDigestDomain "/dav-test/"
    AuthName "DAV access"
    Require valid-user
```

```
        Satisfy Any
    </Directory>
```

Discussion

Because WebDAV operations can modify your server's resources and *mod_dav* runs as part of the server, locations that are WebDAV-enabled need to be writable by the user specified in the server's *User* directive. This means that the same location is writable by any CGI scripts or other modules that run as part of the Apache server. To keep remote modification operations under control, you should enable access controls for WebDAV-enabled locations. If you use weak controls, such as user-level authentication, you should use Digest authentication rather than Basic, as shown in the Solution.

The contents of the *<Directory>* container could be put into a *dav-test/.htaccess* file, as well. Note that the authentication database (specified with the *AuthDigestFile* directive) is not within the server's URI space, and so it cannot be fetched with a browser nor with any WebDAV tools.

Your authentication database and *.htaccess* files should not be modifiable by the server user; you don't want them getting changed by your WebDAV users!

See Also

- Recipe 6.16

6.19 Enabling WebDAV Without Making Files Writable by the Web User

Problem

You want to run WebDAV but don't want to make your document files writable by the Apache server user.

Solution

Run two Web servers as different users. The DAV-enabled server, for example, might run as *User* dav, *Group* dav, whereas the other server, which is responsible for serving your content, might run as *User* nobody, *Group* nobody. Make the Web content writable by the dav user, or the dav group.

Remember that only a single Web server can be handling a particular port/IP address combination. This means that your WebDAV-enabled server will have to be using either a different address, a different port, or both than the non-WebDAV server.

Discussion

A big security concern with DAV is that the content must be modifiable by the Web server user for DAV to be able to update that content. This means that any content also can be edited by CGI programs, SSI directives, or other programs running under the Web server. Although the Apache security guidelines caution against having any files writable by the Web server user, DAV requires it.

By running two Apache servers, you can move around this limitation. The DAV-enabled Web server, running on an alternate port, has the *User* and *Group* directives set to an alternate user and group, such as:

```
User dav
Group dav
```

which is the owner of the Web content in question. The other Web server, which will be responsible for serving content to users, runs as a user who does not have permission to write to any of the documents.

The DAV-enabled Web server should be well authenticated, so that only those who are permitted to edit the site can access that portion of the server. You should probably also set up this server to be very lightweight, both in the modules that you install as well as in the number of child processes (or threads) that you run.

Finally, it should be noted that the *perchild* MPM, under Apache 2.0, supports the idea of running different virtual hosts with different user ids, so that this recipe could be accomplished by enabling DAV just for the one particular vhost. However, as of this writing, the *perchild* MPM is not working yet.

See Also

*   *http://httpd.apache.org/docs-2.0/mod/mod_dav.html*
*   *http://httpd.apache.org/docs-2.0/mod/perchild.html*

6.20 Restricting Proxy Access to Certain URLs

Problem

You don't want people using your proxy server to access particular URLs or patterns of URLs (such as MP3 or streaming video files).

Solution

You can block by keyword:

```
ProxyBlock .rm .ra .mp3
```

You can block by specific backend URLs:

```
<Directory proxy:http://other-host.org/path>
    Order Allow,Deny
    Deny from all
    Satisfy All
</Directory>
```

Or you can block according to regular expression pattern matching:

```
<Directory proxy:*>
    RewriteEngine On
    #
    # Disable proxy access to Real movie and audio files
    #
    RewriteRule "\.(rm|ra)$" "-" [F,NC]
    #
    # Don't allow anyone to access .mil sites through us
    #
    RewriteRule "^[a-z]+://[-.a-z0-9]*\.mil($|/)" "-" [F,NC]
</Directory>
```

Discussion

All of these solutions will result in a client that attempts to access a blocked URL receiving a 403 Forbidden status from the server.

The first solution uses a feature built into the proxy module itself: the *ProxyBlock* directive. It's simple and efficient, and it catches the results so that future accesses to the same URL are blocked with less effort; however, the pattern matching it can perform is extremely limited and prone to confusion. For instance, if you specify:

```
ProxyBlock .mil
```

the server denies access to both *http://www.navy.mil/* and *http://example.com/spec.mil/ list.html*. This is probably not what was intended!

The second method allows you to impose limitations based on the URL being fetched (or gateway, in the case of a *ProxyPass* directive).

The third method, which allows more complex what-to-block patterns to be constructed, is both more flexible and more powerful, and somewhat less efficient. Use it only when the other methods prove insufficient.

 <DirectoryMatch> containers work as well, so more complex patterns may be used.

The flags to the *RewriteRule* directive tell it, first, that any URL matching the pattern should result in the server returning a 403 Forbidden error (F or forbidden), and second that the pattern match is case-insensitive (NC or nocase).

One disadvantage of the *mod_rewrite* solution is that it can be too specific. The first *RewriteRule* pattern can be defeated if the client specifies path-info or a query string, or if the origin server uses a different suffix naming scheme for these types of files. A little cleverness on your part can cover these sorts of conditions, but beware of trying to squeeze too many possibilities into a single regular expression pattern. It's generally better to have multiple *RewriteRule* directives than to have a single all-singing all-dancing one that no one can read—and is, hence, prone to error.

See Also

- The *mod_proxy* and *mod_rewrite* documentation at *http://httpd.apache.org/docs/mod/mod_proxy.html* and *http://httpd.apache.org/docs/mod/mod_rewrite.html*

6.21 Protecting Files with a Wrapper

Problem

You have files to which you want to limit access using some method other than standard Web authentication (such as a members-only area).

Solution

In *httpd.conf*, add the following lines to a *<Directory>* container whose contents should be accessed only through a script:

```
RewriteEngine On
RewriteRule "\.(dll|zip|exe)$" protect.php [NC]
RewriteCond %{REMOTE_ADDR} "!^my.servers.ip"
RewriteRule "\.cgi$" protect.php [NC]
```

And an example *protect.php* that just displays the local URI of the document that was requested:

```php
<?php
/*
 * The URL of the document actually requested is in
 * $_SERVER['REQUEST_URI'].  Appropriate decisions
 * can be made about what to do from that.
 */
Header('Content-type: text/plain');
$body = sprintf("Document requested was: %s\n", $_SERVER['REQUEST_URI']);
Header('Content-length: ' . strlen($body));
print $body;
?>
```

Discussion

In the situation that prompted this recipe, authentication and authorization were completed using a cookie rather than the standard mechanisms built into the Web protocols. Any request for a document on the site was checked for the cookie and redirected to the login page if it wasn't found, was expired, or had some other problem causing its validity to be questioned.

This is fairly common and straightforward. What is needed in addition to this is a way to limit access to files according to the cookie and ensure that no URL-only request could reach them.

To this end, a wrapper is created (called *protect.php* in the Solution), which is invoked any time one of the protected document types is requested. After validating the cookie, the *protect.php* script figures out the name of the file from the environment variables, determines the content-type from the extension, and opens the file and sends the contents.

This is illustrated in the Solution. Any time a document ending in one of the extensions *.dll*, *.zip*, *.exe*, or *.cgi* is requested from the scope covered by the *mod_rewrite* directives, and the request comes from some system other than the Web server system itself (i.e., from a client system), the *protect.php* script will be invoked instead. In the Solution, the script simply displays the local URI of the document that is requested; applying additional access control or other functionality is easily developed from the example.

If access control is the main purpose of the wrapper and the access is granted, the wrapper needs to send the requested document to the client. In this case, the wrapper could either determine the filesystem path to the desired document and use the PHP routine `fpassthru( )` to open it and send it to the client, or it could access the document using PHP's ability to open a URL as though it were a file with the `fopen("http://docurl")` function call. (This latter method is necessary if the document requires server processing, such as if it's a script.)

This would ordinarily trigger the wrapper on the dynamic document again, causing a loop. To prevent this, the wrapper is only applied to dynamic documents if the requesting host isn't the server itself. If it is the Web server making the request, we know the wrapper has already been run and you don't need to run it again. The server processes the document as usual and sends the contents back to the wrapper, which is still handling the original request, and it dutifully passes it along to the client. This is handled by the *RewriteCond* directive, which says "push requests for scripts through the wrapper unless they're coming from the server itself."

This method is perhaps a little less than perfectly elegant and not the best for performance, because each CGI request involves at least two concurrent requests, but it *does* address the problem.

See Also

- Chapter 5

6.22 Protecting Server Files from Malicious Scripts

Problem

Scripts running on your Web server may access, modify, or destroy files located on your Web server if they are not adequately protected. You want to ensure that this cannot happen.

Solution

Ensure that none of your files are writable by the nobody user or the nobody group, and that sensitive files are not readable by that user and group:

```
# find / -user nobody
# find / -group nobody
```

Discussion

The *User* and *Group* directives specify a user and group under whose privileges the Web server will run. These are often set to the values of nobody and nobody, respectively, but they can vary in different setups. It is often advisable to create a completely new user and group for this purpose, so that there is no chance that the user has been given additional privileges of which you are not aware.

Because everything runs with these privileges, any files or directories that are accessible by this user and/or group will be accessible from any script running on the server. This means that a script running under one virtual host may possibly modify or delete files contained within another virtual host, either intentionally or accidentally, if those files have permissions making this possible.

Ideally, no files anywhere on your server should be owned by, or writable by, the server user, unless for the explicit purpose of being used as a datafile by a script. And, even for this purpose, it is recommended that a real database be used, so that the file itself cannot be modified by the server user. And if files simply must be writable by the server, they should definitely not be in some Web-accessible location, such as */cgi-bin/*.

See Also

- Recipe 8.13
- Recipe 6.23

6.23 Setting Correct File Permissions

Problem

You want to set file permissions to provide the maximum level of security.

Solution

The *bin* directory under the *ServerRoot* should be owned by user root, group root, and have file permissions of 755 (`rwxr-xr-x`). Files contained therein should also be owned by root.root and be mode 755.

Document directories, such as *htdocs*, *cgi-bin*, and *icons*, will have to have permissions set in a way that makes the most sense for the development model of your particular Web site, but under no circumstances should any of these directories or files contained in them be writable by the Web server user.

 The solution provided here is specific to Unixish systems. Users of other operating systems should adhere to the principles laid out here, although the actual implementation will vary.

The *conf* directory should be readable and writable only by root, as should all the files contained therein.

The *include* and *libexec* directories should be readable by everyone, writable by no one.

The *logs* directory should be owned and writable by root. You may, if you like, permit other users to read files in this directory, as it is often useful for users to be able to access their logfiles, particularly for troubleshooting purposes.

The *man* directory should be readable by all users.

Finally, the *proxy* directory should be owned by and writable by the server user.

 On most Unixish file systems, a *directory* must have the x bit set in order for the files therein to be visible.

Discussion

You should be aware that if you ask 12 people for the correct ways to set file permissions on your Apache server, you will get a dozen different answers. The recommendations here are intended to be as paranoid as possible. You should feel free to relax these recommendations, based on your particular view of the world and how much you trust your users. However, if you set file permissions any more restrictive than this, your Apache server is likely not to function. There are, of course, exceptions to this, and cases in which you could possibly be more paranoid are pointed out later.

The most important consideration when setting file permissions is the Apache server user—the user as which Apache runs. This is configured with the *User* and *Group* directives in your *httpd.conf* file, setting what user and group the Apache processes will run as. This user needs to have read access to nearly everything but should not have write access to anything.

The recommended permissions for the *bin* directory permit anyone to run programs contained therein. This is necessary in order for users to create password files using the *htpasswd* and *htdigest* utilities, run CGI programs using the *suexec* utility, check the version of Apache using *httpd* -v, or use any of the other programs in this directory. There is no known security risk of permitting this access. The Web server itself cannot be stopped or started by an unprivileged user under normal conditions. These files, or the directory, should never be writable by nonroot users, as this would allow compromised files to be executed with root privileges.

Extra-paranoid server administrators may wish to make the *bin* directory and its contents readable and executable only by root. However, the only real benefit to doing so is that other users cannot run the utilities or *httpd* server, such as on a different port. Some of those utilities, such as *htpasswd* and *htdigest*, are intended to be run by content providers (i.e., users) in addition to the Webmaster.

The *conf* directory, containing the server configuration files, can be locked down as tightly as you like. Although it is unlikely that reading the server configuration files will allow a user to gain additional privileges on the server, more information is always useful for someone trying to compromise your server. You may, therefore, wish to make this directory readable only by root. However, most people will consider this just a little too paranoid.

Document directories are particularly problematic when it comes to making permission recommendations, as the recommended setting will vary from one server to another. On a server with only one content provider, these directories should be owned by that user and readable by the Apache user. On a server with more than one content developer, the files should be owned by a group of users who can modify the files but still be readable by the Apache user. The *icons* directory is a possible exception to this rule, because the contents of that directory are rarely modified and do not need to be writable by any users.

The *include* and *libexec* directories contain files that are needed by the Apache executable at runtime and only need to be readable by root, which starts as root, and by no other users. However, since the *include* directory contains C header files, it may occasionally be useful for users to have access to those files to build applications that need those files.

The *logs* directory should under no circumstances ever be writable by anyone other than root. If the directory is ever writable by another user, it is possible to gain control of the Apache process at start time and gain root privileges on the server. Whether you permit other users to read files in this directory is up to you and is not required. However, on most servers, it is very useful for users to be able to access the logfiles— particularly the *error_log* file, in order to troubleshoot problems without having to contact the server administrator.

The *man* directory contains the manpages for the various utilities that come with Apache. These need to be readable by all users. However, it is recommended that you move them to the system *man* path, or install them there when you install Apache by providing an argument to the ―mandir argument specifying the location of your system *man* directory.

Finally, the *proxy* directory should be owned by, and writable by, the server user. This is the only exception to the cardinal rule that nothing should be writable by this user. The *proxy* directory contains files created by and managed by *mod_proxy*, and they need to be writable by the unprivileged Apache processes. If you are not running a proxy server with *mod_proxy*, you may remove this directory entirely.

See Also

- *Learning the Unix Operating System*, Fifth Edition, by Jerry Peek, Grace Todino-Gonquet, and John Strang (O'Reilly)
- *http://www.onlamp.com/pub/a/bsd/2000/09/06/FreeBSD_Basics.html*

6.24 Running a Minimal Module Set

Problem

You want to eliminate all modules that you don't need in order to reduce the potential exposure to security holes. What modules do you really need?

Solution

For Apache 1.3, you can run a bare-bones server with just three modules (actually, you can get away with not running any modules at all, but it is not recommended):

```
% ./configure --disable-module=all --enable-module=dir \
> --enable-module=mime --enable-module=log_config \
```

For Apache 2.x, this is slightly more complicated, as you must individually disable modules you don't want:

```
% ./configure --disable-access \
> --disable-auth --disable-charset-lite \
> --disable-include --disable-log-config --disable-env --disable-setenvif \
> --disable-mime --disable-status --disable-autoindex --disable-asis \
> --disable-cgid --disable-cgi --disable-negotiation --disable-dir \
> --disable-imap --disable-actions --disable-alias --disable-userdir
```

Note that with 2.x, as with 1.3, you may wish to enable *mod_dir*, *mod_mime*, and *mod_log_config*, by simply leaving them off of this listing.

Discussion

A frequent security recommendation is that you eliminate everything that you don't need; if you don't need something and don't use it, then you are likely to overlook security announcements about it or forget to configure it securely. The question that is less frequently answered is exactly what you do and don't need.

A number of Apache package distributions come with everything enabled, and people end up running modules that they don't really need—or perhaps are not even aware that they are running.

This recipe is an attempt to get to the very smallest Apache server possible, reducing it to the minimum set of modules that Apache will run. That is, if you take any of these out, Apache will not even start up, let alone serve a functional Web site.

Apache 1.3

With Apache 1.3, this question is fairly easy to answer. We've reduced it to a set of three modules, and actually you can eliminate all of the modules if you really want to, as long as you're aware of the implications of doing so.

mod_dir is the module that takes a request for / and turns it into a request for */index.html*, or whatever other file you have indicated with the *DirectoryIndex* directive as the default document for a directory. Without this module, users typing just your hostname into their browser will immediately get a 404 error, rather than a default document. Granted, you could require that users specify a hostname and filename in their URL, in which case you could dispense with this module requirement. This would, however, make your Web site fairly hard to use.

mod_mime enables Apache to determine what MIME type a particular file is and send the appropriate MIME header with that file, enabling the browser to know how to render that file. Without *mod_mime*, your Web server will treat *all* files as having the MIME type set by the *DefaultType* directive. If this happens to match the actual type of the file, well and good; otherwise, this will cause the browser to render the document incorrectly. If your Web site consists only of one type of files, you can omit this module.

Finally, *mod_log_config*, while not technically required at all, is highly recommended. Running your Web server without any activity logfiles will leave you without any idea of how your site is being used, which can be detrimental to the health of your server. However, you should note that it is not possible to disable the *ErrorLog* functionality of Apache, and so, if you really don't care about the access information of your Web site, you could feasibly leave off *mod_log_config* and still have error log information.

The default distributed configuration file will need some adjustment to run under these reduced conditions. In particular, you will probably need to remove *Order*, *Allow*, and *Deny* directives (provided by *mod_access*), and you will need to remove *LogFormat* and *CustomLog* directives if you remove *mod_log_config*. Many other sections of the configuration files are protected by *<IfModule>* sections and will still function in the absence of the required modules.

Apache 2.x

With Apache 2.x, a new configuration utility is used, and so the command-line syntax is more complicated. In particular, there is no single command-line option to let you remove all modules, and so every module must be specified with a `–disable` directive.

The list of modules that are minimally required for Apache 2.x is the same as that for 1.3. *mod_dir*, *mod_mime*, and *mod_log_config* are each recommended, but not mandated, for the same reasons outlined previously.

See Also

- *http://httpd.apache.org/docs/mod/mod_dir.html*
- *http://httpd.apache.org/docs/mod/mod_mime.html*
- *http://httpd.apache.org/docs/mod/mod_log_config.html*

6.25 Restricting Access to Files Outside Your Web Root

Problem

You want to make sure that files outside of your Web directory are not accessible.

Solution

For Unixish systems:

```
<Directory />
    Order deny,allow
    Deny from all
    AllowOverride None
    Options None
</Directory>
```

For Windows systems:

```
<Directory C:/>
    Order deny,allow
    Deny from all
    AllowOverride None
    Options None
</Directory>
```

Repeat for each drive letter on the system.

Discussion

Good security technique is to deny access to everything, and then selectively permit access where it is needed. By placing a *Deny from all* directive on the entire filesystem, you ensure that files cannot be loaded from any part of your filesystem unless you explicitly permit it, using a *Allow from all* directive applied to some other *<Directory>* section in your configuration.

If you wanted to create an *Alias* to some other section of your filesystem, you would need to explicitly permit this with the following:

```
Alias /example /var/example
<Directory /var/example>
    Order allow,deny
    Allow from all
</Directory>
```

See Also

- *http://httpd.apache.org/docs/mod/mod_access.html*

6.26 Limiting Methods by User

Problem

You want to allow some users to use certain methods but prevent their use by others. For instance, you might want users in group A to be able to use both GET and POST but allow everyone else to use only GET.

Solution

Apply user authentication *per* method using the *Limit* directive:

```
AuthName "Restricted Access"
AuthType Basic
AuthUserFile filename
Order Deny,Allow
Allow from all
<Limit GET>
    Satisfy Any
</Limit>
<LimitExcept GET>
    Satisfy All
    Require valid-user
</Limit>
```

Discussion

It is often desirable to give general access to one or more HTTP methods, while restricting others. For example, although you may wish any user to be able to GET certain documents, you may wish for only site administrators to POST data back to those documents.

It is important to use the *LimitExcept* directive, rather than attempting to enumerate all possible methods, as you're likely to miss one.

See Also

- *http://httpd.apache.org/docs/mod/mod_auth.html*
- *http://httpd.apache.org/docs/mod/mod_access.html*
- *http://httpd.apache.org/docs/mod/core.html#limit*
- *http://httpd.apache.org/docs/mod/core.html#limitexcept*

6.27 Restricting Range Requests

Problem

You want to prevent clients from requesting partial downloads of documents within a particular scope, forcing them to request the entire document instead.

Solution

You can overload *ErrorDocument 403* to make it handle range requests. To do this, put the following into the appropriate *<Directory>* container in your *httpd.conf* file or in the directory's *.htaccess* file:

```
SetEnvIf "Range" "." partial_requests
Order Allow,Deny
Allow from all
Deny from env=partial_requests
ErrorDocument 403 /forbidden.cgi
```

Then put the following into a file named *forbidden.cgi* in your server's *DocumentRoot*:

```
#! /usr/bin/perl -w
use strict;
my $message;
my $status_line;
my $body;
my $uri = $ENV{'REDIRECT_REQUEST_URI'} || $ENV{'REQUEST_URI'};
my $range = $ENV{'REDIRECT_HTTP_RANGE'} || $ENV{'HTTP_RANGE'};
if (defined($range)) {
    $body = "You don't have permission to access "
        . $ENV{'REQUEST_URI'}
        . " on this server.\r\n";
```

```perl
        $status_line = '403 Forbidden';
    }
    else {
        $body = "Range requests disallowed for document '"
            . $ENV{'REQUEST_URI'}
            . "'.\r\n";
        $status_line = '416 Range request not permitted';
    }
    print "Status: $status_line\r\n"
        . "Content-type: text/plain;charset=iso-8859-1\r\n"
        . "Content-length: " . length($body) . "\r\n"
        . "\r\n"
        . $body;
    exit(0);
```

Or use *mod_rewrite* to catch requests with a **Range** header. To do this, put the following into the appropriate *<Directory>* container in your *httpd.conf* file or in the directory's *.htaccess* file:

```
RewriteEngine On
RewriteCond "%{HTTP:RANGE}" "."
RewriteRule "(.*)"          "/range-disallowed.cgi" [L,PT]
```

Then put the following into a file named *range-disallowed.cgi* in your server's *DocumentRoot*:

```perl
#! /usr/bin/perl -w
use strict;
my $message = "Range requests disallowed for document '"
    . $ENV{'REQUEST_URI'}
    . "'.\r\n";
print "Status: 416 Range request not permitted\r\n"
    . "Content-type: text/plain;charset=iso-8859-1\r\n"
    . "Content-length: " . length($message) . "\r\n"
    . "\r\n"
    . $message;
exit(0);
```

Discussion

Both of these solutions are a bit sneaky about how they accomplish the goal.

The first overloads an *ErrorDocument 403* script so that it handles both real "access forbidden" conditions *and* range requests. The *SetEnvIf* directive sets the `partial_request` environment variable if the request header includes a **Range** field, the *Deny* directive causes the request to be answered with a 403 Forbidden status if the environment variable is set, and the *ErrorDocument* directive declares the script to handle the 403 status. The script checks to see whether there was a **Range** field in the request header so it knows how to answer—with a "you can't do **Range** requests here" or with a real "document access forbidden" response.

The second solution uses *mod_rewrite* to rewrite any requests in the scope that include a **Range** header field to a custom script that handles only this sort of action; it returns the appropriate status code and message. The "sneaky" aspect of this solution is rewriting a valid and successful request to something that forces the response status to be *unsuccessful*.

See Also

- *http://httpd.apache.org/docs/mod/mod_setenvif.html*
- *http://httpd.apache.org/docs/mod/mod_access.html*
- *http://httpd.apache.org/docs/mod/mod_rewrite.html*

6.28 Rebutting DoS Attacks with mod_evasive

Problem

You want to protect your server from Denial of Service (DoS) attacks.

Solution

Obtain *mod_evasive* from *http://www.zdziarski.com/projects/mod_evasive/* and use a configuration like the following:

```
DOSPageCount       2
DOSPageInterval    1
DOSSiteCount       50
DOSSiteInterval    1
DOSBlockingPeriod  10
```

Discussion

mod_evasive is a third-party module that performs one simple task, and performs it very well. It detects when your site is receiving a Denial of Service (DoS) attack, and it prevents that attack from doing as much damage as it would do if left to run its course.

"Denial of Service" is a fairly broad term used to refer to attacks that consist of connections that cause your server to be so busy handling them that it can't do anything else, such as talk to legitimate clients. Usually, in the case of Apache, this consists of simply making hundreds of HTTP requests per second. Often, the attacker will not even wait for the response, but will immediately disconnect and make another request, leaving Apache making a response to a client that isn't even there anymore.

mod_evasive detects when a single client is making multiple requests in a short period of time, and denies further requests from that client. The period for which the ban is in place can be very short, because it just gets renewed the next time a request is detected from that same host.

This configuration places two restrictions on requests. First, the *DOSPage* directives state that if a single client address requests the same URL more than twice in a single second, it should be blocked. The *DOSSite* directives state that if a single client address requests more than 50 URLs in a single second, it should be blocked. This second value is higher because sometimes a single page will contain a large number of images, and so will result in a larger number of requests from one client.

The *DOSBlockingPeriod* directive sets the interval for which the client will be blocked—in this case, 10 seconds. Although this seems like a very short interval, it can stretch indefinitely, as each time that same client attempts to connect (and is blocked) the denial period will start over again.

See Also

- *http://www.zdziarski.com/projects/mod_evasive*

6.29 Chrooting Apache with mod_security

Problem

You want to chroot Apache to make it more secure.

Solution

There are a number of different ways to chroot Apache. One of the simplest is to use *mod_security*, and add the following directive:

```
SecChrootDir /chroot/apache
```

Discussion

chroot is a Unix command that causes a program to run in a jail. That is to say, when the command is launched, the accessible file system is replaced with another path, and the running application is forbidden to access any files outside of its new file system. By doing this, you are able to control what resources the program has access to and prevent it from writing to files outside of that directory, or running any programs that are not in that directory. This prevents a large number of exploits by simply denying the attacker access to the necessary tools.

The trouble with *chroot* is that it is very inconvenient. For example, when you chroot Apache, you must copy into the new file system any and all libraries or other files that Apache needs to run. For example, if you're running *mod_ssl*, you'd need to copy all of the OpenSSL libraries into the chroot jail so that Apache could access them. And if you had Perl CGI programs, you'd need to copy Perl, and all its modules, into the chroot directory.

mod_security gets around this complexity by chrooting Apache, not when it starts up, but immediately before it forks its child processes. This solves the *mod_ssl* problem mentioned above, but it would not solve the Perl problem because the Perl CGI program is run by the forked child process. However, the number of things that you'll need to move or copy into the chroot jail is greatly reduced, and tends to consist only of things that you're running as CGI programs, rather than all of the libraries that Apache needs while it is starting up. This greatly reduced complexity increases the probability that someone would actually chroot Apache, as otherwise the complexity is such that most of us would never be willing to put up with the inconvenience.

If you're running Apache 1.3, you'll need to make sure that *mod_security* appears first in your *LoadModule* list, so that it can have the necessary level of control over how things are orchestrated. It's important that the chrooting happen at just the right moment, and in order for this to happen, *mod_security* needs to get there first before another module can take over.

If you're running Apache 2.0, this isn't necessary, as the module "knows" when it's supposed to load, and the right thing happens.

See Also

- *http://modsecurity.org*

6.30 Migrating to 2.2 Authentication

Problem

You had authentication working, and then you moved to Apache 2.2, and everything is different.

Solution

Authentication was rearchitected in Apache 2.2 to more completely separate authentication and authorization as separate steps which can be configured independently. Although, at first, it can seem to be change for the sake of change, once you understand this separation, the new configuration syntax makes a lot more sense, and the changes that you'll have to make seem more sensible.

Discussion

These terms—authentication and autorization—are defined in some detail in the introduction to this chapter. Traditionally, Apache has blurred the boundary between these two concepts, making it difficult to configure one without being compelled to configure the other a particular way. For example, if you wanted to use `Digest` authentication, you were required to use a plain text file for the list of users. This is no longer the case with Apache 2.2.

In order to configure authentication and authorization in Apache 2.2, you'll need to make three decisions, which, in practical terms, involves choosing one module from each of three lists.

First, you'll need to determine which authentication type you're going to use. Your choices are Digest and Basic authentication, so you'll need to choose either *mod_auth_basic* or *mod_auth_digest*. This is done with the *AuthType* directive, as it was in versions before 2.2:

```
AuthType Basic
```

Next, you'll need to choose your authentication provider. This means that you're choosing where your authentication information will be stored—in a text file, dbm file, database, and so on. The directive for making this choice will be either *AuthBasicProvider*, if you're using `Basic` authentication, or *AuthDigestProvider*, if you're using `Digest` authentication:

```
AuthBasicProvider dbm
```

Finally, you'll need to provide some authorization requirement, using either a group or a some other method, using the *Require* directive:

```
Require user sarah
```

Thus, as compared to before 2.2, your authentication/authorization configuration directives may be an extra line or two:

```
AuthName "Private"
AuthType Basic
AuthBasicProvider dbm
AuthDBMUserFile /www/passwords/passwd.dbm
Require user sarah isaiah
```

See Also

- *http://httpd.apache.org/docs/2.2/howto/auth.html*

6.31 Blocking Worms with mod_security

Problem

You want to use the *mod_security* third-party module to intercept common probes before they actually reach your Web server's pages.

Solution

If you have *mod_security* installed (see Recipe 2.9), then you can use its basic "core rules" accessory package to intercept many of the most common attack and probe forms that hit Web servers. The core rules package is periodically updated to keep pace with new issues that appear on the Web.

Discussion

Installing the core rules package and following the instructions in the *README* file makes this very simple. In addition, the files in the package make it easy to write your own rules by illustrating the formats.

See Also

- *http://modsecurity.org/projects/rules*

6.32 Mixing Read-Only and Write Access to a Subversion Repository

Problem

You want to protect different portions of your Subversion repository differently, allowing read-access in some paths and write-access in others.

Solution

For a simple solution, you can use the *<LimitExcept>* to protect certain files or paths such that write access requires authentication:

```
<Location "/repos">
    DAV svn
    SVNParentPath "/repository/subversion"
    AuthType Basic
    AuthName "Log in for write access"
    AuthUserFile "/path/to/authfile"
    <LimitExcept GET REPORT OPTIONS PROPFIND>
        Requre valid-user
    </LimitExcept>
</Location>
```

The configuration fragment above applies the restriction to the entire Subversion repository. For more flexible or fine-grained control, combine this with the *mod_authz_svn* module:

```
LoadModule authz_svn_module    modules/mod_authz_svn.so

<Location "/repos">
    DAV svn
    SVNParentPath "/repository/subversion"
    Order Deny,Allow
    Allow from all
    AuthName "Log in for write access"
    AuthType Digest
    AuthDigestDomain "/repos/"
    AuthDigestFile "/path/to/digest-file"
    AuthzSVNAccessFile "/path/to/access-file"
```

```
<Limit GET PROPFIND OPTIONS REPORT>
    Satisfy Any
</Limit>
<LimitExcept GET PROPFIND OPTIONS REPORT>
    Satisfy All
    Require valid-user
</LimitExcept>
</Location>
```

Discussion

The first solution takes a simple approach: it says, in essence, "These methods are harmless, but if you use any others you gotta log in."

The second solution combines this with the functionality of the *mod_authz_svn* module, which allows you to grant (or deny) access selectively according to the path involved. It still provides read access to the entire repository; if you want to limit that to only specific paths according to the username being used, remove the *<LimitExcept>* and *</LimitExcept>* lines, and remove the *<Limit>* container entirely. Then users will be required to log in to access the repository at all, and what they can access—read, write, or not at all—is defined by the SVN auth file identified by the *AuthzSVNAccessFile* directive.

See Also

- *http://httpd.apache.org/docs/2.0/core.html#limitexcept*
- *http://svnbook.red-bean.com/en/1.0/ch06s04.html*

6.33 Using Permanent Redirects to Obscure Forbidden URLs

Problem

When access to a file is forbidden, you don't want the user's browser to show its URL.

Solution

Add an *ErrorDocument* script that issues a permanent redirect to a "document not found" message page:

```
Alias "/not-found" "/path/to/documentroot/not-found.html"
ErrorDocument 403 "/cgi/handle-403
```

And in the *cgi-bin/handle-403* script, something like this:

```
#! /usr/bin/perl -w
#
# Force a permanent redirect
#
print "Location: http://example.com/not-found\r\n\r\n";
exit(0);
```

Discussion

Ordinarily, when access to a document is forbidden, the browser's display of its URL remains when the error is displayed. By using the steps in the Solution, the URL of the actual document being forbidden will be obscured by the server handling it with a redirection—which causes the browser to change its location bar—rather than as a normal error.

 Note that the title of this recipe uses the verb "obscure." That's for a good reason; what's being practiced here is called "security by obscurity," which means, "they can still get at it it if they know exactly what to look for, but we'll hope they don't know it." In a way, it's like sticking your head in the sand and hoping that either the problem will go away or no one will discover it. A savvy user may be able to examine the network traffic and find out the name of the file being forbidden to him.

Because the redirection to the *not-found.html* file is successful, the browser is unaware that it tried to do anything wrong. You can spice this up a bit by making the redirection target a script that uses:

```
print "Status: 403 Forbidden\r\n\r\n";
```

What will happen in this case is that the browser will request a forbidden file, the server will answer, "Go look over there," and when the browser obediently looks, *then* it gets the 403 Forbidden error. But the browser's location field will show the *not-found.html* document's URL rather than that of the actual forbidden document.

See Also

- *http://httpd.apache.org/docs/2.0/core.html#errordocument*
- RFC 3875 sections 6.3.2 and 6.3.3 (*ftp://ftp.rfc-editor.org/in-notes/rfc3875.txt*)

## CHAPTER 7

SSL

Secure Socket Layer (SSL) is the standard way to implement secure Web sites. By encrypting the traffic between the server and the client, which is what SSL does, that content is protected from a third party listening to the traffic going past.

All of the traffic exchanged is encrypted once the SSL session has been set up. This means that even the URLs being requested are encrypted.

The exact mechanism by which this encryption is accomplished is discussed extensively in the SSL specification, which you can read at *http://wp.netscape.com/eng/ssl3*. For a more user-friendly discussion of SSL, we recommend looking through the *mod_ssl* manual, which you can find at *http://httpd.apache.org/docs/2.2/ssl*. This document not only discusses the specific details of setting up *mod_ssl* but also covers the general theory behind SSL and contains pictures illustrating the concepts.

You also may wish to see the TLS 1.0 (RFC 2246) specification, which provides what might be thought of as the next generation of SSL. You can read the full specification at *http://www.ietf.org/rfc/rfc2246.txt*, or you can find a more friendly explanation at *http://en.wikipedia.org/wiki/Transport_Layer_Security*.

In this chapter, we talk about some of the common things that you might want to do with your secure server, including installing it.

7.1 Installing SSL

Problem

You want to install SSL on your Apache server.

Solution

The solutions to this problem fall into several categories, depending on how you installed Apache in the first place (or whether you are willing to rebuild Apache to get SSL).

If you installed a binary distribution of Apache, your best bet is to return to the place from which you acquired that binary distribution and try to find the necessary files for adding SSL to it.

If you built Apache yourself from source, the solution will depend on whether you are running Apache 1.3 or Apache 2.x.

In Apache 1.3, SSL is an add-on module that you must acquire and install from a location different than that from which you obtained Apache. There are two main choices available: *mod_ssl* (*http://www.modssl.org*) and Apache-SSL (*http:// www.apache-ssl.org*); the installation procedure will vary somewhat depending on which one of these you choose.

If you are building Apache 2.x from source, the situation is somewhat simpler; just add *--enable-ssl* to the *./configure* arguments when you build Apache to include SSL as one of the built-in modules.

Consult Chapters 1 and 2 for more information on installing third-party modules, particularly if you have installed a binary distribution of Apache rather than building it yourself from the source code.

If you are attempting to install SSL on Apache for Windows, there is a discussion of this in the Compiling on Windows document, which you can find at *http:// httpd.apache.org/docs/2.0/platform/win_compiling.html* for Apache 2.0. Or if you are using Apache 1.3 on Windows and wish to install SSL, you should consult the file *INSTALL.Win32*, which comes with the SSL distribution, or look at the HowTo at *http://tud.at/programm/apache-ssl-win32-howto.php3*.

Finally, note that the Apache SSL modules are an interface between Apache and the OpenSSL libraries, which you must install before any of this can work. You can obtain the OpenSSL libraries from *http://www.openssl.org*. Although you may already have these libraries installed on your server, it is recommended that you obtain the latest version of the libraries to have the most recent security patches and to protect yourself from exploits.

Discussion

So, why is this so complicated? Well, there are a variety of reasons, most of which revolve around the legality of encryption. For a long time, encryption has been a restricted technology in the United States. Because Apache is primarily based out of the United States, there is a great deal of caution regarding distributing encryption technology with the package. Even though major changes have been made in the laws, permitting SSL to be shipped with Apache 2.0, there are still some gray areas that make it problematic to ship compiled binary distributions of Apache with SSL enabled.

This makes the situation particularly unpleasant on Microsoft Windows, where most people do not have a compiler readily available to them, and so must attempt to acquire binary builds from third parties to enable SSL on their Apache server on Windows. The

URL given previously for compiling Apache 2.0 with SSL on Windows assumes that you do have a compiler, and the document telling you how to build Apache 1.3 with SSL takes great pains to encourage you not to use Apache 1.3 on Windows, where it does not have comparable performance to Apache on Unixish operating systems.

See Also

- *http://httpd.apache.org/docs-2.0/platform/win_compiling.html*
- *http://tud.at/programm/apache-ssl-win32-howto.php3*
- *http://www.openssl.org*
- *http://www.modssl.org*
- *http://www.apache-ssl.org*

7.2 Installing SSL on Windows

Problem

You want to install Apache with SSL on Microsoft Windows.

Solution

Obtain XAMPP from *http://apachefriends.org* and install that.

Discussion

As was mentioned in the previous recipe, it is certainly possible to build Apache with SSL from source on Microsoft Windows. However, to be honest, this is beyond the expertise of most of us.

Fortunately, the kind folks at ApacheFriends have made available a binary distribution called XAMPP, which includes, among other things, Apache with *mod_ssl*. The package also includes MySQL, PHP, and Perl, some of the commonly used tools in Web site development.

So, save yourself some pain, take advantage of the great work that has been done by the ApacheFriends guys, and install the XAMPP package.

7.3 Generating Self-Signed SSL Certificates

Problem

You want to generate a self-signed certificate to use on your SSL server.

Solution

Use the *openssl* command-line program that comes with OpenSSL:

```
% openssl genrsa -out server.key 1024
% openssl req -new -key server.key -out server.csr
% cp server.key server.key.org
% openssl rsa -in server.key.org -out server.key
% openssl x509 -req -days 365 -in server.csr -signkey server.key -out server.crt
```

Then move these files to your Apache server's configuration directory, such as */www/ conf/*, and then add the following lines in your *httpd.conf* configuration file:

```
SSLCertificateFile "/www/conf/server.crt"
SSLCertificateKeyFile "/www/conf/server.key"
```

Discussion

The SSL certificate is a central part of the SSL conversation and is required before you can run a secure server. Thus, generating the certificate is a necessary first step to configuring your secure server.

Generating the key is a multistep process, but it is fairly simple.

Generating the private key

In the first step, we generate the private key. SSL is a private/public key encryption system, with the private key residing on the server and the public key going out with each connection to the server and encrypting data sent back to the server.

The first argument passed to the *openssl* program tells *openssl* that we want to generate an RSA key (*genrsa*), which is an encryption algorithm that all major browsers support.

You may, if you wish, specify an argument telling *openssl* what to use as the source of randomness. The `-rand` flag will accept one or more filenames, which will be used as a key for the random number generator. If no `-rand` argument is provided, OpenSSL will attempt to use */dev/urandom* by default if that exists, and it will try */dev/random* if */dev/ urandom* does not exist. It is important to have a good source of randomness in order for the encryption to be secure. If your system has neither */dev/urandom* nor */dev/random*, you should consider installing a random number generator, such as *egd*. You can find out more information about this on the OpenSSL Web site at *http:// www.openssl.org/docs/crypto/RAND_egd.html*.

The `-out` argument specifies the name of the key file that we will generate. This file will be created in the directory in which you are running the command, unless you provide a full path for this argument. Naming the key file after the hostname on which it will be used will help you keep track of the file, although the name of the file is not actually important.

And, finally, an argument of 1024 is specified, which tells *openssl* how many bytes of randomness to use in generating the key.

Your output should look something like:

```
Generating RSA private key, 1024 bit long modulus
.........................................................++++++
........++++++
e is 65537 (0x10001)
```

Generating the certificate signing request

The next step of the process is to generate a certificate signing request. The reason it is called this is because the resultant file is usually sent to a *certificate authority* (CA) for signing and is, therefore, a signing request. (A certificate is just a signed key, showing that someone certifies it to be valid and owned by the right entity.)

A certificate authority is some entity that can sign SSL certificates. What this usually means is that it is one of the few dozen companies whose business it is to sign SSL certificates for use on SSL servers. When a certificate is signed by one of these certificate authorities browsers will automatically accept the certificate as being valid. If a certificate is signed by a CA that is not listed in the browser's list of trusted CAs, then the browser will generate a warning, telling you that the certificate was signed by an unknown CA and asking you if you are sure that you want to accept the certificate.

This is a bit of an oversimplification of the process but conveys enough of it for the purposes of this recipe.

The alternative is that you sign the certificate yourself, which is what we'll be doing in the coming steps.

The arguments to this command specify the key for which the certificate is being generated (the -**key** argument) and the name of the file that you wish to generate (the -**out** argument).

If you want a certificate that will be accepted without warning or comment by all major browsers, you will send the *csr* file, along with a check or credit card information, to one of these CAs.

During this step, you'll be asked a number of questions. The answers to these questions will become part of the certificate, and will be used by the browser to verify that the certificate is coming from a trusted source. End users may inspect these details any time they connect to your Web site.

The questions will look like the following:

```
Country Name (2 letter code) [GB]: EX
State or Province Name (full name) [Berkshire]: CO
Locality Name (eg, city) [Newbury]: Example City
Organization Name (eg, company) [My Company Ltd]: Institute of Examples
Organizational Unit Name (eg, section) []: Demonstration Services
Common Name (eg, your name or your server's hostname) []: www.example.com
```

```
Email Address []: big-cheese@example.com
Please enter the following 'extra' attributes
to be sent with your certificate request
A challenge password []:
An optional company name []:
```

All of these values are optional, with the exception of the Common Name. You must supply the correct value here, which is the hostname of the server on which this certicate will be used. It is crucial that the hostname that you put in here exactly match the hostname that will be used to access the site. Failure to do this will result in a warning message each time a user connects to your Web site.

Removing the passphrase

In the first step, we put a passphrase on the private key. This makes the key encrypted so that only someone with the passphrase can read the contents of the key.

A side-effect of this is that every time you start up your Apache server, you will need to type in the passprase. This is extremely inconvenient, as it means that starting up the Web server always requires a manual step. This is particularly a problem for reboots or other automated restarts of the Apache server, when there might not be a human handy to type in the passphrase.

Therefore, we're going to remove the passphrase from the key so that this isn't an issue.

The key is copied to a backup location just in case we screw something up, and then the command is issued to remove the passphrase, resulting in an unencrypted key. You must remember to change the permissions on the file so that only root can read this file. Failure to do so may result in someone stealing that file and then being able to run a Web site while pretending to be you.

Signing your key

If you choose not to send the CSR to a Certificate Authority, and, instead, sign your own public key (also called "signing your own certificate," because signing your public key results in a self-signed certificate), this will result in a perfectly usable certificate, and save you a little money. This is especially useful for testing purposes, but it may also be sufficient if you are running SSL on a small site or a server on your internal network.

The process of signing a key means that the signer trusts that the key does indeed belong to the person listed as the owner. If you pay Entrust or one of the other commercial CAs for a certificate, they will actually do research on you and verify, to some degree of certainty, that you really are who you claim to be. They will then sign your public key and send you the resulting certificate, putting their stamp of approval on it and verifying to the world that you are legitimate.

In the example given, we sign the key with the key itself, which is a little silly, as it basically means that we trust ourselves. However, for the purposes of the actual SSL encryption, this is sufficient.

If you prefer, you can use the *CA.pl* script that comes with OpenSSL to generate a CA certificate of your own. The advantage of this approach is that you can distribute this CA certificate to users, who can install it in their browsers, enabling them to automatically trust this certificate and any other certificates that you create with that same CA. This is particularly useful for large companies where you might have several SSL servers using certificates signed by the same CA.

Of the arguments listed in the command, one of the most important ones is the `-days` argument, which specifies how many days the certificate will be good for. If you are planning to purchase a commercial certificate, you should generate your own self-signed key that is good for perhaps 30 days so that you can use it while you are waiting for the commercial certificate to arrive. If you are generating a key for actual use on your server, you may want to make this a year or so, so that you don't have to generate new keys very often.

The `-signkey` argument specifies what key will be used to sign the certificate. This can be either the private key that you generated in the first step or a CA private key generated with the *CA.pl* script, as mentioned earlier.

If this step goes well, you should see some output like the following:

```
Signature ok
subject=/C=US/ST=KY/L=Wilmore/O=Asbury College/OU=Information
Services/CN=www.asbury.edu/Email=rbowen@asbury.edu
Getting Private key
```

Configuring the server

Once you have generated the key and certificate, you can use them on your server using the two lines of configuration shown in the previous solution.

The easy way

Now that we've gone through the long and painful way of doing this, you should know that there is a simpler way. OpenSSL comes with a handy script, called *CA.pl*, which simplifies the process of creating keys. The use of *CA.pl* is described in Recipe 7.4 so you can see it in action. It is useful, however, to know some of what is going on behind the script. At least, we tend to think so. It also gives you considerably more control as to how the certificate is made.

See Also

- The manpage for the *openssl* tool
- The manpage for the *CA.pl* script

- CA.pl documentation at *http://www.openssl.org/docs/apps/CA.pl.html*

7.4 Generating a Trusted CA

Problem

You want to generate SSL keys that browsers will accept without a warning message.

Solution

Issue the following commands:

```
% CA.pl -newca
% CA.pl -newreq
% CA.pl -signreq
% CA.pl -pkcs12
```

Discussion

Recipe 7.3 discusses the lengthy steps that are required to create keys and sign them. Fortunately, OpenSSL comes with a script to automate much of this process so that you don't have to remember all of those arguments. This script, called *CA.pl*, is located where your SSL libraries are installed, for example, */usr/share/ssl/misc/CA.pl*.

The lines in the Solution hide a certain amount of detail, as you will be asked a number of questions in the process of creating the key and the certificate. Note also that you will probably need to be in the directory where this script lives to get successful results from this recipe.

If you want to omit the passphrase on the certificate so that you don't have to provide the passphrase each time you start up the server, use `-newreq-nodes` rather than *-newreq* when generating the certificate request.

After running this sequence of commands, you can generate more certificates by repeating the *-newreq* and *-signreq* commands.

Having run these commands, you will have generated a number of files. The file *newcert.pem* is the file you specify in your *SSLCertificateFile* directive, the file *newreq.pem* is your *SSLCertificateKeyFile*, and the file *demoCA/cacert.pem* is the CA certificate file, which will need to be imported into your users' browsers (for some browsers) so that they can automatically trust certificates signed by this CA. And, finally, *newcert.p12* serves the same purpose as *demoCA/cacert.pem* for certain other browsers.

Importing the CA

If your users are using Internet Explorer, you need to create a special file for them to import. Use the following command:

```
openssl X509 -demoCA/cacert.pem -out cacert.crt -outform DER
```

Then you can send them the *cacert.crt* file.

Clicking on that file will launch the SSL certificate wizard and guide users through installing the CA certificate into their browser.

Other browsers, such as Mozilla, expect to directly import the *cacert.pem* file. Users will navigate through their menus (Edit => Preferences => Privacy and Security => Certificates), then click on Manage Certificates, then on the Authorities tab, and finally on Import, to select the certificate file.

After importing a CA certificate, all certificates signed by that CA should be usable in your browser without receiving any kind of warning.

See Also

- The manpage for the *CA.pl* script
- *CA.pl* documentation at *http://www.openssl.org/docs/apps/CA.pl.html*

7.5 Serving a Portion of Your Site via SSL

Problem

You want to have a certain portion of your site available via SSL exclusively.

Solution

This is done by making changes to your *httpd.conf* file.

For Apache 1.3, add a line such as the following:

```
Redirect /secure/ https://secure.example.com/secure/
```

For Apache 2.0:

```
<Directory /www/secure>
    SSLRequireSSL
</Directory>
```

Note that the *SSLRequireSSL* directive does not issue a redirect. It merely forbids non-SSL requests.

Or for any version of Apache you can accomplish this using *mod_rewrite*:

```
RewriteEngine On
RewriteCond %{HTTPS} !=on
RewriteRule ^/(.*) https://%{SERVER_NAME}/$1 [R,L]
```

Discussion

It is perhaps best to think of your site's normal pages and its SSL-protected pages as being handled by two separate virtual hosts rather than one. Although they may point to the same content, they run on different ports, are configured differently, and, most important, the browser considers them to be completely separate servers. So you should, too.

Don't think of enabling SSL for a particular directory; rather, you should think of it as redirecting requests for one server to another.

Note that the *Redirect* directive preserves path information, which means that if a request is made for */secure/something.html*, then the redirect will be to *https://secure.example.com/secure/something.html*.

Be careful where you put this directive. Make sure that you only put it in the HTTP (non-SSL) virtual host declaration. Putting it in the global section of the *config* file may cause looping, as the new URL will match the *Redirect* requirement and get redirected itself.

Finally, note that if you want the entire site to be available only via SSL, you can accomplish this by simply redirecting all URLs, rather than a particular directory:

```
Redirect / https://secure.example.com/
```

Again, be sure to put that inside the non-SSL virtual host declaration.

You will see various solutions proposed for this situation using *RedirectMatch* or various *RewriteRule* directives. There are special cases in which this is necessary, but in most cases, the simple solution offered here works just fine. In particular, you might be compelled to use this solution when you only have access to your *.htaccess* file, and not to the main server configuration file.

So, the entire setup might look something like this:

```
NameVirtualHost *

<VirtualHost *>
    ServerName regular.example.com
    DocumentRoot /www/docs

    Redirect /secure/ https://secure.example.com/secure/
</VirtualHost>

<VirtualHost _default_:443>
    SSLEngine On
    SSLCertificateFile /www/conf/ssl/ssl.crt
    SSLCertificateKeyFile /www/conf/ssl/ssl.key

    ServerName secure.example.com
    DocumentRoot /www/docs
</VirtualHost>
```

The other two solutions are perhaps more straightforward, although they each have a small additional requirement for use.

The second recipe listed, using *SSLRequireSSL*, will work only if you are using Apache 2.0. It is a directive added specifically to address this need. Placing the *SSLRequireSSL* directive in a particular *<Directory>* section will ensure that non-SSL accesses to that directory are not permitted. It does not redirect users to the SSL host; it merely forbids non-SSL access.

The third recipe, using *RewriteCond* and *RewriteRule* directives, requires that you have *mod_rewrite* installed and enabled. Using the *RewriteCond* directive to check if the client is already using SSL, the *RewriteRule* is invoked only if they are not. In that case, the request is redirected to a request for the same content but using HTTPS instead of HTTP.

See Also

- *http://httpd.apache.org/docs-2.0/mod/mod_ssl.html*
- *http://httpd.apache.org/docs/mod/mod_alias.html*
- *http://httpd.apache.org/docs/mod/mod_rewrite.html*

7.6 Authenticating with Client Certificates

Problem

You want to use client certificates to authenticate access to your site.

Solution

Add the following *mod_ssl* directives to your *httpd.conf* file:

```
SSLVerifyClient require
SSLVerifyDepth 1
SSLCACertificateFile conf/ssl.crt/ca.crt
```

Discussion

If you happen to be lucky enough to have a small, closed user community, such as an intranet, or a Web site for a group of friends or family, it is possible to distribute client certificates so that each user can identify himself.

Create client certificates, signing them with your CA certificate file, and then specify the location of this CA certificate file using the *SSLCACertificateFile* directive, as shown above.

Client certificates are created in the same manner as server certificates, except that the CN (Common Name) on the certificate is the name of the client certificate owner.

See Also

- Recipe 7.3
- *http://httpd.apache.org/docs-2.0/mod/mod_ssl.html*

7.7 SSL Virtual Hosts

Problem

You want to run several SSL hosts on a single IP address.

Solution

There are several possible answers to this problem, depending on your perspective.

The officially correct answer is that you can only run one SSL host per IP address and port. This has to do with the way that SSL works, and is not a limitation specifically of Apache. Attempting to run multiple SSL hosts on the same IP address and port will result in warning messages being displayed by the browser, because it will be receiving the wrong certificate.

One other possible answer is to use a wildcard certificate. This is covered in the next recipe.

Finally, if you don't care about the warning messages, you can set up name-based virtual hosts in the usual way, and simply have Apache use the same certificate for all of them.

In the near future, there will be other solutions to this problem, and there are a considerable number of very smart people working on this problem. Unfortunately, it's still not quite solved.

Discussion

When an https (SSL) request is made by a browser, the first thing that happens is that the certificate is sent to the browser in order for the SSL encryption to be set up. This happens before the browser has told the server what URL it is requesting, so it is impossible to select a particular virtual host. Thus, it is not possible to associate more than one certificate with a particular IP address and port.

There are basically three types of solutions. Either you ignore the problem, you find a way to use one certificate on multiple hostnames, or you use more IP addresses or ports. We'll discuss each of these in turn.

Ignore the problem

In some situations, you may be content to ignore the problem. For test servers, or servers where you have a very small audience and can explain the situation to each person, this may be a perfectly acceptable scenario.

In that case, you can set up name-based virtual hosts, and use the same certificate for each one. However, when you connect to any of them, except for the one for which the hostname matches the Common Name on the certificate, you will get a warning message from the browser. In Firefox, this will look like the image below, and will say something like:

You have attempted to establish a connection with `www.example1.com`. However, the security certificate presented belogs to `www.example2.com`. It is possible, although unlikely, that someone may be trying to intercept your communication with this Web site. If you suspect the certificate shown does not belong to `www.example1.com`, please cancel the connection and notify the site administrator.

At this point you, the site administrator, know that everything is fine, and that there's no actual problem. The person on the other end, however, may have any of a number of different reactions. She may panic, and press "Cancel" immediately. She might ignore the message entirely and click "OK," which is almost as bad because ignoring such warning messages is bound to get one into problems eventually. Or she may indeed take the suggested action and contact you, the site administrator. In any of these cases, you probably can immediately see why this isn't a valid solution when you're running an actual secure Web site and performing tasks like taking credit card transactions.

Use one certificate on several hosts

It is possible to use a single certificate on multiple hostnames if all of those hostnames are in the same domain. This is called a wildcard certificate, and is discussed in the next recipe.

Use more than one address

The recommended solution is that you run each SSL host on its own IP address. Failing that, you can run different sites on different ports on the same IP address. IP-based virtual hosts are discussed in the chapter on Virtual Hosts, as are port-based virtual hosts. Using either one of these solutions, the warning messages will go away.

If you choose to do port-based virtual hosting, remember that you must put the port number in URLs in order for them to work. For example, if you run your SSL host on port 8443, you will need to access the site using a URL like:

```
https://www.example.com:8443/
```

This may be inconvenient for the end user, but if access to the site is all through links and form elements, this is a very fine solution.

7.8 Wildcard Certificates

Problem

You want to use a single certificate for multiple hostnames in the same domain.

Solution

Use a wildcard certificate, which works for any name within a particular domain, such as "*.example.com."

Discussion

Using the technique described in Recipe 7.3, create a certificate with a Common Name of *.example.com, where example.com is the domain for which you wish to use the certificate. This certificate will now work for any hostname in the example.com domain, such as www.example.com or secure.example.com.

On many browsers, however, the certificate will not work for example.com or for one.two.example.com, but only for hostnames strictly of the form *hostname*.example.com.

Most certificate authorities will charge considerably more to sign wildcard certificates. This is not because it is somehow more complicated to sign these certificates, but because it is a simple business decision, based on the fact that buying a wildcard certificate means that you don't need to buy multiple single-host certificates.

See Also

- Recipe 7.3

## CHAPTER 8

Dynamic Content

Very few Web sites can survive without some mechanism for providing dynamic content—content that is generated in response to the needs of the user. The recipes in this chapter guide you through enabling various mechanisms to produce this dynamic content and help you troubleshoot possible problems that may occur.

CGI programs are one of the simplest ways to provide dynamic content for your Web site. They tend to be easy to write because you can write them in any language. Thus, you don't have to learn a new language to write CGI programs. Examples in this chapter will be given in a variety of languages, but it's not necessary that you know these languages in order to see how to configure Apache for their execution.

Although CGI is no longer the preferred mechanism for generating dynamic content, it is the simplest, and understanding how CGI works is a great help in understanding how the more complex dynamic content providers work.

Other dynamic content providers, such as PHP and *mod_perl*, also enjoy a great deal of popularity, because they provide many of the same functions as CGI programs but typically execute faster.

8.1 Enabling a CGI Directory

Problem

You want to designate a directory that contains only CGI scripts.

Solution

Add the following to your *httpd.conf* file:

```
ScriptAlias /cgi-bin/ /www/cgi-bin/
```

Discussion

A CGI directory will usually be designated and enabled in your default configuration file when you install Apache. However, if you want to add additional directories where

CGI programs are located, the *ScriptAlias* directive does this for you. You may have as many *ScriptAlias*'ed directories as you want.

The one line previously introduced is equivalent to these directive lines:

```
Alias /cgi-bin/ /www/cgi-bin/

<Location /cgi-bin/>
    Options ExecCGI
    SetHandler cgi-script
</Location>
```

Note that URLs that map to the directory in question via some other mechanism or URL path, such as another *Alias* or a *RewriteRule*, will not benefit from the *ScriptAlias* setting, as this mapping is by URL (`<Location>`), not by directory. As a result, accessing the scripts in this directory through some other URL path may result in their code being displayed rather than the script being executed.

You also may need to add a *<Directory>* block to permit access to the directory in question, as a *cgi-bin* directory is usually outside of the document directory tree. It is also recommended that you deny the use of *.htaccess* files in *cgi-bin* directories:

```
<Directory /www/cgi-bin>
    Order allow,deny
    Allow from all
    AllowOverride None
</Directory>
```

See also Recipe 8.4 for a discussion of using Windows file extensions to launch CGI programs.

See Also

- Chapter 5
- Recipe 8.2
- *http://httpd.apache.org/docs/2.0/mod/mod_alias.html*

8.2 Enabling CGI Scripts in Non-ScriptAliased Directories

Problem

You want to put a CGI program in a directory that contains non-CGI documents.

Solution

Use *AddHandler* to map the CGI handler to the particular files that you want executed:

```
<Directory "/foo">
    Options +ExecCGI
    AddHandler cgi-script .cgi .py .pl
</Directory>
```

Discussion

Enabling CGI execution via the *ScriptAlias* directive is preferred for a number of reasons over permitting CGI execution in arbitrary document directories. The primary reason is security auditing. It is much easier to audit your CGI programs if you know where they are, and storing them in a single directory ensures that.

However, there are cases in which it is desirable to have access to CGI functionality in other locations. For example, you may want to keep several files together in one directory—some of them static documents, and some of them scripts—because they are part of a single application.

Using the *AddHandler* directive maps certain file extensions to the *cgi-script* handler so they can be executed as CGI programs. In the case of the aforementioned example, programs with a *.cgi*, *.py*, or *.pl* file extension will be treated as CGI programs, whereas all other documents in the directory will be served up with their usual MIME type.

Note that the *+ExecCGI* argument is provided to the *Options* directive, rather than the *ExecCGI* argument—that is, with the + sign rather than without. Using the + sign adds this option to any others already in place, whereas using the option without the + sign will replace the existing list of options. You should use the argument without the + sign if you intend to have only CGI programs in the directory, and with the + sign if you intend to also serve non-CGI documents out of the same directory.

See Also

- Recipe 8.1

8.3 Specifying a Default Document in a CGI Directory

Problem

You want to allow a default file to be served when a CGI directory is requested.

Solution

Rather than using *ScriptAlias* to enable a CGI directory, use the following:

```
Alias /cgi-bin /www/cgi-bin
<Directory /www/cgi-bin>
```

```
        Options ExecCGI
        SetHandler cgi-script
        DirectoryIndex index.pl

        Order allow,deny
        Allow from all
        AllowOverride none
</Directory>
```

Discussion

Using *ScriptAlias* explicitly forbids the use of *DirectoryIndex* to provide a default document for a directory. Because of this, if you attempt to get a default document from a *ScriptAlias*'ed directory, you'll see the following error message in your error log file: `"attempt to invoke directory as script"`.

And, in their browsers, users will see the message:
`Forbidden. You don't have permission to access /cgi-bin/ on this server.`

So, in order to get a default document, you must avoid *ScriptAlias* and use the alternate method of creating a CGI-enabled directory, as discussed in Recipe 8.2.

Once you have created a CGI directory without using *ScriptAlias*, you may use a *DirectoryIndex* directive to display a default document when the directory is requested.

An alternate method is possible if you wish, for some reason, to use *ScriptAlias* rather than this technique. You may use either a *RedirectMatch* directive, or a *RewriteRule* directive, to redirect the request for the CGI directory to the filename desired:

```
ScriptAlias /cgi-bin /www/cgi-bin
RedirectMatch "^/cgi-bin/?$" "http://server.example.com/cgi-bin/index.pl"
```

Or:

```
ScriptAlias /cgi-bin /www/cgi-bin
RewriteEngine On
RewriteRule "^/cgi-bin/?$" "/cgi-bin/index.pl" [PT]
```

The two examples above should go in your main server configuration file. Ordinarily, *.htaccess* files are not enabled in *ScriptAlias* directories. However, if you do have *.htaccess* files enabled in your *ScriptAlias* directory, and wish to use the *RewriteRule* technique in one, remember that the directory path is stripped from the requested URI before the *RewriteRule* is applied, so your rule set should look more like:

```
RewriteEngine On
RewriteBase /cgi-bin/
RewriteRule "^$" "index.pl" [R]
```

See Also

*   Recipe 8.2

8.4 Using Windows File Extensions to Launch CGI Programs

Problem

You want to have CGI programs on Windows executed by the program associated with the file extension. For example, you want *.pl* scripts to be executed by *perl.exe* without having to change the scripts' *#!* line to point at the right location of *perl.exe*.

Solution

Add the following line to your *httpd.conf* file:

```
ScriptInterpreterSource registry
```

Discussion

Because Apache has its roots in the Unixish world, there are a number of things that are done the Unixish way, even on Microsoft Windows. CGI execution is one of these things, but the *ScriptInterpreterSource* directive allows you to have Apache behave more in the way to which Windows users are accustomed.

Usually, on Windows, a file type is indicated by the file extension. For example, a file named *example.pl* is associated with the Perl executable; when a user clicks on this file in the file explorer, Perl is invoked to execute this script. This association is created when you install a particular program, such as Perl or MS Word, and the association is stored in the Windows registry.

On Unixish systems, by contrast, most scripts contain the location of their interpreter in the first line of the file, which starts with the characters #!. This line is often called the *shebang* line (short for sharp bang, which are the shorthand names for the two characters).

For example, a Perl program might start with the line:

```
#!/usr/bin/perl
```

The shell running the script looks in this first line and uses the program at the indicated path to interpret and execute the script. In this way, files with arbitrary file extensions (or no extension at all) may be invoked with any interpreter desired. In the case of Perl, for example, one might have several versions of Perl installed, and the particular version desired may be invoked by using the appropriate #! line.

However, you may be accustomed to Windows' usual way of executing a program based on the file extension, and this Unixism can be somewhat nonintuitive. Thus, in the early days of Apache on Windows, the *ScriptInterpreterSource* directive was added to make Apache behave the way that Windows users expected.

ScriptInterpreterSource may have one of three values. When set to the default value, *script*, Apache will look in the script itself for the location of the interpreter that it is to use.

When it is set to *registry*, it will look in the Windows registry for the mapping that is associated with the file's extension and use this to execute the script.

Setting the value to *registry-strict* will have the same effect as *registry* except that only the subkey `Shell\ExecCGI\Command` will be searched. This requires that the setting be manually configured, and prevents unintentional command execution.

This feature can be very useful for users who are running multiple servers, some on Unixish operating systems and others on Windows, but who want the same CGI programs to run both places. Because Perl, for example, is unlikely to be located at */usr/bin/perl* on your Windows machine, using the *ScriptInterpreterSource* directive allows you to run the script unedited on Windows, simply by virtue of it having a *.pl* file extension.

See Also

- Recipe 8.2
- Recipe 8.5
- *http://httpd.apache.org/docs/2.2/mod/core.html#ScriptInterpreterSource*

8.5 Using Extensions to Identify CGI Scripts

Problem

You want Apache to know that all files with a particular extension should be treated as CGI scripts.

Solution

Add the following to your *httpd.conf* file in a scope covering the areas where it should apply, or in an *.htaccess* file for the appropriate directory:

```
AddHandler cgi-script .cgi
```

Discussion

The *AddHandler* directive shown in this solution tells Apache that any files that have a *.cgi* extension should be treated as CGI scripts, and it should try to execute them rather than treat them as content to be sent.

The directive only affects files with that extension in the same scope as the directive itself. You may replace the common *.cgi* extension with another, or even with a list of space-separated extensions.

Note the use of the term *extension* rather than *suffix*; a file named *foo.cgi.en* is treated as a CGI script unless a handler with the *.en* extension overrides it.

An alternate way of accomplishing this will cause files with a particular extension to be execute as CGI programs regardless of where they appear in the file system:

```
<FilesMatch \.cgi(\.|$)>
    Options +ExecCGI
    SetHandler cgi-script
</FilesMatch>
```

The *FilesMatch* directive allows directives to be applied to any file that matches a particular pattern. In this case, a file with a file extension of *.cgi*. As mentioned above, a file may have several file extensions. Thus, rather than using a pattern of \.*cgi$*, which would require that the filename ended with *.cgi*, we use \.*cgi(\.|$)*. The *(\.|$)* regular expression syntax requires that *.cgi* be followed either by another ., or the end of the string.

See Also

- Recipe 8.2

8.6 Testing that CGI Is Set Up Correctly

Problem

You want to test that you have CGI enabled correctly. Alternatively, you are receiving an error message when you try to run your CGI script and you want to ensure the problem doesn't lie in the Web server before you try to find a problem in the script.

Solution

```
#! /usr/bin/perl
print "Content-type: text/plain\n\n";
print "It's working.\n";
```

And then, if things are still not working, look in the error log.

Discussion

Because Perl is likely to be installed on any Unixish system, this CGI program should be a pretty safe way to test that CGI is configured correctly. In the event that you do not have Perl installed, an equivalent shell program may be substituted:

```
#! /bin/sh
echo Content-type: text/plain
echo
echo It\'s working.
```

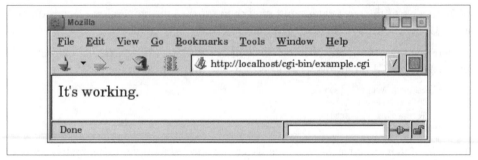

Figure 8-1. Your CGI program worked

And if you are running Apache on Windows, so that neither of the above options works for you, you could also try this with a batch file:

```
echo off
echo Content-type: text/plain
echo.
echo It's working.
```

Make sure that you copy the program code exactly, with all the right punctuation, slashes, and so on, so that you don't introduce additional complexity by having to troubleshoot the program itself.

In either case, once the program is working, you should see something like the screen capture shown in Figure 8-1.

The idea here is to start with the simplest possible CGI program to ensure that problems are not caused by other complexities in your code. We want to ensure that CGI is configured properly, not to verify the correctness of a particular CGI program.

There are a variety of reasons why a particular CGI program might not work. In very general terms, it can be in one of three categories: misconfiguration of the Web server; an error in the program itself; or incorrect permissions on the files and directories in question.

Fortunately, when something goes wrong with one of your CGI programs, an entry is made in your error log. Knowing where your error log is located is a prerequisite to solving any problem you have with your Apache server. The error messages that go to the browser, while vaguely useful, tend to be catch-all messages and usually don't contain any information specific to your actual problem.

Ideally, if you have followed the recipes earlier in this chapter, you will not be having configuration problems with your CGI program, which leaves the other two categories of problems.

If your problem is one of permissions, you will see an entry in your logfile that looks something like the following:

```
[Sun Dec  1 20:31:16 2002] [error] (13)Permission denied: exec of /usr/local/apache/
    cgi-bin/example1.cgi failed
```

The solution to this problem is to make sure that the script itself is executable:

```
# chmod a+x /usr/local/apache/cgi-bin/example1.cgi
```

If the problem is an error in the program itself, then there are an infinite number of possible solutions, as there are an infinite number of ways to make any given program fail. If the example program above works correctly, you can be fairly assured that the problem is with your program, rather than with some other environmental condition.

The error message `Premature end of script headers`, which you will see frequently in your career, means very little by itself. You should always look for other error messages that augment this message. Any error in a CGI program will tend to cause the program to emit warnings and error message prior to the correctly formed HTTP headers, which will result in the server perceiving malformed headers, resulting in this message. The *suexec* wrapper also can confuse matters if it's being used.

One particularly common error message, which can be rather hard to track down if you don't know what you're looking for, is the following:

```
[Sat Jul 19 21:39:47 2003] [error] (2)No such file or directory:
    exec of /usr/local/apache/cgi-bin/example.cgi failed
```

This error message almost always means one of two things: an incorrect path or a corrupted file.

In many cases, particularly if you have acquired the script from someone else, the #! line of the script may point to the wrong location (such as *#!/usr/local/bin/perl*, when perl is instead located at */usr/bin/perl*). This can be confirmed by using the `which` command and comparing its output to the #! line. For example, to find the correct location for Perl, you would type:

```
% which perl
```

The other scenario is that the file has been corrupted somehow so that the #! line is illegible. The most common cause of this second condition is when a script file is transferred from a Windows machine to a Unixish machine, via FTP, in binary mode rather than ASCII mode. This results in a file with the wrong type of end-of-line characters, so that Apache is unable to correctly read the location of the script interpreter.

To fix this, you should run the following one-liner from the command line:

```
% perl -pi.bak -le 's/\r$//;' example.cgi
```

This will remove all of the Windows-style end-of-line characters, and your file will be executable. It also creates a backup copy of the file, with a *.bak* file extension, in case, for some reason, the changes that you make to the file cause any problems.

See Also

- Recipe B.3 in Appendix B
- Appendix B

8.7 Reading Form Parameters

Problem

You want your CGI program to read values from Web forms for use in your program.

Solution

First, look at an example in Perl, which uses the popular *CGI.pm* module:

```perl
#!/usr/bin/perl
use CGI;
use strict;
use warnings;

my $form = CGI->new;

# Load the various form parameters
my $name = $form->param('name') || '-';

# Multi-value select lists will return a list
my @foods = $form->param('favorite_foods');

# Output useful stuff
print "Content-type: text/html\n\n";
print 'Name: ' . $name . "<br />\n";
print "Favorite foods: <ul>\n";
foreach my $food (@foods) {
    print " <li>$food</li>\n";
}
print "</ul>\n";
```

Next, look at a program in C, which does pretty much the same thing, and uses the *cgic* C library:

```c
#include "cgic.h"
/* Boutell.com's cgic library */

int cgiMain() {
    char name[100];

    /* Send content type */
    cgiHeaderContentType("text/html");

    /* Load a particular variable */
    cgiFormStringNoNewlines("name", name, 100);
    fprintf(cgiOut, "Name: ");
    cgiHtmlEscape(name);
    fprintf(cgiOut, "\n");

    return 0;
}
```

For this example, you also will need a *Makefile*, which looks something like this:

```
CFLAGS=-g -Wall
CC=gcc
AR=ar
LIBS=-L./ -lcgic

libcgic.a: cgic.o cgic.h
TAB rm -f libcgic.a
TAB $(AR) rc libcgic.a cgic.o

example.cgi: example.o libcgic.a
TAB gcc example.o -o example.cgi $(LIBS)
```

Discussion

The exact solution to this will vary from one programming language to another, and so examples are given here in two languages. Note that each of these examples uses an external library to do the actual parsing of the form content. This is important, because it is easy to parse forms incorrectly. By using one of these libraries, you ensure that all of the form-encoded characters are correctly converted to usable values, and then there's the simple matter of code readability and simplicity. It's almost always better to utilize an existing library than to reimplement functionality yourself.

The Perl example uses Lincoln Stein's *CGI.pm* module, which is a standard part of the Perl distribution and will be installed if you have Perl installed. The library is loaded using the *use* keyword and is used via the object-oriented (OO) interface.

The *param* method returns the value of a given form field. When called with no arguments, *params()* returns a list of the form field names. When called with the name of a multivalue select form field, it will return a list of the selected values. This is illustrated in the example for a field named favorite_foods.

The example in C uses the *cgic* C library, which is available from *http://boutell.com*. You will need to acquire this library and install it in order to compile the aforementioned code. The *Makefile* provided is to assist in building the source code into a binary file that you can run. Type *make example.cgi* to start the compile. Note that if you are doing this on Windows, you will probably want to replace *.cgi* with *.exe* in the example *Makefile*.

In either case, an HTML form pointed at this CGI program, containing a form field named name, will result in the value typed in that field being displayed in the browser. The necessary HTML to test these programs is as follows:

```
<html>
 <head>
   <title>Example CGI</title>
 </head>
 <body>

   <h3>Form:</h3>

   <form action="/cgi-bin/example.cgi" method="post">
```

```
Name: <input name="name">
<br />
<input type="submit">
</form>

</body>
</html>
```

The examples given in this recipe each use CGI libraries, or modules, for the actual functionality of parsing the HTML form contents. Although many CGI tutorials on the Web show you how to do the form parsing yourself, we don't recommend it. One of the great virtues of a programmer is laziness, and using modules, rather than reinventing the wheel, is one of the most important manifestations of laziness. And it makes good sense, too, because these modules tend to get it right. It's very easy to parse form contents incorrectly, winding up with data that have been translated from the form encoding incompletely or just plain wrongly. These modules have been developed over a number of years, extensively tested, and are much more likely to correctly handle the various cases that you have not thought about.

Additionally, modules handle file uploads, multiple select lists, reading and setting cookies, returning correctly formatted error messages to the browser, and a variety of other functions that you might overlook if you were to attempt to do this yourself. Furthermore, in the spirit of good programming technique, reusing existing code saves you time and tends to prevent errors.

See Also

- *http://search.cpan.org/author/LDS/CGI.pm/CGI.pm*
- *http://www.boutell.com/cgic*

8.8 Invoking a CGI Program for Certain Content Types

Problem

You want to invoke a CGI program to act as a sort of content filter for certain document types. For example, a photographer may wish to create a custom handler to add a watermark to photographs served from his Web site.

Solution

Use the *Action* directive to create a custom handler, which will be implemented by a CGI program. Then use the *AddHandler* directive to associate a particular file extension with this handler:

```
Action watermark /cgi-bin/watermark.cgi
AddHandler watermark .gif .jpg
```

Or if you really want to the server to select your handler based on the type of data rather than the name of the file, you can use:

```
Action image/gif /cgi-bin/watermark.cgi
Action image/jpeg /cgi-bin/watermark.cgi
```

Discussion

This recipe creates a watermark handler that is called whenever a *.gif* or *.jpg* file is requested.

A CGI program, *watermark.cgi*, takes the image file as input and attaches the watermark image on top of the photograph. The path to the image file that was originally requested in the URL is available in the `PATH_TRANSLATED` environment variable, and the program needs to load that file, make the necessary modifications, and send the resulting content to the client, along with the appropriate HTTP headers.

Note that there is no way to circumvent this measure, as the CGI program will be called for any *.gif* or *.jpg* file that is requested from within the scope to which these directives apply.

This same technique may be used to attach a header or footer to HTML pages in an automatic way, without having to add any kind of SSI directive to the files. This can be extremely inefficient, as it requires that a CGI program be launched, which can be a very slow process. It is, however, connstructive to see how it is done. What follows is a very simple implementation of such a footer script:

```perl
#! /usr/bin/perl

print "Content-type: text/html\n\n";

my $file = $ENV{PATH_TRANSLATED};

open FILE, "$file";
print while <FILE>;
close FILE;
print qq~

<p>
FOOTER GOES HERE
</p>
~;
```

An equivalent PHP script might look something like this:

```php
#! /usr/bin/php
$fh = fopen($_SERVER['PATH_TRANSLATED'], 'r');
fpassthru($fh);
print "\n\n<p>\n"
    . "FOOTER GOES HERE\n"
    . "</p>\n";
return;
```

The requested file, located at PATH_TRANSLATED, is read in and printed out, unmodified. Then, at the end of it, a few additional lines of footer are output. A similar technique might be used to filter the contents of the page itself. With Apache 2.0, this may be better accomplished with *mod_ext_filter*.

This script is intended to illustrate the technique, *not* to be used to add footer text to Web pages! It doesn't do any of the checking that would be necessary for such a task ("Is this an HTML file?," "Is it safe to add HTML after all of the content?," and so on).

See Also

- Recipe 8.11
- Recipe 10.7

8.9 Getting SSIs to Work

Problem

You want to enable Server-Side Includes (SSIs) to make your HTML documents more dynamic.

Solution

There are at least two different ways of doing this.

Specify which files are to be parsed by using a filename extension such as *.shtml*. For Apache 1.3, add the following directives to your *httpd.conf* in the appropriate scope:

```
<Directory /www/html/example>
    Options +Includes
    AddHandler server-parsed .shtml
    AddType "text/html; charset=ISO-8859-1" .shtml
</Directory>
```

Or, for Apache 2.0 and later:

```
<Directory /www/html/example>
    Options +Includes
    AddType text/html .shtml
    AddFilter INCLUDES .shtml
</Directory>
```

The second method is to add the *XBitHack* directive to the appropriate scope in your *httpd.conf* file and allow the file permissions to indicate which files are to be parsed for SSI directives:

```
XBitHack On
```

Discussion

SSIs provide a way to add dynamic content to an HTML page via a variety of simple tags. This functionality is implemented by the *mod_include* module, which is documented at *http://httpd.apache.org/docs/mod/mod_include.html*. There is also a how-to-style document available at *http://httpd.apache.org/docs/howto/ssi.html*.

The first solution provided here tells Apache to parse all *.shtml* files for SSI directives. So, to test that the solution has been effective, create a file called *something.shtml*, and put the following line in it:

```
File last modified at '<!--#echo var="LAST_MODIFIED" -->'.
```

 Note the space between the last argument and the closing "-->". This space is surprisingly important; many SSI failures can be traced to its omission.

Accessing this document via your server should result in the page displaying the date and time when you modified (or created) the file.

If you wish to enable SSIs, but do not wish to permit execution of CGI scripts, or other commands using the *#exec* or the *#include virtual* SSI directives, substitute *IncludesNoExec* for *Includes* in the *Options* directive in the solution.

Some Webmasters like to enable SSI parsing for all HTML content on their sites by specifying *.html* instead of *.shtml* in the *AddType*, *AddHandler*, and *AddFilter* directives.

If for some reason you do not wish to rename documents to *.shtml* files, merely because you want to add dynamic content to those files, *XBitHack* gives you a way around this. Of course, you could enable SSI parsing for all *.html* files, but this would probably result in a lot of files being parsed for no reason, which can cause a performance hit.

The *XBitHack* directive tells Apache to parse files for SSI directives if they have the execute bit set on them. So, when you have this directive set to *On* for a particular directory or virtual host, you merely need to set the execute bit on those files that contain SSI directives. This way, you can add SSI directives to existing documents without changing their names, which could potentially break links from other pages, sites, or search engines.

The simplest way of setting (or clearing) the execute permission bit of a file is:

```
# chmod a+x foo.html   # turns it on
# chmod a-x foo.html   # turns it off
```

The *XBitHack* method only works on those platforms that support the concept of execute access to files; this includes Unixish systems but does *not* include Windows.

See Also

- Recipe 8.12
- Recipe 8.11

8.10 Displaying Last Modified Date

Problem

You want your Web page to indicate when it was last modified but not have to change the date every time.

Solution

Use SSI processing by putting a line in the HTML file for which you want the information displayed:

```
<!--#config timefmt="%B %e, %Y" -->
This document was last modified on <!--#echo var="LAST_MODIFIED" -->
```

Discussion

The *config* SSI directive allows you to configure a few settings governing SSI output formats. In this case, we're using it to configure the format in which date/time information is displayed. The default format for date output is `04-Dec-2037 19:58:15 EST`, which is not the most user-friendly style. The recipe provided changes this to the slightly more readable format `December 4, 2002`. If you want another output format, the *timefmt* attribute can take any argument accepted by the C `strftime(3)` function.

See Also

- Recipe 8.9
- The *strftime(3)* documentation

8.11 Including a Standard Header

Problem

You want to include a header (or footer) in each of your HTML documents.

Solution

Use SSI by inserting a line in all your parsed files:

```
<!--#include virtual="/include/headers.html" -->
```

Discussion

By using the SSI *include* directive, you can have a single header file that can be used throughout your Web site. When your header needs to be modified, you can make this change in one place and have it go into effect immediately across your whole site.

The argument to the *virtual* attribute is a local URI and subject to all normal *Alias*, *ScriptAlias*, *RewriteRule*, and other commands, which means that:

```
<!--#include virtual="/index.html" -->
```

will include the file from your *DocumentRoot*, and:

```
<!--#include virtual="/cgi-bin/foo" -->
```

will include the *output* from the *foo* script in your server's *ScriptAlias* directory.

If the argument doesn't begin with a / character, it's treated as being relative to the location of the document using the *#include* directive.

> Be aware that URIs passed to *#include virtual* may *not* begin with ../, nor may they refer to full URLs such as *http://example.com/foo.html*. Documents included using relative syntax (i.e., those not beginning with /) may only be in the same location as the including file, or in some sublocation underneath it. Server processing of the URI may result in the actual included document being located somewhere else, but the restrictions on the *#include virtual* SSI command syntax permit only same-location or descendent-location URIs.

See Also

- Recipe 8.8
- Recipe 8.9

8.12 Including the Output of a CGI Program

Problem

You want to have the output of a CGI program appear within the body of an existing HTML document.

Solution

Use server-side includes by adding a line such as the following to the document (which must be enabled for SSI parsing):

```
<!--#include virtual="/cgi-bin/content.cgi" -->
```

Discussion

The SSI *#include* directive, in addition to being able to include a plain file, can also include other dynamic content, such as CGI programs, other SSI documents, or content generated by any other method.

The *#exec* SSI directive may also be used to produce this effect, but for a variety of historical and security-related reasons, its use is deprecated. The *#include* directive is the preferred way to produce this effect.

See Also

- Recipe 8.9

8.13 Running CGI Scripts as a Different User with suexec

Problem

You want to have CGI programs executed by some user other than nobody (or whatever user the Apache server runs as). For example, you may have a database that is not accessible to anyone except a particular user, so the server needs to temporarily assume that user's identity to access it.

Solution

When building Apache, enable *suexec* by passing the `--enable-suexec` argument to *configure*.

Then, in a virtual host section, specify which user and group you'd like to use to run CGI programs:

```
User rbowen
Group users
```

Also, *suexec* will be invoked for any CGI programs run out of username-type URLs for the affected virtual host.

Discussion

The *suexec* wrapper is a suid (runs as the user ID of the user that owns the file) program that allows you to run CGI programs as any user you specify, rather than as the nobody user that Apache runs as. *suexec* is a standard part of Apache but is not enabled by default.

The *suexec* concept does not fit well into the Windows environment, and so *suexec* is not available under Windows.

When *suexec* is installed, there are two different ways that it can be invoked, as shown in the Solution.

A *User* and *Group* directive may be specified in a *VirtualHost* container, and all CGI programs executed within the context of that virtual host are executed as that user and group. Note that this only applies to CGI programs. Normal documents and other types of dynamic content are still accessed as the user and group specified in the *User* and *Group* directives in the main server configuration, not those in the virtual host, and need to be readable by that user and group.

Second, any CGI program run out of a *UserDir* directory is run with the permissions of the owner of that directory. That is, if a CGI program is accessed via the URL *http:// example.com/~rbowen/cgi-bin/test.cgi*, then that program will be executed, via *suexec*, with a userid of *rbowen*, and a groupid of *rbowen*'s primary group.

 If *UserDir* points to a nonstandard location, you must tell *suexec* about this when you build it. In a default configuration, *suexec* is invoked when CGI programs are invoked in a directory such as */home/username/pub lic_html/* for some *username*. If, however, you move the *UserDir* directory somewhere else, such as, for example, */home/username/www/*, then you could configure *suexec* to be invoked in that directory instead, using the following argument when you build Apache 1.3:

```
--suexec-userdir=www
```

And, for Apache 2.0, you would specify the following:

```
--with-suexec-userdir=www
```

Running CGI programs via *suexec* eliminates some of the security concerns surrounding CGI programs. By default, CGI programs run with the permissions of the user and group specified in the *User* and *Group* directives, meaning that they have rather limited ability to do any damage. However, it also means that CGI programs on one part of your Web server run with all the same permissions as those on another part of your server, and any files that are created or modified by one will be modifiable by another.

By running a CGI program under *suexec*, you allow each user to exercise a little more control over her own file permissions, and in the event that a malicious CGI program is written, it can only damage the files owned by the user in question, rather than having free rein over the entire Web server.

PHP scripts that are run as CGI programs, rather than under the *mod_php* handler, may be run as *suexec* processes in the same way as any other CGI program.

If *suexec* encounters a problem, it reacts in as paranoid a way as possible—which means it won't serve the document. The end user will see an error page, but the only explanation of what *really* went wrong will be found in the server's error log. The messages are pretty self-explanatory. Almost all *suexec* problems are caused by files having the wrong permission or ownership; the entry in *suexec*'s log should make clear which.

See Also

- User directive at *http://httpd.apache.org/docs/mod/core.html#user* or *http://httpd.apache.org/docs-2.0/mod/mpm_common.html#user*
- Group directive at *http://httpd.apache.org/docs/mod/core.html#group* or *http://httpd.apache.org/docs-2.0/mod/mpm_common.html#group*
- The *suexec* documentation at *http://httpd.apache.org/docs/programs/suexec.html* or *http://httpd.apache.org/docs-2.0/programs/suexec.html*

8.14 Installing a mod_perl Handler from CPAN

Problem

You want to install one of the many *mod_perl* handler modules available on CPAN. For example, you want to install the *Apache::Perldoc* module, which generates HTML documentation for any Perl module that you happen to have installed.

Solution

Assuming you already have *mod_perl* installed, you'll just need to install the module from CPAN, and then add a few lines to your Apache configuration file.

To install the module, run the following command from the shell as root:

```
# perl -MCPAN -e 'install Apache::Perldoc'
```

Then, in your Apache configuration file, add:

```
<Location /perldoc>
    SetHandler perl-script
    PerlHandler Apache::Perldoc
</Location>
```

After restarting Apache, you can access the handler by going to a URL such as *http://example.com/perldoc/Apache/Perldoc*.

Discussion

The CPAN shell, which is installed when Perl is installed, gives you an easy way to install Perl modules from CPAN. CPAN, if you're not familiar with it, is the Comprehensive Perl Archive Network, at *http://cpan.org*, a comprehensive archive of Perl stuff, including Perl modules for every purpose you can imagine and several you can't. This includes a substantial number of *mod_perl* handlers.

The module specified in this recipe is a very simple one that gives you HTML documentation for any Perl module you have installed, accessible via your Apache server. Other ones provide photo albums, weblog handlers, and DNS zone management, among other things.

The first time you run the CPAN shell, you will need to answer a series of questions about your configuration, what CPAN server you want to get modules from, where it should find your FTP clients, and so on. This only happens once, and for every use after that it just works.

The specific way that you need to configure Apache to use your newly-installed module will vary from one module to another, but many of them will look like the example given. The *SetHandler perl-script* directive tells Apache that the content will be handled by *mod_perl*, whereas the *PerlHandler* directive specifies what Perl module contains the actual handler code.

See Also

- *http://cpan.org*
- *http://search.cpan.org/author/RBOW/Apache-Perldoc*
- *http://apachegallery.dk*
- *http://dnszone.org*

8.15 Writing a mod_perl Handler

Problem

You want to write your own *mod_perl* handler.

Solution

Here's a simple handler:

```
package Apache::Cookbook::Example;

sub handler {
    my $r = shift;
    $r->send_http_header('text/plain');
    $r->print('Hello, World.');
}

1;
```

Place this code in a file called *Example.pm*, in a directory *Apache/Cookbook/*, somewhere that Perl knows to look for it.

Discussion

The example handler given is fairly trivial and does not do anything useful. More useful examples may be obtained from the *mod_perl* Web site (*http://perl.apache.org*) and from Geoffrey Young's (et al.) excellent book) *mod_perl Developer's Cookbook* (Sams). Also, although it is somewhat dated, the "Eagle book" (*Writing Apache Modules with Perl and C*) by Lincoln Stein and Doug MacEachern (O'Reilly) is an excellent introduction to *mod_perl* and the Apache API.

The real question here, however, is how and where you should install the file that you've created. There are two answers to this question, and which one you choose will be largely personal preference.

When Perl looks for a module, it looks through the list called *@INC* for directories where that module might be. You can either put your module in one of those directories, or you can add a directory to the list.

To find out where Perl is looking, you can examine the values stored in *@INC* with the following:

```
perl -le 'print join "\n", @INC;'
```

This will give you a listing that will look something like:

```
/usr/local/lib/perl5/5.8.0/i686-linux
/usr/local/lib/perl5/5.8.0
/usr/local/lib/perl5/site_perl/5.8.0/i686-linux
/usr/local/lib/perl5/site_perl/5.8.0
/usr/local/lib/perl5/site_perl
.
```

This will of course vary from one system to another, from one version of Perl to another, but will bear some resemblance to that listing.

To install a module called *Apache::Cookbook::Example*, you might put the file *Example.pm* at this location: */usr/local/lib/perl5/site_perl/5.8.0/Apache/Cookbook/Example.pm*.

Alternately, you can tell Perl to look in some other directory by adding a value to the *@INC* list. The best way to do this is to add the following to your *startup.pl* file:

```
use lib '/home/rbowen/perl_libs/';
```

startup.pl should then be loaded by Apache at startup, using the following directive in the Apache server configuration file:

```
PerlRequire /path/to/startup.pl
```

This tells Perl to also look in that directory for Perl modules. This time, if your module is called *Apache::Cookbook::Example*, you would now place it at the location */home/rbowen/perl_libs/Apache/Cookbook/Example.pm*.

See Also

- *mod_perl Developer's Cookbook* by Geoffrey Young et al., which can be accessed at *http://modperlcookbook.org*

8.16 Enabling PHP Script Handling

Problem

You want to enable PHP scripts on your server.

Solution

If you have *mod_php* installed, use *AddHandler* to map *.php* and *.phtml* files to the PHP handler:

```
AddHandler application/x-httpd-php .phtml .php
```

Discussion

This recipe maps all files with *.phtml* or *.php* to the PHP handler. You must ensure that the *mod_php* module is installed and loaded.

 You may find some disagreement as to whether one should use *AddHandler* or *AddType* to enable the module, but the *AddHandler* directive is the correct one.

See Also

- Recipe 2.5
- Installation instructions on the *mod_php* Web site at *http://www.php.net/manual/en/install.apache.php* for Apache 1.3, or go to *http://www.php.net/manual/en/install.apache2.php* for Apache 2.0.

8.17 Verifying PHP Installation

Problem

You want to verify that you have PHP correctly installed and configured.

Solution

Put the following in your test PHP file:

```
<?php phpinfo(); ?>
```

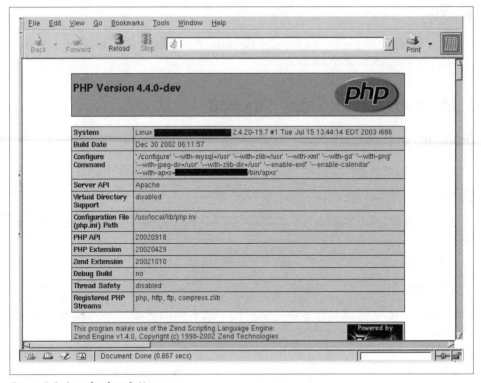

System	Linux ▓▓▓▓▓▓▓▓▓▓▓▓ 2.4.20-19.7 #1 Tue Jul 15 13:44:14 EDT 2003 i686
Build Date	Dec 30 2002 06:11:57
Configure Command	'./configure' '--with-mysql=/usr' '--with-zlib=/usr' '--with-xml' '--with-gd' '--with-png' '--with-jpeg-dir=/usr' '--with-zlib-dir=/usr' '--enable-exif' '--enable-calendar' '--with-apxs=▓▓▓▓▓▓▓▓▓▓▓▓/bin/apxs'
Server API	Apache
Virtual Directory Support	disabled
Configuration File (php.ini) Path	/usr/local/lib/php.ini
PHP API	20020918
PHP Extension	20020429
Zend Extension	20021010
Debug Build	no
Thread Safety	disabled
Registered PHP Streams	php, http, ftp, compress.zlib

Figure 8-2. Sample phpinfo( ) output

Discussion

Place that text in a file called *something.php* in a directory where you believe you have enabled PHP script execution. Accessing that file should give you a list of all configured PHP system variables. The first screen of the output should look something like Figure 8-2.

See Also

- Recipe 8.16

8.18 Parsing CGI Output for Server Side Includes

Problem

You want to include SSI directives in the output from a CGI script and have them processed correctly.

Solution

 This is fully supported only in Apache *httpd* version 2.0 and later.

Put the following into a scope that includes the CGI scripts for which you want the output parsed. Change the `.cgi` suffix to whatever your scripts use:

```
Options +Includes
AddOutputFilter INCLUDES .cgi
```

Discussion

Place this text in the server-wide configuration files or in a *.htaccess* file in the same directory as the scripts. This will cause the server to collect the output from the scripts and examine it for SSI directives before sending it to the client.

See Also

* Recipe 8.19

8.19 Parsing ScriptAlias Script Output for Server-Side Includes

Problem

You want to include SSI directives in the output from one or more of the scripts in your *ScriptAlias* directory and have them processed correctly.

Solution

 This is fully supported only in Apache *httpd* version 2.0 and later.

Put the following into the *<Directory>* container for your *ScriptAlias* directory:

```
Options +Includes
SetOutputFilter INCLUDES
```

Discussion

The above directive will instruct the server to filter all output from scripts in the *ScriptAlias* directory for SSI directives before sending it to the client.

See Also

* Recipe 8.18

8.20 Getting mod_perl to Handle All Perl Scripts

Problem

You want all *.pl* files to always be executed by *mod_perl*.

Solution

Place this line near the top of your *httpd.conf* file, after the module declaration and activation sections:

```
PerlModule Apache::Registry
```

Place this code in the section of your *httpd.conf* file which includes the scope where you want this behavior to occur (such as within a *<Directory>* container:

```
<FilesMatch \.pl$>
    SetHandler perl-script
    PerlHandler Apache::Registry
</FilesMatch>
```

Be sure that you have the Apache module *mod_perl* installed and activated.

Discussion

The *PerlModule* directive ensures that the necessary bits from *mod_perl* are available. The *<FilesMatch>* applies to every file ending in `.pl` and instructs the server to treat it as a script to be handled as CGI scripts by the *Apache::Registry* package.

More information can be found at the *mod_perl* Web site (*http://perl.apache.org*).

These directives will result in *all* `.pl` files being treated as CGI scripts, whether they are or not. If the server tries to execute a non-CGI script using this method, the end-user will get an error page and an entry will be made in the server's error log. The most common error logged refers to "`Premature end of script headers`," which is a pretty sure indicator of either a broken CGI script or a completely non-CGI script being treated like one.

See Also

* The mod_perl Web site at *http://perl.apache.org*
* *mod_perl Developer's Cookbook*, by Geoffrey Young et al., which can be accessed at *http://modperlcookbook.org/*

8.21 Enabling Python Script Handling

Problem

You want to enable Python scripts on your server.

Solution

If you have *mod_python* installed, use the following directives to instruct the server to call it when a Python script is referenced:

```
AddHandler mod_python .py
PythonHandler mod_python.publisher
PythonDebug On
```

Discussion

This recipe maps all files with *.py* to the Python script handler. Whenever a request resolves to a file with a *.py* suffix in the scope of those directives, the server will treat it as a Python script and execute it. You must ensure that the *mod_python* module is installed.

See Also

- Recipe 8.16
- Installation instructions on the *mod_python* Web site at *http://modpython.org/doc_html*

## CHAPTER 9

Error Handling

When you're running a Web site, things go wrong. And when they do, it's important that they are handled gracefully, so that the user experience is not too greatly diminished. In this chapter, you'll learn how to handle error conditions, return useful messages to the user, and capture information that will help you fix the problem so that it does not happen again.

9.1 Handling a Missing Host Field

Problem

You have multiple virtual hosts in your configuration, and at least one of them is name-based. For name-based virtual hosts to work properly, the client must send a valid Host field in the request header. This recipe describes how you can deal with situations in which the field is *not* included.

Solution

Add the following lines to your *httpd.conf* file:

```
Alias /NoHost.cgi /usr/local/apache/cgi-bin/NoHost.cgi
RewriteEngine On
RewriteCond "%{HTTP_HOST}" "^$"
RewriteRule "(.*)" "/NoHost.cgi$1" [PT]
```

The file *NoHost.cgi* can contain something like the following:

```
#! /usr/bin/perl -Tw

my $msg = "To properly direct your request, this server requires that\n"
        . "your web client include the HTTP 'Host' request header field.\n"
        . "The request which caused this response did not include such\n"
        . "a field, so we cannot determine the correct document for you.\n";
print "Status: 400 Bad Request\r\n\"
    . "Content-type: text/plain\r\n\"
    . 'Content-length: ' . length($msg) . "\r\n\"
    . "\r\n\"
```

```
      . $msg;
    exit(0);
```

Discussion

Once the directives in the solution are in place, all requests made of the server that do not include a Host field in the request header will be redirected to the specified CGI script, which can take appropriate action.

The solution uses a CGI script so that the response text can be tailored according to the attributes of the request and the server's environment. For instance, the script might respond with a list of links to valid sites on the server, determined by the script at runtime by examining the server's own configuration files. If all you need is a "please try again, this time with a Host field" sort of message, a static HTML file would suffice. Replace the *RewriteRule* directive in the solution with that below, and create the *nohost.html* accordingly:

```
RewriteRule ".*" "/nohost.html" [PT]
```

A more advanced version of the script approach could possibly scan the *httpd.conf* file for *ServerName* directives, construct a list of possibilities from them, and present links in a 300 Multiple Choices response. Of course, there's an excellent chance they wouldn't work, because the client *still* did not include the Host field.

See Also

- *http://httpd.apache.org/docs/mod/mod_rewrite.html*

9.2 Changing the Response Status for CGI Scripts

Problem

There may be times when you want to change the status for a response—for example, you want 404 Not Found errors to be sent back to the client as 403 Forbidden instead.

Solution

Point your *ErrorDocument* to a CGI script instead of a static file. The CGI specification permits scripts to specify the response status code.

In addition to the other header fields the script emits, like the Content-type field, include one named Status with the value and text of the status you want to return:

```
#! /bin/perl -w
print "Content-type: text/html;charset=iso-8859-1\r\n";
print "Status: 403 Access denied\r\n";
    :
```

Discussion

If Apache encounters an error processing a document, such as not being able to locate a file, by default it will return a canned error response to the client. You can customize this error response with the *ErrorDocument* directive, and Apache will generally maintain the error status when it sends your custom error text to the client.

However, if you want to change the status to something else, such as hiding the fact that a file doesn't exist by returning a Forbidden status, you need to tell Apache about the change.

This requires that the *ErrorDocument* be a dynamic page, such as a CGI script. The CGI specification provides a very simple means of specifying the status code for a response: the `Status` CGI header field. The Solution shows how it can be used.

See Also

- Chapter 8
- *http://httpd.apache.org/docs/mod/core.html#errordocument*
- *http://www.rfc-editor.org/cgi-bin/rfcdoctype.pl?loc=RFC&lets go=3875&type=ftp&file_format=txt*

9.3 Customized Error Messages

Problem

You want to display a customized error message, rather than the default Apache error page.

Solution

Use the *ErrorDocument* directive in *httpd.conf*:

```
ErrorDocument 405 /errors/notallowed.html
```

Discussion

The *ErrorDocument* directive allows you to create your own error pages to be displayed when particular error conditions occur. In the previous example, in the event of a `405` status code (`Method Not Allowed`), the specified URL is displayed for the user, rather than the default Apache error page.

The page can be customized to look like the rest of your Web site. When an error document looks significantly different from the rest of the site, this can leave the user feeling disoriented, or she may think she has left the site that she was on.

See Also

- *http://httpd.apache.org/docs/mod/core.html#errordocument*

9.4 Providing Error Documents in Multiple Languages

Problem

On a multilingual (content-negotiated) Web site, you want your error documents to be content-negotiated as well.

Solution

The Apache 2.0 default configuration file contains a configuration section, initially commented out, that allows you to provide error documents in multiple languages customized to the look of your Web site, with very little additional work.

Uncomment those lines. You can identify the lines by looking for the following comment in your default configuration file:

```
# The internationalized error documents require mod_alias, mod_include
# and mod_negotiation.  To activate them, uncomment the following 30 lines.
```

In Apache 1.3 this is harder, but there's a solution in the works, as of this writing, that will make it similar to the 2.0 implementation. Check the Apache Cookbook Web site for more information.

Discussion

The custom error documents provided with Apache 2.0 combine a variety of techniques to provide internationalized error messages. As of this writing, these error messages are available in German, English, Spanish, French, Dutch, Swedish, Italian, and Portuguese. Based on the language preference set in the client browser, the error message is delivered in the preferred language of the end user.

Using content negotiation, the correct variant of the document (i.e., the right language) is selected for the user, based on her browser preference settings. For more information about content negotiation, see the content negotiation documentation at *http://httpd.apache.org/docs-2.0/content-negotiation.html* (for Apache 2.0) or *http://httpd.apache.org/docs/content-negotiation.html* (for Apache 1.3).

In addition to delivering the error message in the correct language, this functionality also lets you customize the look of these error pages so that they resemble the rest of your Web site. To facilitate this, the files *top.html* and *bottom.html*, located in the *include* subdirectory of the *error* directory, should be modified to look like the standard header and footer content that appears on your Web site. The body of the error message documents is placed between the header and the footer to create a page that is less jarring to users when they transition from your main site to the error pages that are generated.

You also will note that the error documents contain SSI directives, which are used to further customize the error documents for the user. For example, in the case of the 404 (file not found) error document, the page will provide a link back to the page that the user came from, if the environment variable HTTP_REFERER is defined, and if that variable is not found, the page will merely notify the user that the URL was not found. Other SSI directives may be put in these documents, if you wish, to further customize them.

See Also

- *http://httpd.apache.org/docs/content-negotiation.html*
- *http://httpd.apache.org/docs-2.0/content-negotiation.html*
- *http://apache-cookbook.com*
- Recipe 8.9

9.5 Redirecting Invalid URLs to Some Other Page

Problem

You want all "not found" pages to go to some other page instead, such as the front page of the site, so that there is no loss of continuity on bad URLs.

Solution

Use the *ErrorDocument* directive to catch 404 (Not Found) errors:

```
ErrorDocument 404 /index.html
DirectoryIndex index.html /path/to/notfound.html
```

Discussion

The recipe given here will cause all 404 errors—every time someone requests an invalid URL—to return the URL */index.html*, providing the user with the front page of your Web site, so that even invalid URLs still get valid content. Presumably, users accessing an invalid URL on your Web site will get a page that helps them find the information that they were looking for.

By contrast, this behavior may confuse the user who believes she knows exactly where the URL should take her. Make sure that the page that you provide as the global error document does in fact help the user find things on your site, and does not merely confuse or disorient her. You may, as shown in the example, return her to the front page of the site. From there she should be able to find what she was looking for.

When users get good content from bad URLs, they will never fix their bookmarks and will continue to use a bogus URL long after it has become invalid. You will continue to get 404 errors in your log file for these URLs, and the users will never be aware that they are using an invalid URL. If, by contrast, you actually return an error document, they will immediately be aware that the URL they are using is invalid and will update their bookmarks to the new URL when they find it.

Note that, even though a valid document is being returned, a status code of 404 is still returned to the client. This means that if you are using some variety of tool to validate the links on your Web site, you will still get good results, if the tool is checking the status code, rather than looking for error messages in the content.

See Also

- *http://httpd.apache.org/docs/mod/core.html#errordocument*
- *http://httpd.apache.org/docs/mod/mod_dir.html*

9.6 Making Internet Explorer Display Your Error Page

Problem

You have an *ErrorDocument* directive correctly configured, but IE is displaying its own error page, rather than yours.

Solution

Make the error document bigger—at least 512 bytes.

Discussion

Yes, this seems a little bizarre, and it is. In this case, Internet Explorer thinks it knows better than the Web site administrator. If the error document is smaller than 512 bytes, it will display its internal error message page, rather than your custom error page, whenever it receives a 400 or 500 series status code. This size is actually configurable in the browser, so this number may in fact vary from one client to another. "Friendly error messages" also can be turned off entirely in the browser preferences.

This can be extremely frustrating the first time you see it happen, because you just know you have it configured correctly and it seems to work in your other browsers. Furthermore, when some helpful person tells you that your error document just needs to be a little larger, it's natural to think that he is playing a little prank on you, because this seems a little too far-fetched.

But it's true. Make the page bigger. It needs to be at least 512 bytes, or IE will ignore it and gleefully display its own "friendly" error message instead.

Exactly what you fill this space with is unimportant. You can, for example, just bulk it up with comments. For example, repeating the following comment six times would be sufficient to push you over that minimum file size:

```
<!-- message-obscuring clients are an abomination
     and an insult to the user's intelligence -->
```

See Also

- *http://httpd.apache.org/docs/mod/core.html#errordocument*

9.7 Notification on Error Conditions

Problem

You want to receive email notification when there's an error condition on your server.

Solution

Point the *ErrorDocument* directive to a CGI program that sends mail, rather than to a static document:

```
ErrorDocument 404 /cgi-bin/404.cgi
```

404.cgi looks like the following:

```perl
#!/usr/bin/perl
use Mail::Sendmail;
use strict;

my $message = qq~
Document not found: $ENV{REQUEST_URI}
Link was from: $ENV{HTTP_REFERER}
~;

my %mail = (
            To => 'admin@server.com',
            From => 'website@server.com',
            Subject => 'Broken link',
            Message => $message,
            );
sendmail(%mail);

print "Content-type: text/plain\n\n";
print "Document not found. Admin has been notified\n";
```

Discussion

This recipe is provided as an example, rather than as a recommendation. On a Web site of any significant size or traffic level, actually putting this into practice generates a substantial quantity of email, even on a site that is very well maintained. This is because people mistype URLs, and other sites, over which you have no control, will contain incorrect links to your site. It may be educational, however, to put something like this in place, at least briefly, to gain an appreciation for the scale of your own Web site.

The *ErrorDocument* directive will cause all 404 (Document Not Found) requests to be handled by the specified URL, and so your CGI program gets run and is passed environment variables that will be used in the script itself to figure out what link is bad and where the request came from.

The script used the *Mail::Sendmail* Perl module to deliver the email message, and this module should work fine on any operating system. The module is not a standard part of Perl, so you may have to install it from CPAN (*http://www.cpan.org*). A similar effect can, of course, also be achieved in PHP or any other programming language.

The last two lines of the program display a very terse page for the user, telling him that there was an error condition. You may wish, instead, to have the script redirect the user to some more informative and attractive page on your Web site. This could be accomplished by replacing those last two lines with something like the following:

```
print "Location: http://server.name/errorpage.html\n\n";
```

This would send a redirect header to the client, which would display the specified URL to the user.

See Also

- *http://httpd.apache.org/docs/mod/core.html#errordocument*

## CHAPTER 10

Proxies

Proxy means to act on behalf of another. In the context of a Web server, this means one server fetching content from another server, then returning it to the client. For example, you may have several Web servers that hide behind a proxy server. The proxy server is responsible for making sure requests go to the right backend server.

mod_proxy, which comes with Apache, handles proxying behavior. The recipes in this chapter cover various techniques that can be used to take advantage of this capability. We discuss securing your proxy server, caching content proxied through your server, and ways to use *mod_proxy* to map requests to services running on alternate ports.

Additional information about *mod_proxy* can be found at *http://httpd.apache.org/docs/ mod/mod_proxy.html* for Apache 1.3, or *http://httpd.apache.org/docs/2.0/mod/ mod_proxy.html* for Apache 2.0.

Apache 2.2 introduces a number of submodules, such as *mod_proxy_balancer*, which give additional functionality to *mod_proxy*. These will be discussed in this chapter, too.

Please make sure that you don't enable proxying until you understand the security concerns involved and have taken steps to secure your proxy server. (See Recipe 6.20 for details.)

You also may wish to consider a dedicated proxy server, such as Squid (*http:// www.squid-cache.org*), which is focused entirely on one task, and thus has more options related to this task.

10.1 Securing Your Proxy Server

Problem

You want to enable proxying, but you don't want an open proxy that can be used by just anyone.

Solution

For Apache 1.3:

```
<Directory proxy:*>
    Order deny,allow
    Deny from all
    Allow from .yourdomain.com
</Directory>
```

For Apache 2.0:

```
<Proxy *>
    Order Deny,Allow
    Deny from all
    Allow from .yourdomain.com
</Proxy>
```

Discussion

Running an open proxy is a concern because it permits Internet users to use your proxy server to cover their tracks as they visit Web sites. This can be a problem for a numbers of reasons. The user is effectively stealing your bandwidth and is certainly part of the problem. However, perhaps more concerning is the fact that you are probably enabling people to circumvent restrictions that have been put in place by their network administrators, or perhaps you are providing users with anonymity while they visit a Web site, and as a consequence, these visits appear to come from your network.

In these recipes, *.yourdomain.com* should be replaced by the name of your particular domain, or, better yet, the network address(es) that are on your network. (IP addresses are harder to fake than host and domain names.) For example, rather than the line appearing in the recipe, you might use a line such as:

```
Allow from 192.168.1
```

Note that every request for resources that goes through your proxy server generates a logfile entry, containing the address of the client and the resource that she requested through your proxy server. For example, one such request might look like:

```
192.168.1.5 - - [26/Feb/2003:21:26:13 -0500] "GET http://httpd.apache.org/docs/mod/
    mod_proxy.html HTTP/1.1" 200 49890
```

Your users, if made aware of this fact, will no doubt find it invasive, because this will show all HTTP traffic through the proxy server.

It is possible to configure your server not to log these requests. To do this, you need to set an environment variable for proxied requests:

```
<Directory proxy:*>
    SetEnv PROXIED 1
</Directory>
```

Then, in your log directive, specify that these requests are not to be logged:

```
CustomLog /www/logs/access_log common env=!PROXIED
```

See Also

- *http://httpd.apache.org/docs/mod/mod_proxy.html*
- *http://httpd.apache.org/docs/mod/mod_log_config.html*

10.2 Preventing Your Proxy Server from Being Used as an Open Mail Relay

Problem

If your Apache server is set up to operate as a proxy, it is possible for it to be used as a mail relay unless precautions are taken. This means that your system may be functioning as an "open relay" even though your mail server software is securely configured.

Solution

Use *mod_rewrite* to forbid proxy requests to port 25 (SMTP):

```
<Directory proxy:*>
    RewriteEngine On
    RewriteRule "^proxy:[a-z]*://[^/]*:25(/|$)" "-" [F,NC,L]
</Directory>
```

Discussion

To use the Apache proxy as an SMTP relay is fairly trivial, but then so is preventing it. The solution simply tells the server to respond with a **403 Forbidden** to any attempts to use it to proxy to a remote mail server (port 25). Other ports, such as HTTP (port 80), HTTPS (port 443), and FTP (ports 20 and 21), which are commonly permitted proxy access, will not be affected.

See Also

- *http://httpd.apache.org/docs/mod/mod_proxy.html*
- *http://httpd.apache.org/docs/mod/core.html#directory*
- *http://httpd.apache.org/docs/mod/mod_rewrite.html*

10.3 Forwarding Requests to Another Server

Problem

You want requests for particular URLs to be transparently forwarded to another server.

Solution

Use *ProxyPass* and *ProxyPassReverse* directives in your *httpd.conf*:

```
ProxyPass /other/ http://other.server.com/
ProxyPassReverse /other/ http://other.server.com/
```

Discussion

These directives will cause requests to URLs starting with */other/* to be forwarded to the server *other.server.com*, with the path information preserved. That is to say, a request for *http://www.server.com/other/something.html* will be translated into a request for *http://other.server.com/something.html*. Content obtained from this other server will be returned to the client, who will be unable to determine that any such technique was employed. The *ProxyPassReverse* directive ensures that any redirect headers sent from the backend server (in this case, *other.server.com*) will be modified so that they appear to come from the main server.

This method is often used to have the dynamic portion of the site served by a server running *mod_perl*—often even on the same machine, but on a different port—while the static portions of the site are served from the main server, which can be lighter weight, and so run faster.

Note that URLs contained within documents are not rewritten as they pass through the proxy, and links within documents should be relative, rather than absolute, so that they work correctly.

Use this recipe when you have a frontend server and one or more backend servers, inaccessible from the Internet, and you wish to serve content from them. In the example given, when a request is made for a URL starting with /other/, Apache makes a request for the URL *http://other.server.com*, and returns the content obtained by the client. For example, a request for the URL /other/example.html results in a request for the URL *http://other.server.com/example.html*.

The *ProxyPassReverse* directive ensures that any header fields returned by the secondary server (which contain the name of the server, such as Location headers) will be rewritten to contain the URL that the end user will actually be using, ensuring that the redirect actually functions as desired.

Note that links within HTML documents on the secondary site should all be relative, rather than absolute, so that these links work for users using the content via the proxy server. In the recipe given, for example, a link to */index.html* removes the /other/ portion of the URL, causing the request to no longer hit the proxied portion of the server.

Using this technique, you can have content for one Web site actually served by multiple Web server machines. This can be used as a means to traverse the border of your network, or it can be used as a load-sharing technique to lessen the burden on your primary Web server.

See Also

- *http://httpd.apache.org/docs/mod/mod_proxy.html*
- Recipe 11.12

10.4 Blocking Proxied Requests to Certain Places

Problem

You want to use your proxy server as a content filter, forbidding requests to certain places.

Solution

Use *ProxyBlock* in the *httpd.conf* to deny access to particular sites:

```
ProxyBlock forbiddensite.com www.competitor.com monster.com
```

Discussion

This example forbids proxied requests to the sites listed. These arguments are substring matches; `example.com` will also match `www.example.com`, and an argument of `example` would match both.

If you want more fine-grained control of what content is requested through your proxy server, you may want to use something more sophisticated, such as Squid, which is more full-featured in that area.

See Also

- The Squid proxy server, found at *http://www.squid-cache.org*

10.5 Proxying mod_perl Content to Another Server

Problem

You want to run a second HTTP server for dynamically generated content and have Apache transparently map requests for this content to the other server.

Solution

First, install Apache, running on an alternate port, such as port 90, on which you will generate this dynamic content. Then, on your main server:

```
ProxyPass /dynamic/ http://localhost:90/
ProxyPassReverse /dynamic/ http://localhost:90/
```

Discussion

Most dynamic content generation techniques use a great deal more system resources than serving static content. This can slow down the process of serving static content from the same server, because child processes will be consumed with producing this dynamic content, and thus unable to serve the static files.

By giving the dynamic content its own dedicated server, you allow the static content to be served much more rapidly, and the dynamic content has a dedicated server. Each server can have a smaller set of modules installed than it would otherwise require because it'll be performing a smaller subset of the functionality needed to do both tasks.

This technique can be used for a *mod_perl* server, a PHP server, or any other dynamic content method. Or you could reverse the technique and have, for example, a dedicated machine for serving image files using *mod_mmap_static* to serve the files very rapidly out of an in-memory cache.

In the example, all URLs starting with */dynamic/* will be forwarded to the other server, which will, presumably, handle only requests for dynamic content. URLs that do not match this URL, however, will fall through and be handled by the frontend server.

See Also

- *http://httpd.apache.org/docs/mod/mod_proxy.html*
- Chapter 8

10.6 Configuring a Caching Proxy Server

Problem

You want to run a caching proxy server.

Solution

Configure your server to proxy requests and provide a location for the cached files to be placed:

```
ProxyRequests on
CacheRoot /var/spool/httpd/proxy
```

Discussion

Running a caching proxy server allows users on your network to have more rapid access to content that others have already requested. They will perhaps not be getting the most recent version of the document in question, but since they are retrieving the content from a local copy rather than from the remote Web server, they will get it much more quickly.

With the contents of the WWW growing ever more dynamic, running a caching proxy server perhaps makes less sense than it once did, when most of the Web was composed of static content. However, because *mod_proxy* is fairly smart about what it caches and what it does not cache, this sort of setup will still speed things up by caching the static portions of documents, such as the image files, while retrieving the most recent version of those documents that change over time.

The directory specified in the *CacheRoot* directive specifies where cached content will be stored. This directory must be writable by the user that Apache is running as (typically nobody), so that it is able to store these files there.

Finally, note that, while in Apache 1.3, the functions discussed here are provided by *mod_proxy*; in Apache 2.0, the proxying and caching functionalities have been split into the modules *mod_proxy* and *mod_cache*, respectively. In either case, these modules are not enabled by default.

See Also

- *http://httpd.apache.org/docs/mod/mod_proxy.html*

10.7 Filtering Proxied Content

Problem

You want to apply some filter to proxied content, such as altering certain words.

Solution

In Apache 2.0 and later, you can use *mod_ext_filter* to create output filters to apply to content before it is sent to the user:

```
ExtFilterDefine naughtywords mode=output intype=text/html cmd="/bin/sed s/darned/
    blasted/g"

<Proxy *>
    SetOutputFilter naughtywords
</Proxy>
```

Discussion

The recipe offered is a very simple-minded "naughty word" filter, replacing the naughty word "darned" with the sanitized alternate "blasted." This could be expanded to a variety of more sophisticated content modification, because the *cmd* argument can be any command line, such as a Perl script, or arbitrary program, which can filter the content in any way you want. All proxied content will be passed through this filter before it is delivered to the client.

Note that this recipe will work only in Apache 2.0, as the module *mod_ext_filter*, the *SetOutputFilter* directive, and the *<Proxy>* directive are available only in Apache 2.0.

Note also that there are ethical and legal issues surrounding techniques like these, which you may need to deal with. We don't presume to take a position on any of them. In particular, modifying proxied content that does not belong to you may be a violation of the owner's copyright and may be considered by some to be unethical. Thankfully, this is just a technical book, not a philosophical one. We can tell you how to do it, but whether you should is left to your conscience and your lawyers.

See Also

- *http://httpd.apache.org/docs-2.0/mod/mod_proxy.html*
- *http://httpd.apache.org/docs-2.0/mod/mod_ext_filter.html*

10.8 Requiring Authentication for a Proxied Server

Problem

You wish to proxy content from a server, but it requires a login and password before content may be served from this proxied site.

Solution

Use standard authentication techniques to require logins for proxied content:

```
ProxyPass "/secretserver/" "http://127.0.0.1:8080"
<Directory "proxy:http://127.0.0.1:8080/">
    AuthName SecretServer
    AuthType Basic
    AuthUserFile /path/to/secretserver.htpasswd
    Require valid-user
</Directory>
```

Discussion

This technique can be useful if you are running some sort of special-purpose or limited-function Web server on your system, but you need to apply Apache's rich set of access control and its other features to access it. This is done by using the *ProxyPass* directive to make the special-purpose server's URI space part of your main server, and using the special proxy:*path* <Directory> container syntax to apply Apache settings only to the mapped URIs.

See Also

- Recipe 6.7

10.9 Load Balancing with mod_proxy_balancer

Problem

You want to balance the load between several backend servers.

Solution

Use *mod_proxy_balancer* to create a load-balanced cluster:

```
<Proxy balancer://mycluster>
    BalancerMember http://192.168.1.50:80
    BalancerMember http://192.168.1.51:80
</Proxy>
ProxyPass /application balancer://mycluster/
```

Discussion

mod_proxy_balancer is an exciting new module that provides load balancing between multiple backend servers. This kind of functionality has traditionally been associated with expensive and complex commercial solutions. This module makes this simple to configure, and it's included in the standard installation of the Apache Web server.

The example given above sets up a two-member balanced cluster and proxies the URL /application to that cluster.

mod_proxy_balancer offers a wide variety of options, which you can find in detail in the documentation, available here: *http://httpd.apache.org/docs/2.2/mod/mod_proxy_balancer.html*.

For example, you can indicate that a particular server is more powerful than another, and so should be allowed to assume more of the load than other machines in the cluster. In the following configuration line, we indicate that one particular machine should receive twice as much traffic as other machines:

```
BalancerMember http://192.168.1.51:80 loadfactor=2
```

Traffic may be balanced by traffic (bytes transferred) or by request (number of requests made per host) by putting additional arguments on the *ProxyPass* directive:

```
ProxyPass /application balancer://mycluster/ lbmethod=bytraffic
```

See the *mod_proxy* documentation for more information on this point.

And there is a Web-based balancer manager tool, which can be configured as follows:

```
<Location /balancer-manager>
    SetHandler balancer-manager
</Location>
```

The balancer manager lets you set servers available or unavailable, and change their load factor, without restarting the server. This allows you to take servers offline for maintenance, do whatever needs to be done, and bring them back up, without ever affecting the end user.

See Also

- *http://httpd.apache.org/docs/2.2/mod/mod_proxy_balancer.html*

10.10 Proxied Virtual Host

Problem

You want to have an entire virtual host proxied to a different server.

Solution

Place a *ProxyPass* directive in your *VirtualHost* configuration block:

```
<VirtualaHost *:80>
    ServerName server2.example.com
    ProxyPass / http://192.168.1.52:80
    ProxyPassReverse / http://192.168.1.52:80
</VirtualHost>
```

Discussion

This recipe will pass all requests to this virtual host to the specified backend server and serve the content from there. The *ProxyPassReverse* directive ensures that redirects issued from the backend server will be correctly rewritten to the front-end server, rather than having clients try to request content directly from the backend server.

It can be useful to collect logfiles on the frontend server, rather than on the backend server. Requests to the backend server will appear to come from the proxy server, rather than from the original client address. However, logfiles collected on the proxy (frontend) server will have the original client address.

See Also

- *http://httpd.apache.org/docs/2.2/mod/mod_proxy.html*

10.11 Refusing to Proxy FTP

Problem

You want to make sure that FTP (or, perhaps, other protocols) are not proxied through your server.

Solution

Make sure that *mod_proxy_ftp* isn't loaded:

```
# LoadModule proxy_ftp_module modules/mod_proxy_ftp.so
```

Discussion

mod_proxy has several helper modules that provide the protocol-specific proxying functionality. These modules are *mod_proxy_http*, for proxying HTTP requests; *mod_proxy_ftp*, for proxying FTP requests; and *mod_proxy_connect*, for support for the CONNECT HTTP method, used primarily for tunneling SSL requests through proxy servers.

If you want *mod_proxy* to never proxy FTP requests, you need merely to ensure that the *LoadModule* directive for *mod_proxy_ftp* is commented out, as shown above.

See Also

- *http://httpd.apache.org/docs/2.2/mod/mod_proxy_ftp.html*
- *http://httpd.apache.org/docs/2.2/mod/mod_proxy.html*

## CHAPTER 11

Performance

Your Web site can probably be made to run faster if you are willing to make a few trade-offs and spend a little time benchmarking your site to see what is really slowing it down.

There are a number of things that you can configure differently to get a performance boost. Although, there are other things to which you may have to make more substantial changes. It all depends on what you can afford to give up and what you are willing to trade off. For example, in many cases, you may need to trade performance for security, or vice versa.

In this chapter, we make some recommendations of things that you can change, and we warn against things that can cause substantial slow-downs. Be aware that Web sites are very individual, and what may speed up one Web site may not necessarily speed up another Web site.

Topics covered include hardware considerations, configuration file changes, and dynamic content generation, which can all be factors in getting every ounce of performance out of your Web site.

Very frequently, application developers create programs in conditions that don't accurately reflect the conditions under which they will run in production. Consequently, the application that seemed to run adequately fast with the test database of 100 records, runs painfully slowly with the production database of 200,000 records.

By ensuring that your test environment is at least as demanding as your production environment, you greatly reduce the chances that your application will perform unexpectedly slow when you roll it out.

11.1 Determining How Much Memory You Need

Problem

You want to ensure that you have sufficient RAM in your server.

Solution

Find the instances of Apache in your process list, and determine an average memory footprint for an Apache process. Multiply this number by your peak load (maximum number of concurrent Web clients you'll be serving).

Discussion

Because there is very little else that you can do at the hardware level to make your server faster, short of purchasing faster hardware, it is important to make sure that you have as much RAM as you need.

Determining how much memory you need is an inexact science, to say the least. In order to take an educated guess, you need to observe your server under load, and see how much memory it is using.

The amount of memory used by one Apache process will vary greatly from one server to another, based on what modules you have installed and what the server is being called upon to do. Only by looking at your own server can you get an accurate estimate of what this quantity is for your particular situation.

Tools such as *top* and *ps* may be used to examine your process list and determine the size of processes. The `server-status` handler, provided by *mod_status*, may be used to determine the total number of Apache processes running at a given time.

If, for example, you determine that your Apache processes are using 4 MB of memory each, and under peak load, you find that you are running 125 Apache processes, then you will need, at a bare minimum, 500 MB of RAM in the server to handle this peak load. Remember that memory is also needed for the operating system, and any other applications and services that are running on the system, in addition to Apache. So in reality you will need more than this amount to handle this peak load.

If, by contrast, you are unable to add more memory to the server, for whatever reason, you can use the same technique to figure out the maximum number of child processes that you are capable of serving at any one time, and use the *MaxClients* directive to limit Apache to that many processes:

```
MaxClients 125
```

See Also

- *http://httpd.apache.org/docs/misc/perf-tuning.html*

11.2 Benchmarking Apache with ab

Problem

You want to benchmark changes that you are making to verify that they are in fact making a difference in performance.

Solution

Use *ab* (Apache bench), which you will find in the *bin* directory of your Apache installation:

```
ab -n 1000 -c 10 http://www.example.com/test.html
```

Discussion

Apache bench is a command-line utility that comes with Apache and lets you do very basic performance testing of your server. It is especially useful for making small changes to your configuration and testing server performance before and after the change.

The arguments given in the previous example tell *ab* to request the resource *http://www.example.com/test.html* 1000 times (-n **1000** indicates the number of requests) and to make these requests 10 at a time (-c **10** indicates the concurrency level).

Other arguments that may be specified can be seen by running *ab* with the -h flag. Of particular interest is the -k flag, which enables keepalive mode. See the following keepalive recipe for additional details on this matter.

There are a few things to note about *ab* when using it to evaluate performance.

Apache bench does not mimic Web site usage by real people. It requests the same resource repeatedly to test the performance of that one thing. For example, you may use *ab* to test the performance of a particular CGI program, before and after a performance-related change was made to it. Or you may use it to measure the impact of turning on *.htaccess* files, or content negotiation, for a particular directory. Real users, of course, do not repeatedly load the same page, and so performance measurements made using *ab* may not reflect actual real-world performance of your Web site.

You should probably not run the Web server and *ab* on the same machine, as this will introduce more uncertainty into the measurement. With both *ab* and the Web server itself consuming system resources, you will receive significantly slower performance than if you were to run *ab* on some other machine, accessing the server over the network. However, also be aware that running *ab* on another machine will introduce network latency, which is not present when running it on the same machine as the server.

Finally, there are many factors that can affect performance of the server, so you will not get the same numbers each time you run the test. Network conditions, other processes running on the client or server machine, and a variety of other things may influence your results slightly one way or another. The best way to reduce the impact of environmental changes is to run a large number of tests and average your results. Also, make sure that you change as few things as possible—ideally, just one—between tests, so that you can be more sure what change has made any differences you can see.

Finally, you need to understand that, while *ab* gives you a good idea of whether certain changes have improved performance, it does not give a good simulation of actual users. Actual users don't simply fetch the same resource repeatedly; they obtain a variety of different resources from various places on your site. Thus, actual site usage conditions may produce different performance issues than those revealed by *ab*.

See Also

- The manpage for the *ab* tool
- *http://httpd.apache.org/docs/2.2/programs/ab.html*

11.3 Tuning KeepAlive Settings

Problem

You want to tune the keepalive-related directives to the best possible setting for your Web site.

Solution

Turn on the *KeepAlive* setting, and set the related directives to sensible values:

```
KeepAlive On
MaxKeepAliveRequests 0
KeepAliveTimeout 15
```

Discussion

The default behavior of HTTP is for each document to be requested over a new connection. This causes a lot of time to be spent opening and closing connections. *KeepAlive* allows multiple requests to be made over a single connection, thus reducing the time spent establishing socket connections. This, in turn, speeds up the load time for clients requesting content from your site.

In addition to turning keepalive on using the *KeepAlive* directive, there are two directives that allow you to adjust the way that it is done.

The first of these, *MaxKeepAliveRequests*, indicates how many keepalive requests should be permitted over a single connection. There is no reason to have this number set low. The default value for this directive is 100, and this seems to work pretty well for most sites. Setting this value to 0 means that an unlimited number of requests will be permitted over a single connection. This might allow users to load all of their content from your site over a single connection, depending on the value of *KeepAliveTimeout* and how quickly they went through the site.

KeepAliveTimeout indicates how long a particular connection will be held open when no further requests are received. The optimal setting for this directive depends entirely on the nature of your Web site. You should probably think of this value as the amount of time it takes users to absorb the content of one page of your site before they move on to the next page. If the users move on to the next page before the *KeepAliveTimeout* has expired, when they click on the link for the next page of content, they will get that next document over the same connection. If, however, that time has already expired, they will need to establish a new connection to the server for that next page.

You also should be aware that if users load a resource from your site and then go away, Apache will still maintain that open connection for them for *KeepAliveTimeout* seconds, which makes that child process unable to serve any other requests during that time. Therefore, setting *KeepAliveTimeout* too high is just as undesirable as setting it too low.

In the event that *KeepAliveTimeout* is set too high, you will see (i.e., with the *server-status* handler—see Recipe 11.4) that a significant number of processes are in keepalive mode, but are inactive. Over time, this number will continue to grow, as more child processes are spawned to take the place of child processes that are in this state.

Conversely, setting *KeepAliveTimeout* too low will result in conditions similar to having *KeepAlive* turned off entirely, when a single client will require many connections over the course of a brief visit. This is harder to detect than the opposite condition. In general, it is probably better to err on the side of setting it too high, rather than too low.

Because the length of time that any given user looks at any given document on your site is going to be as individual as the users themselves, and varies from page to page around your Web site, it is very difficult to determine the best possible value of this directive for a particular site. However, it is unlikely that this is going to make any large impact on your overall site performance when compared to other things that you can do. Leaving it at the default value of 5 tends to work pretty well for most sites.

See Also

- *http://httpd.apache.org/docs/2.2/mod/core.html#keepalive*
- *http://httpd.apache.org/docs/2.2/mod/core.html#maxkeepaliverequests*
- *http://httpd.apache.org/docs/2.2/mod/core.html#keepalivetimeout*

11.4 Getting a Snapshot of Your Site's Activity

Problem

You want to find out exactly what your server is doing.

Solution

Enable the `server-status` handler to get a snapshot of what child processes are running and what each one is doing. Enable *ExtendedStatus* to get even more detail:

```
<Location /server-status>
    SetHandler server-status
    Order deny,allow
    Deny from all
    Allow from 192.168.1
</Location>

ExtendedStatus On
```

Then, view the results at the URL *http://servername/server-status*.

Discussion

Provided by *mod_status*, which is enabled by default, the `server-status` handler provides a snapshot of your server's activity. This snapshot includes some basic details, such as when the server was last restarted, how long it has been up, and how much data it has served in that time. Following that, there will be a list of the child processes and what each one is doing. At the bottom of the page is a detailed explanation of the terms used and what each column of the table represents.

 The server status display shows activity across the entire server—including virtual hosts. If you are providing hosting services for others, you may not want them to be able to see this level of detail about each other.

It is recommended that, as in the default configuration file that comes with Apache, you restrict access to this handler. Part of the information contained on this page is a list of client addresses and the document that they are requesting. Some users feel that it is a violation of their privacy for you to make this information readily available on your Web site. Additionally, it may provide information such as `QUERY_STRING` variables, `PATH_INFO` variables, or simply URLs that you wished to not be made public. It is therefore recommended that you add to the above recipe some lines such as:

```
Order deny,allow
Deny from all
Allow from 192.168.1
```

This configuration allows access only from the 192.168.1 network, or whatever network you put in there, and denies access from unauthorized Internet users.

See Also

- *http://httpd.apache.org/docs/2.2/mod/mod_status.html*
- *http://httpd.apache.org/server-status/*

11.5 Avoiding DNS Lookups

Problem

You want to avoid situations where you have to do DNS lookups of client addresses, as this is a very slow process.

Solution

Always set the *HostNameLookups* directive to Off:

```
HostNameLookups Off
```

Make sure that, whenever possible, *Allow* from and/or *Deny* from directives use the IP address, rather than the hostname of the hosts in question.

Discussion

DNS lookups can take a very long time—anywhere from 0 to 60 seconds—and should be avoided at all costs. In the event that a client address cannot be looked up at all, it can take up to a minute for the lookup to time out, during which time the child process that is doing the lookup cannot do anything else.

There are a number of cases in which Apache will need to do DNS lookups, and so the goal here is to completely avoid those situations.

HostNameLookups

Before Apache 1.3, *HostNameLookups*, which determines whether Apache logs client IP addresses or hostnames, defaulted to on, meaning that each Apache log entry required a DNS lookup to convert the client IP address to a hostname to put in the logfile. Fortunately, that directive now defaults to off, and so this is primarily an admonition to leave it alone.

If you need to have these addresses converted to hostnames, this should be done by another program, preferably running on a machine other than your production Web server. That is, you really should copy the file to some other machine for the purpose of processing, so that the effort required to do this processing does not negatively effect your Web server's performance.

Apache comes with a utility called *logresolve*, which will process your logfile, replacing IP addresses with hostnames. Additionally, most logfile analysis tools will also perform this name resolution as part of the log analysis process.

Allow and Deny from hostnames

When you do host-based access control using the *Allow* from and *Deny* from directives, Apache takes additional precautions to make sure that the client is not spoofing its hostname. In particular, it does a DNS lookup on the IP address of the client to obtain the name to compare against the access restriction. It then looks up the name that was obtained, just to make sure that the DNS record is not being faked.[*]

For the sake of better performance, therefore, it is much better to use an IP address, rather than a name, in *Allow* and *Deny* directives.

See Also

- Chapter 3

11.6 Optimizing Symbolic Links

Problem

You wish to balance the security needs associated with symbolic links with the performance impact of a solution, such as using *Options* `SymLinksIfOwnerMatch`, which causes a server slowdown.

Solution

For tightest security, use *Options* `SymlinksIfOwnerMatch`, or *Options* `-FollowSymLinks` if you seldom or never use symlinks.

For best performance, use *Options* `FollowSymlinks`.

Discussion

Symbolic links are an area in which you need to weigh performance against security and make the decision that makes the most sense in your particular situation.

In the normal everyday operation of a Unixish operating system, symbolic links are considered to be the same as the file to which they link.[†] When you *cd* into a directory, you don't need to be aware of whether that was a symlink or not. It just works.

---

[*] For example, the owner of the IP address could very easily put a PTR record in his reverse-DNS zone, pointing his IP address at a name belonging to someone else.

[†] Of course, this is not true at the filesystem level, but we're just talking about the practical user level.

Apache, by contrast, has to consider whether each file and directory is a symlink or not, if the server is configured not to follow symlinks. And, additionally, if *Option* `SymlinksIfOwnerMatch` is turned on, Apache not only has to check if the particular file is a symlink, but also has to check the ownership of the link itself and of the target, in the event that it is a symlink. Although this enforces a certain security policy, it takes a substantial amount of time and so slows down the operation of your server.

In the trade-off between security and performance, in the matter of symbolic links, here are the guidelines.

If you are primarily concerned about security, never permit the following of symbolic links. It may permit someone to create a link from a document directory to content that you would not want to be on a public server. Or, if there are cases in which you really need symlinks, use *Options* `SymlinksIfOwnerMatch`, which requires that someone may only link to files that they own and will presumably protect you from having a user link to a portion of the filesystem that is not already under her control.

If you are concerned about performance, always use *Options* `FollowSymlinks`, and never use *Options* `SymlinksIfOwnerMatch`. *Options* `FollowSymlinks` permits Apache to follow symbolic links in the manner of most Unixish applications—that is, Apache does not even need to check to see if the file in question is a symlink or not.

See Also

- *http://httpd.apache.org/docs/2.2/mod/core.html#options*

11.7 Minimizing the Performance Impact of .htaccess Files

Problem

You want *per*-directory configuration but want to avoid the performance hit of *.htaccess* files.

Solution

Turn on *AllowOverride* only in directories where it is required, and tell Apache not to waste time looking for *.htaccess* files elsewhere:

```
AllowOverride None
```

Then use <*Directory*> sections to selectively enable *.htaccess* files only where needed.

Discussion

.htaccess files cause a substantial reduction in Apache's performance, because it must check for a *.htaccess* in every directory along the path to the requested file to be assured of getting all of the relevant configuration overrides. This is necessary because Apache configuration directives apply not only to the directory in which they are set, but also

to all subdirectories. Thus, we must check for .htaccess files in parent directories, as well as in the current directory, to find any directives that would trickle down the current directory.

For example, if, for some reason, you had *AllowOverride* `All` enabled for all directories and your *DocumentRoot* was */usr/local/apache/htdocs*, then a request for the URL *http:// example.com/events/parties/christmas.html* would result in the following files being looked for and, if found, opened and searched for configuration directives:

```
/.htaccess
/usr/.htaccess
/usr/local/.htaccess
/usr/local/apache/.htaccess
/usr/local/apache/htdocs/.htaccess
/usr/local/apache/htdocs/events/.htaccess
/usr/local/apache/htdocs/events/parties/.htaccess
```

Now, hopefully, you would never have *AllowOverride* `All` enabled for your entire filesystem, so this is a worst-case scenario. However, occasionally, when people do not adequately understand what this configuration directive does, they will enable this option for their entire filesystem and suffer poor performance as a result.

The recommended solution is by far the best way to solve this problem. The *<Directory>* directive is specifically for this situation, and .htaccess files should really only be used in the situation where configuration changes are needed and access to the main server configuration file is not readily available.

For example, if you have a .htaccess file in */usr/local/apache/htdocs/events* containing the directive:

```
AddEncoding x-gzip tgz
```

You should instead simply replace this with the following in your main configuration file:

```
<Directory /usr/local/apache/htdocs/event>
    AddEncoding x-gzip tgz
</Directory>
```

Which is to say, anything that appears in a .htaccess can, instead, appear in a *<Directory>* section, referring to that same directory.

If you are compelled to permit .htaccess files somewhere on your Web site, you should only permit them in the specific directory where they are needed. For example, if you particularly need to permit .htaccess files in the directory */www/htdocs/users/leopold/*, then you should explicitly allow then for only this directory:

```
<Directory /www/htdocs/users/leopold>
    AllowOverride All
</Directory>
```

One final note about the *AllowOverride* directive: this directive lets you be very specific about what types of directives you permit in .htaccess files, and you should make an effort only to permit those directives that are actually needed. That is, rather than using the `All` argument, you should allow specific types of directives as needed. In particular, the `Options` argument to *AllowOverride* should be avoided, if possible, as it may enable users to turn on features that you have turned off for security reasons.

See Also

- *http://httpd.apache.org/docs/2.2/howto/htaccess.html*

11.8 Disabling Content Negotiation

Problem

Content negotiation causes a big reduction in performance.

Solution

Disable content negotiation where it is not needed. If you do require content negotiation, use the `type-map` handler, rather than the `MultiViews` option:

```
Options -MultiViews
AddHandler type-map var
```

Discussion

If at all possible, disable content negotiation. However, if you must do content negotiation—if, for example, you have a multilingual Web site—you should use the `type-map` handler, rather than the `MultiViews` method.

When `MultiViews` is used, Apache needs to get a directory listing each time a request is made. The resource requested is compared to the directory listing to see what variants of that resource might exist. For example, if *index.html* is requested, the variants *index.html.en* and *index.html.fr* might exist to satisfy that request. Each matching variant is compared with the user's preferences, expressed in the various `Accept` headers passed by the client. This information allows Apache to determine which resource is best suited to the user's needs.

However, this process can be very time-consuming, particularly for large directories or resources with large numbers of variants. By putting the information in a *.var* file and allowing the `type-map` handler to be used instead, you eliminate the requirement to get a directory listing, and greatly reduce the amount of work that Apache must do to determine the correct variant to send to the user.

The *.var* file just needs to contain a listing of the variants of a particular resource and describe their important attributes.

If you have, for example, English, French, and Hebrew variants of the resource *index.html*, you may express this in a *.var* file called *index.html.var* containing information about each of the various variants. This file might look like the following:

```
URI: index.html.en
Content-language: en
Content-type: text/html

URI: index.html.fr
Content-language: fr
Content-type: text/html

URI: index.html.he.iso8859-8
Content-language: he
Content-type: text/html;charset=ISO-8859-8
```

This file should be placed in the same directory as the variants of this resource, which are called *index.html.en*, *index.html.fr*, and *index.html.he.iso8859-8*.

Note that the Hebrew variant of the document indicates an alternate character set, both in the name of the file itself, and in the `Content-type` header field.

Enable the *.var* file by adding a *AddHandler* directive to your configuration file, as follows:

```
AddHandler type-map .var
```

 Each of the file extensions used in these filenames should have an associated directive in your configuration file. This is not something that you should have to add—these should appear in your default configuration file. Each of the language indicators will have an associated *AddLanguage* directive, while the character set indicator will have an *AddCharset* directive.

In contrast to `MultiViews`, this technique gets all of its information from this *.var* file instead of from a directory listing, which is much less efficient.

You can further reduce the performance impact of content negotiation by indicating that negotiated documents can be cached. This is accomplished by the directive:

```
CacheNegotiatedDocs On
```

Caching negotiated documents can cause unpleasant results, such as people getting files in a language that they cannot read or in document formats that they don't know how to render.

If possible, you should completely avoid content negotiation in any form, as it will greatly slow down your server no matter which technique you use.

See Also

- *http://httpd.apache.org/docs/2.2/mod/mod_negotiation.html*

- *http://httpd.apache.org/docs/2.2/mod/mod_mime.html#addhandler*
- *http://httpd.apache.org/docs/2.2/mod/mod_mime.html#addcharset*
- *http://httpd.apache.org/docs/2.2/mod/mod_mime.html#addlanguage*
- *http://httpd.apache.org/docs/2.2/mod/core.html#optionsr*

11.9 Optimizing Process Creation

Problem

You're using Apache 1.3, or Apache 2.0 with the *prefork* MPM, and you want to tune *MinSpareServers* and *MaxSpareServers* to the best settings for your Web site.

Solution

Will vary from one site to another. You'll need to watch traffic on your site and decide accordingly.

Discussion

The *MinSpareServers* and *MaxSpareServers* directives control the size of the server pool so that incoming requests will always have a child process waiting to serve them. In particular, if there are fewer than *MinSpareServers* idle processes, Apache will create more processes until that minimum is reached. Similarly, if there are ever more than *MaxSpareServers* processes, Apache will kill off processes until there are fewer than that maximum. These things will happen as the site traffic fluctuates on a normal day.

The best values for these directives for your particular site depends on the amount and the rate at which traffic fluctuates. If your site is prone to large spikes in traffic, *MinSpareServers* needs to be large enough to absorb those spikes. The idea is to never have a situation where requests come in to your site, and there are no idle server processes waiting to handle the request. If traffic patterns on your site are fairly smooth curves with no abrupt spikes, the default values may be sufficient.

The best way to watch exactly how much load there is on your server is by looking at the `server-status` handler output. (See Recipe 11.4.)

You also should set *MaxClients* to a value such that you don't run out of server resources during heavy server loads. For example, if your average Apache process consumes 2 MB of memory and you have a total of 256 MB of RAM available, allowing a little bit of memory for other processes, you probably don't want to set *MaxClients* any higher than about 120. If you run out of RAM and start using swap space, your server performance will abruptly go downhill and will not recover until you are no longer using swap. You can watch memory usage by running a program such as *top*, which shows running processes and how much memory each is using.

See Also

- Recipe 11.10

11.10 Tuning Thread Creation

Problem

You're using Apache 2.0 with one of the threaded MPMs, and you want to optimize the settings for the number of threads.

Solution

Will vary from server to server.

Discussion

The various threaded MPMs on Apache 2.0 handle thread creation somewhat differently. In Apache 1.3, the Windows and Netware versions are threaded, whereas the Unixish version is not. Tuning the thread creation values will vary from one of these versions to another.

Setting the number of threads on single-child MPMs

On MPMs that run Apache with a single threaded child process, such as the Windows MPM (*mpm_winnt*) and the Windows and Netware versions of Apache 1.3, there are a fixed number of threads in the child process. This number is controlled by the *ThreadsPerChild* directive and must be large enough to handle the peak traffic of the site on any given day. There really is no performance tuning that can be done here, as this number is fixed throughout the lifetime of the Apache process.

Number of threads when using the worker MPM

The *worker* MPM has a fixed number of threads per child process but has a variable number of child processes so that increased server load can be absorbed. A typical configuration might look like the following:

```
StartServers 2
MaxClients 150
MinSpareThreads 25
MaxSpareThreads 75
ThreadsPerChild 25
ServerLimit 16
```

The *MinSpareThreads* and *MaxSpareThreads* directives control the size of the idle pool of threads, so that incoming clients will always have an idle thread waiting to serve their request. The *ThreadsPerChild* directive indicates how many threads are in each child process so when the number of available idle threads drops below *MinSpareThreads*,

Apache will launch a new child process populated with *ThreadsPerChild* threads. Similarly, when server load is reduced and the number of idle threads is greater than *MaxSpareThreads*, Apache will kill off one or more child processes to reduce the idle pool to that number or less.

The goal, when setting these values, is to ensure that there are always idle threads ready to serve any incoming client's request without having to create a new one. The previous example will work for most sites, as it will ensure that there is at least one completely unused child process, populated with 25 threads, waiting for incoming requests. As soon as threads within this process start to be used, a new child process will be launched for future requests.

The values of *MaxClients* and *ServerLimit* should be set so that you will never run out of RAM when a new child process is launched. Look at your process list, using *top* or a similar utility, and ensure that *ServerLimit*, multiplied by the size of an individual server process, does not exceed your available RAM. *MaxClients* should be less than, or equal to, *ServerLimit* multiplied by *ThreadsPerChild*.

Setting the number of threads when using netware or the perchild MPM

Whereas with most of the other MPMs the *MinSpareThreads* and *MaxSpareThreads* directives are server-wide, in the *perchild* and *netware* MPMs, these directives are assessed per child process. Of course, with the *netware* MPM, there is only one child process, so it amounts to the same thing.

With the *netware* MPM, threads are created and reaped as needed to keep the number of spare threads between the limits imposed by *MinSpareThreads* and *MaxSpareThreads*. The total number of threads must be kept at all times below the limit imposed by the *MaxThreads* directive.

See Also

- *http://httpd.apache.org/docs/2.2/mpm.html*

11.11 Caching Frequently Viewed Files

Problem

You want to cache files that are viewed frequently, such as your site's front page, so that they don't have to be loaded from the filesystem every time.

Solution

Use *mod_mmap_static* or *mod_file_cache* (for Apache 1.3 and 2.0, respectively) to cache these files in memory:

```
MMapFile /www/htdocs/index.html
MMapFile /www/htdocs/other_page.html
```

For Apache 2.0, you can use either module or the *CacheFile* directive. *MMapFile* caches the file contents in memory, while *CacheFile* caches the file handle instead, which gives slightly poorer performance but uses less memory:

```
CacheFile /www/htdocs/index.html
CacheFile /www/htdocs/other_page.html
```

Discussion

For files that are frequently accessed, it is desirable to cache that file in some fashion to save disk access time. The *MMapFile* directive loads a file into RAM, and subsequent requests for that file are served directly out of RAM, rather than from the filesystem. The *CacheFile* directive, by contrast, opens the file and caches the file handle, saving time on subsequent file opens.

In Apache 1.3, this functionality is available with the *mod_mmap_static* module, which is labelled as experimental and is not built into Apache by default. To enable this module, you need to specify the –enable-module=mmap_static flag to *configure* when building Apache. *mod_mmap_static* provides only the *MMapFile* directive.

In Apache 2.0, this functionality is provided by the *mod_file_cache* module, which is labelled as experimental, and is not built into Apache by default. To enable this module, you need to specify the --enable-file-cache flag to *configure* when building Apache. *mod_file_cache* provides both the *MMapFile* and *CacheFile* directives.

These directives take a single file as an argument, and there is not a provision for specifying a directory or set of directories. If you wish to have the entire contents of a directory mapped into memory, the documentation provides the following suggestion. For the directory in question, you would run the following command:

```
% find /www/htdocs -type f -print \
> | sed -e 's/.*/mmapfile &/' > /www/conf/mmap.conf
```

In your main server configuration file, you would then load the file created by that command, using the *Include* directive:

```
Include /www/conf/mmap.conf
```

This would cause every file contained in that directory to have the *MMapFile* directive invoked on it.

Note that when files are cached using one of these two directives, any changes to the file will require a server restart before they become visible.

See Also

- *http://httpd.apache.org/docs/2.2/mod/mod_mmap_static.html*
- *http://httpd.apache.org/docs/2.2/mod/mod_file_cache.html*

11.12 Distributing Load Evenly Between Several Servers

Problem

You want to serve the same content from several servers and have hits distributed evenly among the servers.

Solution

Use DNS round-robin to have requests distributed evenly, or at least fairly evenly, among the servers:

```
www.example.com.    86400    IN    A    192.168.10.2
www.example.com.    86400    IN    A    192.168.10.3
www.example.com.    86400    IN    A    192.168.10.4
www.example.com.    86400    IN    A    192.168.10.5
www.example.com.    86400    IN    A    192.168.10.6
www.example.com.    86400    IN    A    192.168.10.7
```

Add the following to your configuration file:

```
FileETag MTime Size
```

Discussion

This example is an excerpt from a BIND zone file. The actual syntax may vary, depending on the particular name server software you are running.

By giving multiple addresses to the same hostname, you cause hits to be evenly distributed among the various servers listed. The name server, when asked for this particular name, will give out the addresses listed in a round-robin fashion, causing requests to be sent to one server after the other. The individual servers need be configured only to answer requests from the specified name.

Running the *host* command on the name in question will result in a list of possible answers, but each time you run the command, you'll get a different answer first:

```
% host www.example.com
www.example.com has address 192.168.10.2
www.example.com has address 192.168.10.3
www.example.com has address 192.168.10.4
www.example.com has address 192.168.10.5
www.example.com has address 192.168.10.6
www.example.com has address 192.168.10.7
% host www.example.com
www.example.com has address 192.168.10.7
www.example.com has address 192.168.10.2
www.example.com has address 192.168.10.3
www.example.com has address 192.168.10.4
www.example.com has address 192.168.10.5
www.example.com has address 192.168.10.6
```

Make sure that when you update your DNS zone file, you also update the serial number and restart or reload your DNS server.

One of the document aspects used to determine cache freshness is the `ETag` value the server associates with it. This usually includes a calculation based on the document's actual disk location, which may be different on the different backend hosts. The *FileETag* settings cause that information to be omitted, so if the documents are truly identical they should all be given the same `ETag` value, and be indistinguishable when it comes to caching them.

See Also

- *DNS and Bind* by Paul Albitz and Cricket Liu (O'Reilly)
- Recipe 10.3

11.13 Caching Directory Listings

Problem

You want to provide a directory listing but want to reduce the performance hit of doing so.

Solution

Use the `TrackModified` argument to *IndexOptions* to allow browsers to cache the results of an auto-generated directory index:

```
IndexOptions +TrackModified
```

Discussion

When sending a directory listing to a client, Apache has to open that directory, obtain a directory listing, and determine various attributes of the files contained therein. This is very time consuming, and it would be nice to avoid this when possible.

By default, the Last Modified time sent with a directory listing is the time that the content is being served. Thus, when a client, or proxy server, makes a *HEAD* or conditional *GET* request to determine if it can use the copy that it has in cache, it will always decide to get a fresh copy of the content. The `TrackModified` option to *IndexOptions* cause *mod_autoindex* to send a Last Modified time corresponding to the file in the directory that was most recently modified. This enables browsers and proxy servers to cache this content, rather than retrieving it from the server each time, and also ensures that the listing that they have cached is in fact the latest version.

Note that clients that don't implement any kind of caching will not benefit from this directive. In particular, testing with *ab* will show no improvement from turning on this setting, as *ab* does not do any kind of content caching.

See Also

- The manpage for the *ab* tool
- *http://httpd.apache.org/docs/2.2/programs/ab.html*

11.14 Speeding Up Perl CGI Programs with mod_perl

Problem

You have existing functional Perl CGI programs and want them to run faster.

Solution

If you have the *mod_perl* module installed, you can configure it to run your Perl CGI programs instead of running *mod_cgi*. This gives you a big performance boost, without having to modify your CGI code.

There are two slightly different ways to do this.

For Apache 1.3 and *mod_perl* version 1:

```
Alias /cgi-perl/ /usr/local/apache/cgi-bin/
<Location /cgi-perl>
    Options ExecCGI
    SetHandler perl-script
    PerlHandler Apache::PerlRun
    PerlSendHeader On
</Location>

Alias /perl/ /usr/local/apache/cgi-bin/
<Location /perl>
    Options ExecCGI
    SetHandler perl-script
    PerlHandler Apache::Registry
    PerlSendHeader On
</Location>
```

For Apache 2.0 and *mod_perl* version 2, the syntax changes slightly:

```
PerlModule ModPerl::PerlRun
Alias /cgi-perl/ /usr/local/apache2/cgi-bin/
<Location /cgi-perl>
    SetHandler perl-script
    PerlResponseHandler ModPerl::PerlRun
    Options +ExecCGI
</Location>

PerlModule ModPerl::Registry
```

```
Alias /perl/ /usr/local/apache2/cgi-bin/
<Location /perl>
    SetHandler perl-script
    PerlResponseHandler ModPerl::Registry
    Options +ExecCGI
</Location>
```

Discussion

By using *mod_perl*'s CGI modes, you can improve the performance of existing CGI programs without modifying the CGI code itself in any way. Given the previous configuration sections, a CGI program that was previously accessed via the URL *http://www.example.com/cgi-bin/program.cgi* will now be accessed via the URL *http://www.example.com/cgi-perl/program.cgi* to run it in *PerlRun* mode or via the URL *http://www.example.com/perl/program.cgi* to run it in *Registry* mode.

The primary difference between *PerlRun* and *Registry* is that, in *Registry*, the program code itself is cached after compilation, whereas in *PerlRun* mode, it is not. While this means that code run under *Registry* is faster than that executed under *PerlRun*, it also means that a greater degree of code quality is required. In particular, global variables and other careless coding practices may cause memory leaks, which, if run in cached mode, could eventually cause the server to run out of available memory.

When writing Perl CGI code to run under *mod_perl*, and, in general, when writing any Perl code, it is recommended that you place the following two lines at the top of each program file, following the #! line:

```
use strict;
use warnings;
```

Code that runs without error messages, with these two lines in them, runs without problems under *Registry*.

 strict is not available before Perl 5, and *warnings* is not available before Perl 5.6. In versions of Perl earlier than 5.6, you can get behavior similar to *warnings* by using the -w flag to Perl. This is accomplished by adding it to the #! line of your Perl programs:

```
#!/usr/bin/perl -w
```

See Also

- *Programming Perl*, Third Edition, by Larry Wall, Tom Christiansen, and Jon Orwant (O'Reilly)

11.15 Caching Dynamic Content

Problem

You want to cache dynamically generated documents that don't actually change very often.

Solution

In Apache 2.2, use the following recipe:

```
CacheEnable disk /
CacheRoot /var/www/cache
CacheIgnoreCacheControl On
CacheDefaultExpire 600
```

In 2.3 and later, you can use something like this:

```
CacheEnable disk /
CacheRoot /var/www/cache
CacheDefaultExpire 600
CacheMinExpire 600
```

Discussion

Caching is usually explicitly disabled for dynamic content. Dynamic content, by definition, is content that is generated on demand—that is, created fresh each time it is requested. Thus, caching it is contrary to its very nature

However, it is often—even usually—the case that dynamically generated content doesn't actually change very much from one minute to the next. This means that you end up wasting an awful lot of time generating content that hasn't actually changed since the last time it was requested. If you're doing this several times per second, you're probably causing your server a great deal more work than is really necessary.

The recipes above solve this problem in two slightly different ways. The solution for 2.3 is better, but, as of this writing, 2.3 hasn't been released yet, so it's not a terribly practical solution yet.

The recipe for Apache 2.2 takes the approach of disabling cache control—that is, it tells Apache to ignore the request made by the dynamic content that it not be cached, and caches it anyway. Then, for good measure, a default cache expiration time of 5 minutes (600 seconds) is set, so that any content that is cached will be retained at least that long.

The solution for 2.3 is slightly more elegant. It sets a minimum cache expiration time of five minutes, as well as setting the default expiration time. This ensures that all content is cached at least for five minutes, but the content itself may specify a longer time, if desired. The main difference here is that in the 2.2 solution if the content itself sends a request that it be cached longer this will be ignored, whereas in the 2.3 solution it will be honored.

You'll first see the 2.3 solution working when the 2.4 version of the server is released. 2.3 is a development branch, and it will be called 2.4 when it is ready for general use.

Make sure that the directory specified as the CacheRoot exists and is writeable by the Apache user.

See Also

- *http://httpd.apache.org/docs/2.2/caching.html*

## CHAPTER 12

Directory Listings

The default Apache HTTP Server package includes a module, *mod_autoindex*, for displaying a directory listing as a Web page. The default display is simple and informative, but the module provides all sorts of controls to let you tweak and customize the output.

12.1 Generating Directory/Folder Listings

Problem

You want to see a directory listing when a directory is requested.

Solution

Turn on *Options Indexes* for the directory in question:

```
<Directory /www/htdocs/images>
    Options +Indexes
</Directory>
```

Discussion

When a URL maps to a directory or folder in the filesystem, Apache will respond to the request in one of three ways:

1. If *mod_dir* is part of the server configuration, *and* the mapped directory is within the scope of a *DirectoryIndex* directive, *and* the server can find one of the files identified in that directive, then the file will be used to generate the response.

2. If *mod_autoindex* is part of the server configuration and the mapped directory is within the scope of an *Options* directive that has enabled the *Indexes* keyword, then the server will construct a directory listing at runtime and supply it as the response.

3. The server will return a 404 ("`Resource Not Found`") status.

Enabling directory listings

The real keys to enabling the server's ability to automatically generate a listing of files in a directory are the inclusion of *mod_autoindex* in the configuration and the `Indexes` keyword to the *Options* directive. This can be done either as an absolute form, as in:

```
Options FollowSymLinks Indexes
```

Or in a selective or relative form such as:

```
Options -ExecCGI +Indexes
```

Enabling directory listings should be done with caution. Because of the scope inheritance mechanism (see *http://httpd.apache.org/docs/2.2/sections.html#mergin* for more details), directories farther down the tree also will be affected; and because the server will apply the sequence of rules listed at the beginning of this section in an effort to provide some sort of response, a single missing file can result in inadvertent exposure of your filesystem's contents.

Disabling directory indexing below an enabled directory

There are essentially two ways to work around this issue and ensure that the indexing applies only to the single directory:

- Add an "*Options* -`Indexes`" to *.htaccess* files in each subdirectory.
- Add an "*Options* -`Indexes`" to a *<Directory>* container that matches all the subdirectories.

For example, to permit directory indexes for directory */usr/local/htdocs/archives* but not any subdirectories thereof:

```
<Directory /usr/local/htdocs/archives>
    Options +Indexes
</Directory>

<Directory /usr/local/htdocs/archives/*>
    Options -Indexes
</Directory>
```

If this needs to apply only to certain subdirectories, the task becomes a little more complex. You may be able to accomplish it with a *<DirectoryMatch>* directive if the list of subdirectories is reasonably small:

```
<Directory /usr/local/htdocs/archives>
    Options +Indexes
</Directory>

<DirectoryMatch /usr/local/htdocs/archives/(images|video|audio)>
    Options -Indexes
</DirectoryMatch>
```

- *http://httpd.apache.org/docs/2.2/mod/core.html#options*
- *http://httpd.apache.org/docs/2.2/mod/mod_dir.html*
- *http://httpd.apache.org/docs/2.2/mod/mod_autoindex.html*

12.2 Display a Standard Header and Footer on Directory Listings

Problem

You want to display a header above and a footer below your directory listing.

Solution

```
# Remove the standard HTML header, if desired
IndexOptions +SuppressHTMLPreamble
HeaderName /includes/header.html
ReadmeName /includes/footer.html
```

Discussion

The directives *HeaderName* and *ReadmeName* specify the URI of files to be used as a header and footer, respectively, for directory listings.

If your *HeaderName* file contains an HTML `<head>` tag, `<title>` tag, or other things associated with the start of an HTML document, you will want to use the *IndexOptions +SuppressHTMLPreamble* directive to disable *mod_autoindex*'s automatically generated HTML heading. Failure to do so will result in an HTML document with two heading elements, with the result that any heading attributes set in your header will probably be ignored by the browser.

The argument to both *HeaderName* and *ReadmeName* is a URI relative to the current directory. That is, if there is no leading slash, it is interpreted as a path relative to the current directory, but if there is a leading slash, it is interpreted as a URI path—that is, relative to the *DocumentRoot*.

Your *HeaderName* and *ReadmeName* can be arbitrarily complex to produce whatever page layout you like wrapped around the auto-generated directory listing. You could, for example, open `<table>` or `<div>` sections in the header, which you then close in the footer, in order to produce page layout effects.

See Also

- *http://httpd.apache.org/docs/2.2/mod/mod_autoindex.html*

12.3 Applying a Stylesheet

Problem

You want to apply a CSS stylesheet to a directory listing without supplying a whole *HeaderName* document.

Solution

```
IndexStyleSheet /styles/listing.css
```

Discussion

The *IndexStyleSheet* directive sets the name of the file that will be used as the CSS for the index listing.

See Also

- *http://httpd.apache.org/docs/2.2/mod/mod_autoindex.html*

12.4 Hiding Things from the Listing

Problem

You want to omit certain files from the directory listing.

Solution

```
IndexIgnore *.tmp *.swp .svn secret.txt
```

Discussion

Certain files should be ommitted from directory listings. Temporary files, swap files, and various other generated files don't need to be shown to users visiting your Web site. Revision control directories, such as the *CVS* directory created by CVS, or the *.svn* directory created by Subversion, also should not be displayed, as they are un-likely to contain any information that would be of use to your visitors.

 Although this technique can be used to hide private or secret documents, it must be understood that these files can still be accessed by someone who knows, or guesses, the filename. The files are hidden from the directory listing, but they are still accessible. Do not use this technique with an expectation of security.

Files that are password-protected are automatically omitted from directory listings.

See Also

- Recipe 12.19
- *http://httpd.apache.org/docs/2.2/mod/mod_autoindex.html*

12.5 Searching for Certain Files in a Directory Listing

Problem

You want to provide a way to filter the listing by filename.

Solution

Use a P (pattern) argument in the *QUERY_STRING* of the URL:

> *http://servername/directory/?P=a**

Or place the following HTML form in a *HeaderName* file to provide a search feature on a directory listing.

```
<form action="" method="get">
Show files matching <input type="text" name="P" value="*" />
<input type="submit" value="Go" />
<form>
```

Discussion

In Apache 2.0.23, a number of new options were added to *mod_autoindex*, which allowed for more client control over the output of directory listings. By inserting options in the *QUERY_STRING* of the URL, changes can be made to the sort order, output formatting, and, as shown in this recipe, the files that are shown in the listing.

Using the *?P= QUERY_STRING*, the file listing is filtered by the supplied argument. For example, with a URL of: *http://servname/directory/?P=a**, any file starting with *a* will be listed.

Because this functionality is new with 2.0, there is no way to achieve the same outcome with earlier versions of Apache.

See Also

- Recipe 12.16
- Recipe 12.2

12.6 Sorting the List

Problem

You want to sort the directory listing by something other than the defaults.

Solution

```
IndexOrderDefault Descending Date
```

Discussion

The *IndexOrderDefault* directive allows you to specify, in your configuration file or *.htaccess* file, the order in which the directory listing will be displayed, by default. If, for example, you wish to have files displayed with the most recent one first, you could use the directive shown in the Solution above.

The possible arguments to *IndexOrderDefault* are:

- Name—the file or directory name
- Date—the date and time that the file was most recently modified
- Size—the size of the file, in bytes
- Description—the file description, if any, set with the *AddDescription* directive

Any of these may be ordered *Ascending* or *Descending*.

The value of *IndexOrderDefault* may be overridden by the end user by supplying *QUERY_STRING* arguments, unless you explicitly forbid it using *IndexOptions IgnoreClient*.

See Also

- Recipe 12.17
- Recipe 12.7

12.7 Allowing a Client-Specified Sort Order

Problem

You want to allow the end user to specify the order in which the listing should be ordered.

Solution

Users can supply *QUERY_STRING* arguments to modify the sort order:

http://servername/directory/?C=D&O=D

Or you can provide a form allowing the user to select the sort order, by placing the following form in a *HeaderName* file:

```
<form action="" method="get">
Order by by <select name="C">
<option value="N" selected="selected"> Name</option>
<option value="M"> Date Modified</option>
<option value="S"> Size</option>
<option value="D"> Description</option>
</select>
<select name="O">
<option value="A" selected="selected"> Ascending</option>
<option value="D"> Descending</option>
</select>
<input type="submit" value="Go" />
</form>
```

Discussion

Allowing the end user to control his experience is a powerful way to make your Web content more useful.

Unless this feature has been explicitly disabled using the *IgnoreClient* argument to *IndexOptions*, you will always be able to reorder the directory listing using the *?C=* and *?O= QUERY_STRING* options.

O (order) can be set to either A, for Ascending, or D, for Descending, and C (column) may be set to one of the following:

- N—name of the file or directory
- M—the last modified date of the file or directory
- S—the size of the file in bytes
- D—the description of the file, set with the *AddDescription* directive

The argument parsing routine will quit if it encounters an invalid argument.

With Apache 1.3, the syntax is, instead:

http://servername/directory/?X=Y

where X is one of **n**, **m**, **s**, or **d**, as described earlier, and Y is either **a**, for ascending, or **d**, for descending.

See Also

- Recipe 12.16
- Recipe 12.17
- Recipe 12.2

12.8 Specifying How the List Will Be Formatted

Problem

You want to specify different levels of formatting on the listing.

Solution

There are three levels of formatting that can be set. The list may be unformatted, formatted, or can be rendered in an HTML table.

To enable fancy indexing, do the following:

```
IndexOptions FancyIndexing
IndexOptions FancyIndexing HTMLTables
```

Discussion

The "fancy" formatting is the one that you're most used to seeing because it's the default setting in most configurations of Apache.

The *HTMLTable* formtting is rather less common, and gives a slightly less plain look to the listing.

See Also

- *http://httpd.apache.org/docs/2.2/mod/mod_autoindex.html#indexoptions*

12.9 Allowing the Client to Specify the Formatting

Problem

You want to allow the end user to specify how the list will be formatted.

Solution

The user may specify which of the formatting options she wishes to use by adding an F argument to the query string.

To specify a plain bulleted list:

```
http://www.example.com/icons/?F=0
```

To specify a formatted list:

```
http://www.example.com/icons/?F=1
```

To specify a list arranged in an HTML table:

```
http://www.example.com/icons/?F=2
```

Discussion

Unless *IndexOptions IgnoreClient* is in effect, the end user may apply a number of layout customizations by adding query string arguments. The F argument controls the formatting of the list.

See Also

- Recipe 12.16

12.10 Adding Descriptions to Files

Problem

You want to put a brief description of files in the listing.

Solution

Use the *AddDescription* directive to add a description to certain files or groups of files:

```
AddDescription "GIF image" .gif
```

Discussion

You may set a description for a particular file, or for any file that matches a particular pattern. The first argument to *AddDescription* is the description that you want to use, and the second is a substring that will be compared to file names. Any file that matches the pattern will have the description used for it.

By default, you have 23 characters available for this description. That space can be altered explicitly by setting *IndexOptions DescriptionWidth*, or by suppressing one of the other columns.

You should ensure that the description isn't too long, or it will be truncated when it reaches the width limit. This can be annoying when the description is truncated and therefore unreadable. Also, because you're permitted to use HTML in the description, it's possible that the HTML could be truncated, leaving unclosed HTML tags.

See Also

- *http://httpd.apache.org/docs/2.2/mod/mod_autoindex.html#adddescription*

12.11 Autogenerated Document Titles

Problem

You want to have the description of HTML files autogenerated.

Solution

Place the following in the *<Directory>* scope where you want to have descriptions automatically loaded from the *<Title>* tags of HTML files:

```
IndexOptions ScanHTMLTitles
```

Discussion

If generating a directory listing of a directory full of HTML files, it is often convenient to have the titles of those documents automatically displayed in the description column.

The *ScanHTMLTitles* option has *mod_autoindex* look in each HTML file for the contents of the *<Title>* tag, and use that value for the description.

This process is, of course, rather file-access intensive, and so will cause a significant performance degradation proportional to the number of HTML files that are in the directory.

See Also

- *http://httpd.apache.org/docs/2.2/mod/mod_autoindex.html#indexoptions*

12.12 Changing the Listing Icons

Problem

You want to use different icons in the directory listing.

Solution

Use *AddIcon* and its variants to specify which icons are to be used by different kinds of files:

```
AddIcon /icons/image.gif .gif .jpg .png
```

Discussion

There are a number of variants of the *AddIcon* directive that allow you to associate certain icons with various files, groups of files, or types of files.

The *AddIcon* directive sets an icon to be used for files that match a particular pattern. The first argument is the URI of the icon file to be used. The argument or arguments following this are file extensions, partial filenames, or complete filenames, with which this icon should be used.

You also can specify the argument ^^DIRECTORY^^ for directories, or ^^BLANKICON^^ to be used for blank lines, to ensure correct spacing.

To specify an icon to be used for the parent directory link, use an argument of "..":

```
AddIcon /icons/up_one.gif ".."
```

You also may use *AddIconByEncoding* to specify an icon to be used for files with a particular encoding such as, x-gzip:

```
AddIconByEncoding /icons/gzip.gif x-gzip
```

Use *AddIconByType* for associating an icon with a particular MIME type:

```
AddIconByType /icons/text.gif text/*
AddIconByType /icons/html.gif text/html
```

Finally, you can specify the default icon to be used if nothing else matches:

```
DefaultIcon /icons/unknown.png
```

With any of these directives, you also may specify an alternate text to be displayed for clients that have image loading turned off. The syntax for this is to include the alt text in parentheses before the image path:

```
AddIcon (IMAGE,/icons/image.gif) .gif .png .jpg
```

See Also

• *http://httpd.apache.org/docs/2.2/mod/mod_autoindex.html#addicon*

12.13 Listing the Directories First

Problem

You want to have the folders (directories) listed at the top of the directory listing.

Solution

To have the directories displayed first in the directory listing, rather than in alphabetical order with the rest of the files, place the following in your configuration file:

```
IndexOptions FoldersFirst
```

Discussion

By default, directory listings are displayed in alphabetical order, including the directories. However, some people are used to having the directories at the top, followed by the files. This allows for faster navigation through deep directory structures.

Adding the *FoldersFirst* option puts the folders at the top of the listing, followed by the files in alphabetical order.

See Also

• *http://httpd.apache.org/docs/2.2/mod/mod_autoindex.html#indexoptions*

12.14 Ordering by Version Number

Problem

You want to have files ordered by version number so that 1.10 comes after 1.9 rather than before 1.2.

Solution

To have files sorted in version number order, add the following to your configuration file:

```
IndexOptions VersionSort
```

Discussion

Sites that distribute software will often have multiple versions of the software in the directory, and it is useful to have them ordered by version number rather than alphabetically. In this way, *httpd-1.10.tar.gz* will be listed after *httpd-1.9.tar.gz*, rather than between *httpd-1.1.tar.gz* and *httpd-1.2.tar.gz*, as it would be in alphabetical order.

See Also

- *http://httpd.apache.org/docs/2.2/mod/mod_autoindex.html#addicon*

12.15 Allowing the End User to Specify Version Sorting

Problem

You want to let the end user enable or disable version sorting.

Solution

The user may specify whether to enable or disable the version ordering by adding a V query string argument to the URL:

To enable version ordering:

```
http://www.example.com/download/?V=1
```

To disable it:

```
http://www.example.com/download/?V=0
```

Discussion

Like the F argument, the V argument allows the user to impose his own custom formatting on a directory listing.

See Also

- *http://httpd.apache.org/docs/2.2/mod/mod_autoindex.html*

12.16 Complete User Control of Output

Problem

You want to combine some of the above techniques to give the end user full control of the output of a directory listing.

Solution

Place the following HTML in a file and use it as the header for your directory listing:

```
<form action="" method="get">
Show me a <select name="F">
<option value="0"> Plain list</option>
<option value="1" selected="selected"> Fancy list</option>
<option value="2"> Table list</option>
<select>
Sorted by <select name="C">
<option value="N" selected="selected"> Name</option>
<option value="M"> Date Modified</option>
<option value="S"> Size</option>
<option value="D"> Description</option>
<select>
<select name="O">
<option value="A" selected="selected"> Ascending</option>
<option value="D"> Descending</option>
<select>
<select name="V">
<option value="0" selected="selected"> in Normal
order</option>
<option value="1"> in Version order</option>
<select>
Matching <input type="text" name="P" value="*" />
<input type="submit" value="Go" />
<form>
```

Discussion

Several of these recipes show how to let the end user specify formatting options in the query string. However, they're likely not going to know about this.

This recipe allows you to give the end user the full bag of tricks, and lets her select various formatting options right there in the page. If you save the above HTML as *header.html*, you can use this in your directory listing with the *HeaderName* directive:

```
HeaderName /header.html
```

The user can than select various options, reorder the listing, search for various strings, and alter the formatting of the output to his heart's content.

See Also

- *http://httpd.apache.org/docs/2.2/mod/mod_autoindex.html*

12.17 Don't Allow the End User to Modify the Listing

Problem

You don't want the end user to be able to modify the output of the directory listing.

Solution

Place the following *IndexOptions* directive in the *<Directory>* scope where you wish this restriction to be in place:

```
IndexOptions +IgnoreClient
```

Discussion

Although it is generally preferable to allow the end user to have some control over her user experience, there may be times when you wish for a particular directory listing to be presented in a particular way, without the option of a user to modify that display.

Although most users will probably be unaware of the ability to do so, by default any user can modify the output of the directory listing with a combination of *QUERY_STRING* arguments. With the recipe shown above, this feature is disabled.

When *IgnoreClient* is set, *SuppressColumnSorting* is also put into effect. That is, the clickable header at the top of each column is removed so that the user isn't misled into thinking that he can alter the sort order by these links.

IgnoreClient can be used in conjunction with *IndexOrderDefault* to enforce a certain nondefault directory listing order.

See Also

- *http://httpd.apache.org/docs/2.2/mod/mod_autoindex.html*

12.18 Suppressing Certain Columns

Problem

You don't want to show certain columns in the directory listing.

Solution

Various columns can be suppressed with one of the *Suppress** arguments to the *IndexOptions* directive. For example, to suppress the last modified date column:

```
IndexOptions SuppressLastModified
```

Discussion

With the exception of the filename, all of the columns in a directory listing may be suppressed using one of the following *IndexOptions* arguments:

- *SuppressDescription*—hide the description column.
- *SuppressIcon*—don't display the icon usually shown next to the filename.
- *SuppressLastModified*—hide the column that lists the file datestamp.
- *SuppressSize*—hide the column showing the file size.

See Also

- *http://httpd.apache.org/docs/2.2/mod/mod_autoindex.html*

12.19 Showing Forbidden Files

Problem

Password-protected files and directories don't show up in the directory listing.

Solution

If you're running Apache 2.2, place the following *IndexOptions* directive in a *<Directory>* block referring to the directory in question, or in a *.htaccess* file in that directory:

```
IndexOptions +ShowForbidden
```

If you're running Apache 2.0, there is no solution.

Discussion

Starting with Apache 2.0, directory listings attempt to protect protected documents. So if a file or directory requires password authentication, it is not shown in a directory listing.

In Apache 2.0, this is simply how things work. There is no way to have forbidden files or directories shown in directory listings.

In Apache 2.2, the *ShowForbidden* argument was added for the *IndexOptions* directive, specifically to address this request.

See Also

- *http://httpd.apache.org/docs/2.2/mod/mod_autoindex.html*

12.20 Aliases in Directory Listings

Problem

Aliases don't show up in directory listings.

Solution

In the directory to be listed, put a file or directory named the same as the *Alias*. It will be displayed in the listing, but clicking on it will invoke the *Alias*.

Discussion

Aliases don't show up in directory listings, because *mod_autoindex* generates the listing by asking the filesystem for an actual directory listing. The filesystem doesn't know about the aliases.

There is no way to get *mod_autoindex* to pick up on these *Alias*es and list them.

You can, however, place items in the directory that act as placeholders for the *Alias*. Because an *Alias* is consulted before the filesystem, when you actually click on the file the *Alias* will be invoked and the file ignored.

See Also

- *http://httpd.apache.org/docs/2.2/mod/mod_autoindex.html*
- *http://httpd.apache.org/docs/2.2/mod/mod_alias.html*

Miscellaneous Topics

With its hundreds of configuration directives, and dozens upon dozens of modules providing additional functionality, the Apache Web server can be terrifically complex. So, too, can the questions about how to use it. We have collected many of the most common questions we have seen and categorized them, putting related topics into their own chapters when there were enough of them.

However, some of the questions that come up don't fall readily into one of the categories we have chosen, and some are more fundamental so we've collected them into this catch-all chapter of "questions that don't belong anywhere else."

13.1 Placing Directives Properly

Problem

You know what directive you need but aren't sure where to put it.

Solution

If you wish the scope of the directive to be global (i.e., you want it to affect all requests to the Web server), then it should be put in the main body of the configuration file or it should be put in the section starting with the line *<Directory />* and ending with *</Directory>*.

If you wish the directive to affect only a particular directory, it should be put in a *<Directory>* section that specifies that directory. Be aware that directives specified in this manner also affect subdirectories of the stated directory.

Likewise, if you wish the directive to affect a particular virtual host or a particular set of URLs, then the directive should be put in a *<VirtualHost>* section, *<Location>* section, or perhaps a *<Files>* section, referring to the particular scope in which you want the directive to apply.

In short, the answer to "Where should I put it?" is "Where do you want it to be in effect?"

Discussion

This question is perhaps the most frequently asked question in every Apache help venue. It is usually answered in a way that is relevant to the specific situation but not in a general all-purpose kind of way.

The situation is further complicated by the fact that the configuration file is frequently split over several files, which are loaded via *Include* directives, and the (usually) mistaken impression that it will make a difference whether a directive is put in one file or another.

Knowing exactly where to put a particular directive comes from understanding how Apache deals with sections (such as *<Directory>* and *<Location>*). There is seldom one magic place that a directive must be placed to make it work. However, there are usually a number of places where you can put a directive and have it produce an undesired effect.

There are two main situations in which a directive, when added to your configuration file, will not have the desired effect. These are when a directive is overridden by a directive appearing in the same scope but later in the configuration, and when there is a directive in a more specific scope.

For the first of these two situations, it is important to understand that the Apache configuration file is parsed from top to bottom. Files that use *Include* are considered to appear in their entirety in the location where the *Include* directive appears. Thus, if you have the same directive appearing twice but with different values, the last one appearing will be the one that is actually in effect.

In the other situation, it's important to understand that, while directives in one directory apply to subdirectories, a *<Directory>* section referring to a more specific or "deeper" directory will have precedence over sections referring to "shallower" directories. For example, consider the following configuration:

```
<Directory /www/docs>
    Options ExecCGI
</Directory>

<Directory /www/docs/mod>
    Options Includes
</Directory>
```

Files accessed from the directory */www/docs/mod/misc/* will have *Options Includes* in effect but will not have *Options ExecCGI* in effect, because the more specific directory section is the configuration that applies.

Finally, you must consider *.htaccess* files as well, which can override settings in the main server configuration file and cause situations that are confusing and difficult to track.

See Also

For *.htaccess* files:

> *http://httpd.apache.org/docs/howto/htaccess.html*
> *http://httpd.apache.org/docs/2.2/howto/htaccess.html*

For directories:

> *http://httpd.apache.org/docs/mod/core.html#directory*
> *http://httpd.apache.org/docs/mod/core.html#directorymatch*
> *http://httpd.apache.org/docs/2.2/mod/core.html#directory*
> *http://httpd.apache.org/docs/2.2/mod/core.html#directorymatch*

For location:

> *http://httpd.apache.org/docs/mod/core.html#location*
> *http://httpd.apache.org/docs/mod/core.html#locationmatch*
> *http://httpd.apache.org/docs/2.2/mod/core.html#location*
> *http://httpd.apache.org/docs/2.2/mod/core.html#locationmatch*

For Apache:

> *http://httpd.apache.org/docs/mod/core.html#files*
> *http://httpd.apache.org/docs/mod/core.html#filesmatch*
> *http://httpd.apache.org/docs/2.2/mod/core.html#files*
> *http://httpd.apache.org/docs/2.2/mod/core.html#filesmatch*

13.2 Renaming .htaccess Files

Problem

You want to change the default name of *per*-directory configuration files on a Windows system, because filenames beginning with a dot can cause problems.

Solution

Use the *AccessFileName* directive to specify the new name:

```
AccessFileName ht.access
```

Discussion

In addition to the server-wide configuration files, you can add directives to special files in individual directories. These are called *.htaccess* (*aitch tee access*) files because that's the default name for them.

However, the Unixish convention of filenames that begin with a dot doesn't play well on all platforms; on Windows in particular it can be difficult to edit files with such names.

Apache allows you to change the name it will use when looking for these *per*-directory files with the *AccessFileName* directive (which can only appear in the server-wide configuration files). You can use any name that's valid on your platform.

If you use the *AccessFileName* directive, be sure to make any additional appropriate changes to your configuration such as the *<FilesMatch "^\.ht">* container that keeps the files from being fetchable over the Web:

```
<FilesMatch "^ht\.">
    Order deny,allow
    Deny from all
</FilesMatch>
```

See Also

- Recipe 11.7
- *http://httpd.apache.org/docs/howto/htaccess.html*
- *http://httpd.apache.org/docs/2.2/howto/htaccess.html*

13.3 Generating Directory/Folder Listings

Problem

You want to see a directory listing when a directory is requested.

Solution

Turn on *Options Indexes* for the directory in question:

```
<Directory /www/htdocs/images>
    Options +Indexes
</Directory>
```

Discussion

When a URL maps to a directory or folder in the filesystem, Apache will respond to the request in one of three ways:

- If *mod_dir* is part of the server configuration, the mapped directory is within the scope of a *DirectoryIndex* directive, and the server can find one of the files identified in that directive, then the file will be used to generate the response.
- If *mod_autoindex* is part of the server configuration and the mapped directory is within the scope of an *Options* directive that has enabled the *Indexes* keyword, then the server will construct a directory listing at runtime and supply it as the response.
- The server will return a 404 (`Resource Not Found`) status.

Enabling directory listings

The real keys to enabling the server's ability to automatically generate a listing of files in a directory are the inclusion of *mod_autoindex* in the configuration and the Indexes keyword to the *Options* directive. This can be done either as an absolute form, as in:

```
Options FollowSymLinks Indexes
```

or in a selective or relative form, such as:

```
Options -ExecCGI +Indexes
```

Enabling directory listings should be done with caution. Because of the scope inheritance mechanism, directories farther down the tree also will be affected; because the server will apply the sequence of rules listed at the beginning of this section in an effort to provide some sort of response, a single missing file can result in the inadvertent exposure of your filesystem's contents.

Disabling directory indexing below an enabled directory

There are essentially two ways to work around this issue and ensure that the indexing applies only to the single directory:

- Add an *Options* -Indexes to *.htaccess* files in each subdirectory.
- Add an *Options* -Indexes to a *<Directory>* container that matches all the subdirectories.

For example, to permit directory indexes for directory */usr/local/htdocs/archives* but not any subdirectories, use:

```
<Directory /usr/local/htdocs/archives>
    Options +Indexes
</Directory>

<Directory /usr/local/htdocs/archives/*>
    Options -Indexes
</Directory>
```

See Also

- *http://httpd.apache.org/docs/mod/core.html#options*
- *http://httpd.apache.org/docs/mod/mod_dir.html*
- *http://httpd.apache.org/docs/mod/mod_autoindex.html*

13.4 Solving the "Trailing Slash" Problem

Problem

Loading a particular URL works with a trailing slash but does not work without it.

Solution

Make sure that *ServerName* is set correctly and that none of the *Alias* directives have a trailing slash.

Discussion

The "trailing slash" problem can be caused by one of two configuration problems: an incorrect or missing value of *ServerName*, or an *Alias* with a trailing slash that doesn't work without it.

Incorrect ServerName

An incorrect or missing *ServerName* seems to be the most prevalent cause of the problem, and it works something like this: when you request a URL such as *http://example.com/something*, where *something* is the name of a directory, Apache actually sends a redirect to the client telling it to add the trailing slash.

The way that it does this is to construct the URL using the value of *ServerName* and the requested URL. If *ServerName* is not set correctly, then the resultant URL, which is sent to the client, will generate an error on the client end when it can't find the resulting URL.

If, by contrast, *ServerName* is not set at all, Apache will attempt to guess a reasonable value when you start it up. This will often lead it to guess incorrectly, using values such as 127.0.0.1 or localhost, which will not work for remote clients. Either way, the client will end up getting a URL that it cannot retrieve.

Invalid Alias directive

In the second incarnation of this problem, a slightly malformed *Alias* directive may cause a URL with a missing trailing slash to be an invalid URL entirely.

Consider, for example, the following directive:

```
Alias /example/ /home/www/example/
```

The *Alias* directive is very literal, and aliases URLs starting with */example/*, but it does not alias URLs starting with */example*. Thus, the URL *http://example.com/example/* will display the default document from the directory */home/www/example/*, while the URL *http://example.com/example* will generate a "file not found" error message, with an error log entry that will look something like:

```
File does not exist: /usr/local/apache/htdocs/example
```

The solution to this is to create *Alias* directives without the trailing slash, so that they will work whether or not the trailing slash is used:

```
Alias /example /home/www/example
```

See Also

- *http://httpd.apache.org/docs/misc/FAQ-E.html#set-servername*

13.5 Setting the Content-Type According to Browser Capability

Problem

You want to set `Content-Type` headers differently for different browsers, which may render the content incorrectly otherwise.

Solution

Check the `Accept` headers with *RewriteCond* and then set the `Content-Type` header with a T flag:

```
RewriteCond "%{HTTP_ACCEPT}" "application/xhtml\+xml"
RewriteCond "%{HTTP_ACCEPT}" "!application/xhtml\+xml\s*;\s*q=0+(?:\.0*[^0-9])"
RewriteRule . - [T=application/xhtml+xml;charset=iso-8859-1]
```

Discussion

Different browsers tend to deal with content differently and sometimes need a nudge in the right direction. In this example, for browsers that specify (using the `HTTP_ACCEPT` header) that they prefer XHTML content, we want to send a `Content-Type` header specifying that the content we are sending fulfills that requirement.

The T (Type) flag sets the `Content-Type` for the response.

See Also

- *http://httpd.apache.org/docs/mod/mod_rewrite.html*

13.6 Handling Missing Host: Header Fields

Problem

You want to treat differently all requests that are made without a `Host` request header field.

Solution

```
SetEnvIf Host "^$" no_host=1
Order Allow,Deny
Allow from all
Deny from env=no_host
RewriteCond "%{HTTP_HOST}" "^$"
RewriteRule ".*"          -    [F,L]
```

Discussion

The `Host:` request header field is essential to correct handling of name-based virtual hosts (see Recipe 4.1). If the client doesn't include it, the chances are very good that the request will be directed to the wrong virtual host. All modern browsers automatically include this field, so only custom-written or very old clients are likely to encounter this issue.

The solutions given will cause such requests to be rejected with a `403 Forbidden` status; the exact text of the error page can be tailored with an *ErrorDocument 403* directive.

The first solution is slightly more efficient.

See Also

- Recipe 4.1

13.7 Alternate Default Document

Problem

You want to have some file other than *index.html* appear by default.

Solution

Use *DirectoryIndex* to specify the new name:

```
DirectoryIndex default.htm
```

Discussion

When a directory is requested—that is, a URL ending in a / rather than in a filename—*mod_dir* will select the index document from that directory and serve that file in response. By default, the index file is assumed to be *index.html*, but this can be configured to something else with the *DirectoryIndex* directive.

Note also that *DirectoryIndex* can be set to several files, which are listed in order of precedence:

```
DirectoryIndex index.html index.htm index.php default.htm
```

Finally, note that you also can provide a relative URL if you want to load content from some other directory, such as a CGI program:

```
DirectoryIndex /cgi-bin/index.pl
```

See Also

- *http://httpd.apache.org/docs/mod/mod_dir.html*

13.8 Setting Up a Default "Favicon"

Problem

You want to define a default favorite icon, or "favicon," for your site, but allow individual sites or users to override it.

Solution

Put your default *favicon.ico* file into the */icons/* subdirectory under your *ServerRoot*, and add the following lines to your server configuration file in the scope where you want it to take effect (such as inside a particular *<VirtualHost>* container or outside all of them):

```
AddType image/x-icon .ico
<Files favicon.ico>
    ErrorDocument 404 /icons/favicon.ico
</Files>
```

Discussion

favicon.ico files allow Web sites to provide a small (16 × 16 pixels) image to clients for use in labeling pages; for instance, the Mozilla browser will show the favicon in the location bar and in any page tabs. These files are typically located in the site's *DocumentRoot* or in the same directory as the pages that reference them.

What the lines in the solution do is trap any references to *favicon.ico* files that don't exist and supply a default instead. An *ErrorDocument* is used instead of a *RewriteRule* because we want the default to be supplied *only* if the file isn't found where expected. A rewrite, unless carefully crafted, would force the specified file to be used regardless of whether a more appropriate one existed.

See Also

- Chapter 5

13.9 Directory Listings in ScriptAliased Directories

Problem

You want to allow directory indexing in a directory named in a *ScriptAlias* directive.

 This is considered a bad idea because it can reveal to strangers the names of specific scripts that may be subvertible.

Solution

Add the following lines to the *<Directory>* container that defines the characteristics of your *ScriptAlias*ed directory:

```
<Files ".">
    Options Indexes FollowSymLinks
    SetHandler httpd/unix-directory
</Files>
```

Discussion

The *ScriptAlias* directive imposes a lot of restrictions on directories to which it is applied, primarily for reasons of security. After all, such directories contain scripts of arbitrary code that will be executed on your system; if you should happen to be using a well-known and popular script in which a vulnerability is subsequently detected, anyone on the Web may be able to take advantage of it.

One of the restrictions imposed explicitly by design is disallowing directory listings in *ScriptAlias*ed parts of the filesystem. This amounts to what's called "security through obscurity"—namely, hiding an issue and hoping that no one discovers it even though it's easily accessible—but it's better than advertising what scripts your server can execute.

However, under some circumstances you may want to allow directory listings in such directories—or at least the use of pseudolistings provided by files named in a *DirectoryIndex* directive. To do this you need to override the special protections. In particular, you need to indicate that they *don't* apply to the directory itself (indicated by the *<Files ".">* container), and that the directory should be treated as a directory (the *AddHandler* directive) and not a script.

This is actually playing rather fast and loose with Apache's internal mechanisms, and taking advantage of an unintentional feature. As a consequence, it may not continue to work in future versions of the software.

See Also

- Chapter 12

13.10 Enabling .htaccess Files

Problem

You want to enable the use of *.htaccess* files in directories on your server.

Solution

Add the following line to your *httpd.conf* file in a scope that applies to the directory (or directories) for which you want to enable *.htaccess* files:

```
AllowOverride keyword ...
```

Discussion

As long as the *keyword* you specify isn't *None*, this will instruct the server to process *.htaccess* files in the relevant scope. Which keyword or keywords you use depends on what sort of things you want the *.htaccess* file to be able to affect.

 Some platforms, such as Microsoft Windows, object to filenames that begin with a dot. To placate this particular idiosyncrasy, you can use the *AccessFileName* directive to tell the server to use a different name for these files, such as:

```
AccessFileName ht.access
```

If Apache seems to be ignoring an *.htaccess* file, you can verify this by putting some normal text into the file and browsing to a document in the same directory:

```
This is not an Apache directive
```

If the server is reading the *.htaccess* file, it will complain about the text (because it isn't an Apache directive); you'll get both a message in the server's error log and an "Internal Server Error" page in your browser. If neither of these happens, then the file *is* being ignored, and you should check your scoping and *AllowOverride* directives.

See Also

- *http://httpd.apache.org/docs/mod/core.html#allowoverride*

13.11 Converting IBM/Lotus Server-Side Includes to Apache

Problem

You are migrating documents from a Web server running IBM's Web Traffic Express or Lotus Domino Go Webserver to a server running Apache.

Solution

Most of the WTE/LDGW server side include directives that are directly portable to Apache's format, but there are a few that either have no parallel or need to be modified to work properly. Here is a list of the exceptions:

- *config cmntmsg*—there is no Apache equivalent for this setting.

- *echo* directive variables `SSI_DIR`, `SSI_FILE`, `SSI_INCLUDE`, `SSI_PARENT`, and `SSI_ROOT` —there are no built-in Apache equivalents for these automatic variables.

- *global*—there is no direct equivalent for this SSI directive. Variables set in the current file may be referenced later in the file, but they are not available to included documents.

- *set* directive—Apache's version of this directive is roughly the same as WTE's/ LDGW's, except that it *does not* understand the `&varname;` type of SSI variable substitution.

Discussion

Apache's *mod_include* module implements the canonical list of SSI directives, but WTE and LDGW have added extensions to the "standard" list. Because SSI is now largely considered a legacy technology for providing dynamic content, the usual recommendation is to use servlets, template engines, or scripting languages to provide equivalent functionality. It is extremely unlikely that Apache's implementation will be extended, so if you're taking advantage of some of the WTE/LDGW extensions, your time would probably be better spent migrating to a newer technology instead of trying to duplicate the original effect with Apache's SSI implementation.

See Also

- *http://httpd.apache.org/docs/mod/mod_include.html*

Using Regular Expressions in Apache

A number of the Apache Web server's configuration directives permit (or require!) the use of what are called *regular expressions*. Regular expressions are used to determine if a string, such as a URL or a user's name, matches a pattern.

There are numerous resources that cover regular expressions in excruciating detail, so this Appendix is not designed to be a tutorial for their use. Instead, it documents the specific features of regular expressions used by Apache—what's available and what isn't. Even though there are quite a number of regular expression packages, with differing feature sets, there are some commonalities among them. The Perl language, for instance, has a particularly rich set of regular expressions, which have been mostly available in the Apache regex library since version 2.0 of the server.

Regular expressions, as mentioned, are a language that allows you to determine if a particular string or variable looks like some pattern. For example, you may wish to determine if a particular string is all uppercase, or if it contains at least three numbers, or perhaps if it contains the word "monkey" or "Monkey." Regular expressions provide a vocabulary for talking about these sort of tests. Most modern programming languages contain some variety of regular expression library, and they tend to have a large number of things in common, although they may differ in small details.

Apache 1.3 uses a regular expression library called *hsregex*, so called because it was developed by Henry Spencer. Note that this is the same regular expression library that has been used in the *egrep*.

Apache 2.0 uses a somewhat more full-featured regular expression library called Perl Compatible Regular Expressions (PCRE), so called because it implements many of the features available in the regular expression engine that comes with the Perl programming language. Although this appendix does not attempt to communicate all the differences between these two implementations, you should know that *hsregex* is a subset of PCRE, as far as functionality goes, so everything you can do with regular expressions in Apache 1.3, you can do in 2.0, but not necessarily the other way around.

To grossly simplify, regular expressions implement two kinds of characters. Some characters mean exactly what they say (for example, a G appearing in a regular expression will usually mean the literal character G), whereas some characters have special significance (for example, the period [.] will match any character at all—a wild-card character). Regular expressions can be composed of these characters to represent (almost) any desired pattern appearing in a string. (Recursive patterns, for example, are not possible.)

What Directives Use Regular Expressions?

Two main categories of Apache directives use regular expressions. Any directive with a name containing the word *Match*, such as FilesMatch, can be assumed to use regular expressions in its arguments. And directives supplied by the module *mod_rewrite* use regular expressions to accomplish their work.

For more about *mod_rewrite*, see Chapter 5.

SomethingMatch directives each implement the same functionality as their counterpart without the *Match*. For example, the *RedirectMatch* directive does essentially the same thing as the *Redirect* directive, except that the first argument, rather than being a literal string, is a regular expression, which will be compared to the incoming request URL.

Regular Expression Basics

To get started in writing your own regular expressions, you'll need to know a few basic pieces of vocabulary, such as shown in Tables A-1 and A-2. These constitute the bare minimum that you need to know. Although this will hardly qualify you as an expert, it will enable you to solve many of the regex scenarios you will find yourself faced with.

Table A-1. A basic regex vocabulary

Character	Meaning
.	Matches any character. This is the wildcard character.
+	Matches one or more of the previous character. For example, M+ would match one or more Ms; "+" would match one or more characters of any kind.
*	Matches zero or more of the previous character. For example, M* would match zero or more Ms. This means that it will not only match M, MM, and MMM, it will also match a string that doesn't have any Ms in it at all.
?	Makes the previous character optional. For example, the regular expression monkeys? will match a string containing either monkey or monkeys.
^	Indicates that the following characters must appear at the beginning of the string being tested. Thus, a regular expression of ^zim requires that the string being tested start with the characters zim. ^ is referred to as an anchor because it anchors the match to the beginning of the string. In the context of a character class (see below), the ^ character has another special meaning.
$	Indicates that the characters to be matched must appear at the end of the string. Thus, a regular expression of gif$ requires that the string being tested end with the characters gif. $ is referred to as an anchor because it anchors the match to the end of the string.

Character	Meaning
\	Escapes the following character, meaning that it removes the "specialness" of the character. For example, a pattern containing \. would match a literal . character, since the \. removes the special meaning of the . character.
[]	Character class. Match one of the things contained in the square brackets. For example, [abc] will match either an a, or b, or c. [abc]+, on the other hand, would match a sequence of a's, b's, and c's, or any combination of them. Note that within a character class, the ^ character doesn't have its normal anchor status but means any character *except* those in the class. Thus, a character class of [^abc] will match any character that is *not* an a, b, nor c. A character class containing a - between two characters means an entire range of characters. For example, the character class [a-q] means all of the lowercase letters starting from a and ending with q. [a-zA-Z] would be all uppercase and all lowercase letters. In addition to character classes that you form yourself, there are a number of special predefined character classes to represent commonly used groups of characters. See Table A-2 for a list of these predefined character classes.
()	Groups a set of characters together. This allows you to consider them as a single unit. For example, you could apply a + or ? to an entire group of characters, rather than just a single character. The expression (monkeys)?, for example, would make the entire word monkeys an optional part of the match. In some regular expression libraries, the ( ) characters also capture the contents of the match so that they can be used later. (The regex libraries used by the Apache HTTP server *always* do this.)

Two Common Mistakes

A common pitfall when constructing regular expression (also called "RE" or "regex" [pronounced "rej-eks"]) patterns is overlooking that * matches *zero* or more occurrences. This means that a pattern of `^firstfield:*lastfield$`, intended to match things like `firstfield:blah:foo:blah:lastfield`, will *also* match `firstfieldlast field`. Often, you actually want to use a + meaning *one* or more occurrences.

Another fact often forgotten is that pattern characters that match a variable number of occurrences—*, +, and ?—apply to the single pattern expression they immediately follow. And unless you've grouped several together with parentheses, that usually means a single character. `foo+` will match `foo` and `foooooo`, *not* `foofoofoofoo`. To match the latter, group the characters like this: `(foo)+`.

Table A-2. Predefined regular expression character classes

Character class	Meaning
\d	Any decimal digit ("0" through "9").
\D	Any character that is *not* a decimal digit.
\s	Any whitespace character except VT (vertical TAB). This matches space, HT, CR, LF, and FF. (Note that this differs from the POSIX class [:space:] described elsewhere in this table, which matches all of those characters *and* VT.)
\S	Any nonwhitespace character (that is, anything that doesn't match \s).

Character class	Meaning
\w	Any "word" character; that is, an underscore or any character with an ordinal value less than 255 that is a letter or decimal digit. (This has restrictions and ideosyncrasies which are affected by the current locale. See the PCRE documentation for details.)
\W	Any nonword character.
[:alnum:]	Any alphanumeric character.
[:alpha:]	Any alphabetical character.
[:blank:]	A space or horizontal tab.
[:cntrl:]	A control character.
[:digit:]	A decimal digit.
[:graph:]	A nonspace, noncontrol character.
[:lower:]	A lowercase letter.
[:print:]	Same as graph, but also space and tab.
[:punct:]	A punctuation character.
[:space:]	Any whitespace character, including newline and return.
[:upper:]	An uppercase letter.
[:xdigit:]	A valid hexadecimal digit.

[ ] and [: :]

The POSIX classes (the ones using [: :]) are shorthand names for multiple matching characters, and the [: and :] are part of their syntax. As classes, they can only be used within a class expression (i.e., between [and]), which can make things look a little weird and confusing. For instance, to match any single hexadecimal digit, you'd use:

    [[:xdigit:]]

To match more than one, you'd use:

    [[:xdigit:]]+

To match any hexidecimal digit *or* whitespace character:

    [[:xdigit:][:space:]]

Or maybe:

    [[:xdigit:]\s]

To match any character *except* a hexidecimal digit, use:

    [^[:xdigit:]]

(The PCRE implementation of POSIX classes also allows:

    [[:^xdigit:]]

but that's an extension syntax and not universally supported.)

Examples

The previous concepts can best be illustrated by a few examples of regular expressions in action.

Redirecting several URLs

We'll start with something fairly simple. In this scenario, we're getting a new Web server to handle the customer support portion of our Web site. So, all requests that previously went to *http://www.example.com/support* will now go to the new server, *http://support.example.com*. Ordinarily, this could be accomplished with a simple *Redirect* statement, but it appears that our Web site developer has been careless and has been using *mod_speling* (see Recipe 5.9), so there are links throughout the site to *http://www.example.com/support* and to *http://www.example.com/Support*, which requires not one but two *Redirect* statements.

So, instead of using the two *Redirect* statements, we will use the following one *RedirectMatch* directive:

```
RedirectMatch ^/[sS]upport/(.*) http://support.example.com/$1
```

The square brackets indicate a character class, causing this one statement to match requests with either the upper- or lowercase s.

Note also the ^ on the front of the argument, causing this directive to apply only to URLs that *start* with the specified pattern, rather than URLs that simply happen to contain that pattern somewhere in them.

The parentheses on the end of the regular expression capture the remainder of the requested URI, putting it in the variable $1 for later use. We use it in the redirect target to retain the remainder of the requested URI.

Catching common misspellings

While watching the logfiles, we see that a number of people are misspelling support as suport. This is easily fixed by slightly altering our *RedirectMatch* directive:

```
RedirectMatch ^/[sS]upp?ort/(.*) http://support.example.com/$1
```

The ? makes the second p optional, thus catching those requests that are misspelled and redirecting them to the appropriate place anyway.

For More Information

By far the best resources for learning about regular expressions are Jeffrey Friedl's book *Mastering Regular Expressions* and Tony Stubblebine's book *Regular Expression Pocket Reference*, both published by O'Reilly. They cover regular expressions in many languages, as well as the theory behind regular expressions in general.

For a free resource on regular expressions, you should see the Perl documentation on the topic. Just type `perldoc perlre` on any system that has Perl installed. Or you can view this documentation online at *http://perldoc.perl.org/perlre.html*. But be aware that there are subtle (and not-so-subtle) differences between the regular expression vocabulary of Perl and that of the PCRE library (the one used by Apache). These differences are described on the Web at *http://www.pcre.org/pcre.txt*.

Troubleshooting

The Apache Web server is a very complex beast. The vanilla package includes over 30 functional modules and more than 12 dozen configuration directives. This means that there are significant opportunities for interactions that produce unexpected or undesirable results. This Appendix covers some of the more common issues that cause problems, as culled from various support forums.

Troubleshooting Methodology

In the Error Log

The Apache software does quite a reasonable job of reporting the details when it encounters problems. The reports are recorded in the server's error log, which is usually stored in one of the following places:

- */usr/local/apache/logs/error_log*
- */var/log/apache/error_log*
- */var/log/httpd-error.log*
- */var/log/httpd/error_log*
- *C:\Program Files\Apache Group\error.log*

Where the error log is put depends on how you installed and configured the server; the wealth of possible locations in the list above is because popular prepackaged installation kits (from Red Hat, SuSE, etc.) each has its own preferred location. Of course, the definitive location can be determined by examining your *httpd.conf* file for the *ErrorLog* directive(s).

So the very first thing you should do when Apache appears to be misbehaving is see if the server has any comments to make.

If the messages in the error log don't make the cause of the problem immediately clear, or if there aren't any messages that seem to relate to the problem, it's a good idea to crank the logging level up by changing the *LogLevel* setting in the *httpd.conf* file:

```
LogLevel debug
```

The **debug** setting enables all possible error messages and makes the server extremely verbose, so it's a good idea to set it back to **warning** or **error** after it has helped you locate the cause of your problem.

Characterize the Problem

When you're trying to diagnose a problem, here is a question you should ask yourself: "What is the current behavior, and in what ways is it different from the expected or desired behavior?"

If you ask this question, a natural successive question is: "What could cause the current behavior?"

Between the answers to these two questions often lies a "Eureka!" moment. At the very least, they narrow your area of research.

Debugging the Configuration

When diagnosing a problem by examining your server's configuration, be sure to examine all of the files involved. In particular, look for files identified in Include directives, as well as those in the main *httpd.conf* file and in *.htaccess* files.

If you're editing the server-wide configuration files, be sure to restart the server afterward to make the changes take effect!

If editing a configuration or *.htaccess* file seems to have no effect, test that it's actually being processed by putting a line of gibberish into the file and trying again.

If it seems that a *.htaccess* file is being ignored, even when you insert gibberish, it indicates that it's within the scope of an *AllowOverride None* directive.

Debugging Premature End of Script Headers

When you're working with CGI scripts, certain messages can quickly become extremely familiar and tiresome; typically the output in the browser window will be either a blank page or an Internal Server Error page.

This message has several different possible causes. These include, but are not necessarily limited to:

- The CGI script is either not emitting any output at all, or it is emitting content before the required header lines, or it's neglecting to emit the obligatory blank line between the header and the content.

- The script encountered an error and emitted the error message instead of its expected output.

- You're using *suexec* and one or more of the *suexec* constraints has been violated.

To test to see if the problem is an error condition or improper CGI response formatting, run the script interactively from the command line to verify that it is emitting content in compliance with the CGI rules.

If you're using *suexec*, check the *suexec* logfile to see if there are security constraints being violated.

You can tell if you're using *suexec* with the following command:

```
% httpd -l
Compiled-in modules:
  http_core.c
  mod_so.c
suexec: disabled; invalid wrapper /var/www/apache/bin/suexec
```

If you get a message that says that *suexec* is disabled, you can ignore that as a possible cause of the script's execution problems.

If *suexec* is enabled, though, you should look at its logfile to get more details about the problem. You can find the logfile with:

```
# suexec -V
 -D DOC_ROOT="/usr/local/apache/htdocs"
 -D GID_MIN=100
 -D HTTPD_USER="www"
 -D LOG_EXEC="/usr/local/apache/logs/suexec.log"
 -D SAFE_PATH="/usr/local/bin:/usr/bin:/bin"
 -D UID_MIN=100
 -D USERDIR_SUFFIX="public_html"
```

The important line is `-D LOG_EXEC="/usr/local/apache/logs/suexec.log"`; it tells you *exactly* where *suexec* is recording its errors.

You can find out more about CGI and *suexec* here:

- The CGI specification at *http://www.ietf.org/rfc/rfc3875*
- Recipe 8.13
- The *suexec* manpage

Common Problems on Windows

Windows has its own distinct set of problem areas that don't apply to Unixish environments.

Cannot Determine Hostname

When trying to start Apache from a DOS window, you receive a message like, "Cannot determine hostname. Use *ServerName* directive to set it manually."

If you don't explicitly supply Apache with a name for your system, it tries to figure it out. This message is the result of that process failing.

The cure for this is really quite simple: edit your *conf\httpd.conf* file, look for the string ServerName, and make sure there's an uncommented directive such as:

```
ServerName localhost
```

or:

```
ServerName www.foo.com
```

in the file. Correct it if there is one there with wrong information, or add one if you don't already have one.

Also, make sure that your Windows system has DNS enabled. See the TCP/IP setup component of the Networking or Internet Options control panel.

After verifying that DNS is enabled and that you have a valid hostname in your *ServerName* directive, try to start the server again.

Finding WS2_32.DLL on Windows

When trying to start Apache on Windows 95, a message like, "Unable To Locate WS2_32.DLL..." appears. This file is necessary for Apache to function properly.

Prior to Version 1.3.9, Apache for Windows used Winsock 1.1. Beginning with Version 1.3.9, Apache began using Winsock 2 features (specifically, WSADuplicateSocket()). *WS2_32.DLL* implements the Winsock 2 API. Winsock 2 ships with Windows NT 4.0 and Windows 98. Some of the earlier releases of Windows 95 did not include Winsock 2.

To fix it, install Winsock 2, which is available at *http://www.microsoft.com/windows95/downloads/*. Then restart your server, and the problem should be gone.

Fixing WSADuplicateSocket Errors

If, when trying to start Apache on Windows, it fails and the Apache error log contains this message:

```
[crit] (10045) The attempted operation is not supported for the type of object
    referenced: Parent: WSADuplicateSocket failed for socket ###
```

it indicates that your system is using a firewall product that has inserted itself into the network software but doesn't fully provide all the functionality of the native network calls.

To get rid of the problem, you need to reconfigure, disable, or remove the firewall product that is running on the same box as the Apache server.

This problem has been seen when Apache is run on systems along with Virtual Private Networking (VPN) clients such as *Aventail Connect*. *Aventail Connect* is a Layered Service Provider (LSP) that inserts itself, as a *shim*, between the Winsock 2 API and

Windows' native Winsock 2 implementation. The *Aventail Connect* shim does not implement `WSADuplicateSocket`, which is the cause of the failure.

The shim is not unloaded when *Aventail Connect* is shut down. Once observed, the problem persists until the shim is either explicitly unloaded or the machine is rebooted.

Another potential solution (not tested) is to add *apache.exe* to the *Aventail Connect* exclusion list (see below).

Apache is affected in a similar way by any firewall program that isn't correctly configured. Assure you exclude your Apache server ports (usually port 80) from the list of ports to block. Refer to your firewall program's documentation for the how-to.

Relevant information specific to *Aventail Connect* can be found at *How to Add an Application to Aventail Connect's Application Exclusion List* at *http://support.aventail.com/akb/article00586.html*.

Handling System Error 1067

Sometimes, when starting Apache on Windows, you might get a message like "`System error 1067 has occurred. The process terminated unexpectedly.`" This uninformative message means that the Web server was unable to start correctly as a service for one reason or another.

As with any error, the first step should be to check your Apache error log. If that doesn't reveal anything useful, try checking the Windows application event log to find out why Apache won't start. If that doesn't help, try:

```
D:\>c:
C:\>cd "\Program Files\Apache Group\Apache"
C:\Program Files\Apache Group\Apache>apache
```

(If you don't get the prompt back, hit Ctrl-C to cause Apache to exit.)

This will run Apache interactively rather than as a service; any error messages should show up on your screen rather than being concealed behind a `System Error 1067` alert box.

Fixing Build-Time Error Messages

__inet Symbols

If you have installed BIND-8, then this is normally because of a conflict between your include files and your libraries. BIND-8 installs its include files and libraries in */usr/local/include/* and */usr/local/lib/*, whereas the resolver that comes with your system is probably installed in */usr/include/* and */usr/lib/*.

If your system uses the header files in */usr/local/include/* before those in */usr/include/* but you do not use the new resolver library, then the two versions will conflict. To resolve this, you can either make sure you use the include files and libraries that came with your system, or make sure to use the new include files and libraries.

If you're using Apache 2.0 or later, or Apache 1.3 with the APACI build script, you can make changes to the library search lists by defining them on the *./configure* command line:

```
% LIBS=-lbind ./configure ...
```

If you're using Apache 1.3 or earlier and controlling the build process by editing the *Configuration* file directly, just add `-lbind` to the `EXTRA_LDFLAGS` line in the file.

After making the appropriate change to your build configuration process, Apache should build with the correct library.

 Apache versions 1.2 and earlier use `EXTRA_LFLAGS` in the *Configuration* file instead.

As of BIND 8.1.1, the *bind* libraries and files are installed under */usr/local/bind* by default, so you should not run into this problem. Should you want to use the bind resolvers, you'll have to add the following to the respective lines:

- For Apache 1.3 with APACI, or 2.0 and later:

```
% CFLAGS=-I/usr/local/bin/include \
> LDFLAGS=/usr/local/bind/lib LIBS=-lbind \
> ./configure ...
```

- For Apache 1.2 or 1.3 with direct editing of *Configuration*, add/change the following lines in the file:

```
EXTRA_CFLAGS=-I/usr/local/bind/include
EXTRA_LDFLAGS=-L/usr/local/bind/lib
EXTRA_LIBS=-lbind
```

Getting Server-Side Includes to Work

The solution is to make sure that *Options Includes* is turned on and that either *XBitHack* is turned *On*, or that you have the appropriate *AddHandler* directives set on the file type that you are using.

As discussed in Recipe 8.9, there are a number of ways to enable SSI. If the unparsed SSI directives are appearing in the HTML when the page is loaded, this is a clear indication that SSI execution is not enabled for the document in question.

If the server has difficulty parsing an SSI directive, it will substitute the phrases "An error occurred while processing this directive" in its place in the response. If this happens, the cause of the problem should be listed in the server's error log. See also Recipe 8.13.

Debugging Rewrites That Result in "Not Found" Errors

If your *RewriteRule* directives keep resulting in 404 Not Found error pages, add the PT (PassThrough) flag to the *RewriteRule* line. Without this flag, Apache won't process a lot of other factors that might apply, such as *Alias* settings.

You can verify that this is the cause of your problem by cranking the *mod_rewrite* logging level up to 9 and seeing that the entries relating to the *RewriteRule* mention something about prefixes with document_root:

```
RewriteLog logs/rewrite-log
RewriteLogLevel 9

% tail logs/rewrite_log
ip-address - - [date] [reqid] (2) prefixed with document_root to
/usr/local/apache/htdocs/robots.text
ip-address - - [date] [reqid] (1) go-ahead with
/usr/local/apache/htdocs/robots.text [OK]
```

 Don't forget to turn off the *RewriteLog* directive, or possibly just turn down the logging level, after you've done your checking! Otherwise, your disk space may disappear like the snows of yesteryear.

Without the PT flag, *mod_rewrite* assumes that any rewriting it does will be the last URL manipulation the server needs to do for the request. Because *mod_rewrite* directives are handled very early in request processing, this can mean that *Alias*, *ScriptAlias* and other URL manipulations may not get executed. Specifying the flag tells *mod_rewrite* to not short-circuit processing but to let it continue as usual.

.htaccess Files Having No Effect

Make sure that *AllowOverride* is set to an appropriate value. Then, to make sure that the *.htaccess* file is being parsed at all, put the following line in the file and ensure that it causes a server error page to show up in your browser:

```
Garbage Goes Here
```

.htaccess files override the settings in the main server configuration file. Because this is frequently an undesired thing, *.htaccess* files are frequently disabled, which will cause your *.htaccess* file to be ignored.

.htaccess files are enabled using the *AllowOverride* directive, which lists categories of directives that may appear in an *.htaccess* file. For example, if you wish to put

authentication-related directives in an *.htaccess* file, you will need to put the following line in the main server configuration file:

```
AllowOverride AuthConfig
```

AllowOverride All permits any directive to be put in the *.htaccess* file, while the directive *AllowOverride None* means, "Please ignore my *.htaccess* files."

Thus, the most common cause of an *.htaccess* file being ignored is simply that your configuration file tells Apache to ignore it.

If you put garbage in your *.htaccess* file, this should generate a Server Error message in the browser, which will verify that Apache is indeed looking at the contents of your file. However, if such a message is not displayed, this is a sure sign that your *.htaccess* file is being completely ignored.

Address Already in Use

If, when attempting to start your Apache server, you get the following error message:

```
[Thu May 15 01:23:40 2003] [crit] (98)Address already in use: make_sock: could not
    bind to port 80
```

one of three things is happening:

- You are attempting to start the server as a nonroot user. Become the root user and try again.
- There is already some process running (perhaps another Apache server) using port 80. Run *netstat*, or perhaps look at the process list and kill any process that seems to fill this role.
- You have more than one *Listen* directive in your configuration file pointing to the same port number. Find the offending duplicate directive and remove it.

In the case of the first condition, you will need to become the root user in order to start Apache. By long tradition, only the root user may bind to any port lower than 1025. Because Apache typically runs on port 80, this requires root privileges.

The second condition can be a little trickier. Sometimes a child process will refuse to die and will remain running after Apache has been shut down. There are numerous reasons this might happen. Most of the time, you can kill this process forcibly using *kill* or *kill -9* while logged in as root. As long as this process is running and has the port occupied, you will be unable to start anything else wanting to bind to that same port.

In the case of the third condition, the second *Listen* directive attempts to bind to port 80, which has already been taken by the first *Listen* directive. Simply removing one of the *Listen* directives will clear up this problem.

Index

We'd like to hear your suggestions for improving our indexes. Send email to *index@oreilly.com*.

About the Authors

Ken Coar is a member of the Apache Software Foundation, the body that oversees Apache development. He is the author of *Apache Server for Dummies* (Wiley) and co-author of *Apache Server Unleashed* (Sams). Ken has been responsible for fielding email sent to the Apache project, and his experience with that mailing list provided a foundation for this book.

Rich Bowen is a member of the Apache Software Foundation, working primarily on the documentation for the Apache Web Server. He is a coauthor of *Apache Administrator's Handbook*. Rich lives in Lexington, Kentucky, where he spends his free time GeoCaching. He also enjoys flying kites and reading stuff by Charles Dickens and his contemporaries.

Rich, or DrBacchus—his handle on IRC—also spends entirely too much time on #apache. You can find him on the web at *http://www.drbacchus.com/journal*.

Colophon

The animal on the cover of *Apache Cookbook*, Second Edition, is a moose. The moose roams the forests of North America, Europe, and Russia. It's the largest of the deer family, and the largest moose of all—*Alces alces gigas*—is found throughout Alaska. That particular moose, in fact, is so ubiquitous that it has played an important role in the development of the state—although the relationship between moose and men is often adversarial.

Moose have a high reproductive potential and can quickly fill a range to capacity. In Alaska, the removal of mature timber through logging and fire has benefited them by providing new stands of young timber—high-quality moose food. Unfortunately, moose get to be a pain when they eat crops, stand on airfields, wander the city streets, and collide with cars and trains.

But, in general, these animals are good for the state's economy. Moose are an essential part of the Alaskan landscape, providing tourista with photo opportunities when the animals feed along the highway. Residents and out-of-state hunters harvest 6,000 to 8,000 moose annually—approximately 3.5 million pounds of meat. The future for these animals in Alaska is reasonably bright because humans are learning how to manage moose habitat with wildlife and how to mitigate factors that affect moose populations, such as hunting and predation by wolves and bears.

The cover image is an original engraving from *The Illustrated Natural History: Mammalia*. The cover font is Adobe's ITC Garamond. The text font is Linotype Birka, the heading font is Adobe Myriad Condensed, and the code font is LucasFont's TheSans Mono Condensed.

Related Titles from O'Reilly

Web Authoring and Design

ActionScript 3.0 Cookbook

Ajax Hacks

Ambient Findability

Creating Web Sites: The Missing Manual

CSS Cookbook, *2nd Edition*

CSS Pocket Reference, *2nd Edition*

CSS: The Definitive Guide, *3rd Edition*

CSS: The Missing Manual

Dreamweaver 8: Design and Construction

Dreamweaver 8: The Missing Manual

Dynamic HTML: the Definitive Reference, *3rd Edition*

Essential ActionScript 3.0

Flex 8 Cookbook

Flash 8: Projects for Learning Animation and Interactivity

Flash 8: The Missing manual

Flash 9 Design: Motion Graphics for Animation & User Interfaces

Flash Hacks

Head First HTML with CSS & XHTML

Head Rush Ajax

Head First Web Design

High Performance Web Sites

HTML & XHTML: The Definitive Guide, *6th Edition*

HTML & XHTML Pocket Reference, *3rd Edition*

Information Architecture for the World Wide Web, *3rd Edition*

Information Dashboard Design

JavaScript: The Definitive Guide, *5th Edition*

JavaScript & DHTML Cookbook, *2nd Edition*

Learning ActionScript 3.0

Learning JavaScript

Learning Web Design, *3rd Edition*

PHP Hacks

Programming Collective Intelligence

Programming Flex 2

Web Design in a Nutshell, *3rd Edition*

Web Site Measurement Hacks

O'REILLY®

Our books are available at most retail and online bookstores.

To order direct: 1-800-998-9938 • *order@oreilly.com* • *www.oreilly.com*

Online editions of most O'Reilly titles are available by subscription at *safari.oreilly.com*